Business Goes Virtual

Business Goes Virtual

Realizing the Value of Collaboration, Social and Virtual Strategies

John P. Girard, PhD

Minot State University

Cindy Gordon, PhD

Helix Commerce International Inc.

JoAnn L. Girard

Sagology

Business Goes Virtual: Realizing the Value of Collaboration, Social and Virtual Strategies

First published in 2011 by
Business Expert Press, LLC
222 East 46th Street, New York, NY 10017
www.businessexpertpress.com

ISBN-13: 978-1-60649-076-1 (paperback)
ISBN-13: 978-1-60649-077-8 (e-book)

10.4128/9781606490778

A publication of the Business Expert Press Strategic Management collection

Collection ISSN: 2150-9611 (print)
Collection ISSN: 2150-9646 (electronic)

Cover design by Jonathan Pennell
Interior design by Scribe Inc.

First edition: July 2011

10 9 8 7 6 5 4 3 2 1

Printed in the United States of America.

Abstract

As business leaders look to the future, especially in troubling economic times, many are considering how to remain competitive in an era of scarce resources. For most, capital projects are constrained and the idea of growing the workforce is a distant dream. So what can business leaders do about this? Some savvy leaders are recognizing the potential of virtual business and more specifically, many are implementing a virtual business strategy to build a sustainable competitive advantage. *Business Goes Virtual* combines real-world practitioner success stories, augmented with proven academic theory, to arm executives with proven leading practices to accelerate growth capabilities.

Despite several false starts, the concept of virtual business is finally coming to fruition. A melding of four critical enablers drives this new reality: social technology, visionary leadership, an increasing recognition of the value of a collaboration culture, plus virtual worlds. This so-called TLC+V (technology, leadership, collaboration, and the virtual) of virtual business has suddenly combined to create exciting and uncharted business opportunities waiting to be harnessed. Fortunately, some pioneering leaders have blazed the path and demonstrated the untapped potential of this new domain.

Many definitions exist for the term "virtual business," and although we do not want to engage in a lengthy discussion of which is best, we do believe we should explain what we mean by the term. From our study of businesses in the domain, we define the term as follows: "A virtual business provides innovative solutions to new and traditional business challenges by exploiting social technology, leadership, and collaboration in both the real and virtual words."

This book examines four virtual business strategies that are showing unprecedented opportunity. The "any place, any time" strategy focuses on providing high quality service 24/7 by ignoring traditional geographic challenges. The "people know best" strategy harnesses the power of everyday people to create value. The "everyone has a stake" strategy considers the stakeholder view of the organization and guides leaders in tapping this vast store of wisdom. Finally, the "real in the virtual world" strategy offers incredible opportunity for real businesses to sell their wares in the virtual world.

As with all innovative strategies, some potential pitfalls will demand the attention of virtual business leaders. The first is developing a social media policy that enables creating a collaborative culture while guarding corporate intellectual capital—this is often a difficult balancing act. Equally important and just as challenging is the difficult issue of not succumbing to the forces we plan to tap. Social technology is a double-edged sword and an angry consumer group can quickly become a network army with incredible power: witness the Twitter Moms who took on a large corporation and won.

Throughout the book, we present a collection of best practices derived from our case studies of real virtual business successes. We include a healthy dose of not-so-successful stories to remind us that these strategies are not a quick win but rather the product of sound strategic planning combined with focused and skilled execution expertise. Finally, we gaze into the future to consider what is on the horizon. This uncharted territory will be of great interest to early adopters who are looking for the next big thing. What we have learned from researching and writing this book is the future of work is here now, and more leaders simply need to embrace it. The reality is *Business Goes Virtual* is here to stay; we hope you are action-oriented leaders taking advantage of what others have achieved. *Collaborate or Die* was one of the titles we were toying with earlier. This is not an "if we should" or "when" question, it is a business imperative and those that get it will succeed, those that don't will lag and many will face demise.

Keywords

Virtual business, business strategy, virtual worlds, collaboration, digital media, social media, social technology, leadership, web 2.0

Contents

Acknowledgments

Creating this book has been an interesting journey! It seemed every time we were close to finishing a section, something big would happen that impacted the subject we were studying. We quickly learned that in the dynamic world of the virtual organizations in action, it was necessary to be agile and adapt to the changing times. We also recognized that often we learn as much from organizations that are no longer operating. Almost certainly, by the time you read this book, many more of the organizations we profiled will be distant memories or operating in a very different way. Such is the case of the fast-paced virtual world. We have done our best to represent the organizations as they existed when we studied them. We apologize in advance if the facts of the future are different from those of today.

We would be remiss if we did not acknowledge that many people helped us with this book, some directly and others indirectly. First, we thank the team at Business Expert Press, especially David Parker and Mason Carpenter, for advice and patience as we developed the manuscript. We would also like to thank Sandy Lambert who coauthored the appendix on organizational storytelling. This material was previously included in our book *The Leader's Guide to Knowledge Management*.

Many people, real pioneers in the virtual business space, have generously volunteered their stories. These leadership tales provide a first-person narrative of the successes and challenges of operating in the virtual space. We would like to thank Jimmy van Tonder, the proprietor of An African Villa in Cape Town, South Africa; Chris Ducker, the full-time Virtual CEO, originally from the United Kingdom but currently living in the Philippines; Jo Khalifa, President of MoJo Roast of Westhope, North Dakota; Dr. Lori Willoughby, professor at Minot State University and the architect of the first virtual business undergraduate program; Alex Blom, a serial entrepreneur, born and raised in Australia, now living in Toronto; and Spencer Thompson, a true millennial entrepreneur who aspires to help every single person put on this planet do something amazing.

Cindy Gordon would like to first thank her family, Normal Gordon, Benjamin Gordon, Perry Muhlbier, Bryce Muhlbier, and Jessica Muhlbier, for their lifelong support of my writing passion. With 12 books completed and two more in development, their confidence in my aspiration for communicating what others often fail to see has always been an inspiration and the flame to my heart! To my Helix family team, thank you for your leadership support; to Alex Blom, my Helix business partner, for your always turned-on, go-virtual vision and leadership in shaping all we do. Also, special thanks goes to Andrew Weir and Kathryn Gibson for their virtual world research support, Cathy Koop for her research support from RIM and Molson Coors Brewing Company, and Kristina Tan for her research support. To our Helix Board Advisors— Bill Hutchison, Chair iWATERFRONT; Kelvin Cantafio, President CIO Association; Dave Revell, Former Senior Vice President, Bank of Montreal; Rick Stuckey, former Senior Partner, Accenture—thank you for your many gifts of wisdom and inspiration. To our clients who have provided primary interview and case study contributions from Research In Motion (RIM): Rex Lee, Director eCollaboration; Kathy Alexander, Senior Manager; Nastaran Bisheban, Senior Project Manager; Seema Gupta, Senior Manager; from MTS Allstream: Craig Brown, Senior Director; from Molson Coors Brewing Company: Ferg Devins, Chief Public Affairs Officer; Tonia Hammer, Social Media Manager; Andrew Moffat; Director, Public Communications; from Cisco: Ayelet Baron, VP Business Strategy and Transformation—thank you for your invaluable contributions. Thanks to many industry leaders that openly shared their collaboration and social media journey stories in the community during this research to help brew this book's insights: from CIBC: Takis Spiropoulos, Head of Electronic Banking; Ben Alexander, Senior Director Portals; Abdullah Malik, Vice President of Information Technology; from IBM: Eileen Brown, David Ransom, Debbie Granger, Dionne Duncan, Tom Papagiannopoulos; from MTS Allstream: Dean Prevost, CEO; Gary Davenport, CIO, Suzanne Harrison, Senior Director, and Craig Brown, Senior Manager; from ING Direct: Peter Aceto, CEO; Herman Tange, Senior Vice President, from OpenText: Eugene Roman, CTO, and former CIO, Bell Canada, for his social networking pioneering leadership and relentless innovation inspiration at OpenText; from Procter & Gamble: Susan Doniz, CIO; from RBC: Avi Pollock, Head of IT Strategy and Social Media; from TD: Sue McVey, former Vice President of Marketing now currently at BMO as VP of Employee Communications; Wendy Arnott, Vice President Communications and Social Media; Glenda Crisp, Vice President of Information Technology Collaboration Applications; Michael Loftus, Vice President, Collaboration Infrastructure; Dave Codack, Senior Vice President, Networks and Infrastructure; Gerald Jennabian, Senior Manager; Rogers Communications: Kevin Pennington, Executive Vice President, Human Resources for his tenacity in leadership development at Rogers, from the Ontario Government: Ron McKerlie, Bryan Hammer, Natasha Milijasevic, and Andeen Drayton. To our Helix partners at IT World, in particular, Fawn Annan, CEO, and to the University of Waterloo Stratford Institute (new social media program) leaders: Ken Coates, Paul Doherty, and Tobi-Day Hamilton an indebtedness to the journey of lifelong learning. To my Canadian Advanced Technology Association (CATA) and iCANADA leaders, John Reid, CEO, CATA, and Barry Gander, Joanne Stanley, Bill Hutchison—thank you for your vision for diversity in leadership and in creating a stronger intelligent nation in Canada. I would be remiss if I did not acknowledge my former Accenture partner: Dr. Bill Ives for his sustaining knowledge management vision and leadership. To my former collaboration coauthors, Dr. Jose Claudio Terra and Heidi Collins, thank you for your incredible inspiration in constantly striving to shift forward the world of work, and to Claudio for your enduring support of me in life. To my knowledge management, social media and collaboration fellow thought leaders: Dr. Verna Allee, Alex Blom, Dr. Nick Bontis, Dr. John Seeley Brown, Dr. Timothy Chou, Dr. Carla O'Dell, Ester Dyson, Dr. Thomas Davenport, Rick Levine, Ross Dawson, Seth Godin, John Hagel, Christopher Locke, Dr. James Noiree, Hubert St. Onge, Dave Snowden, Doc Searles, Thomas Stewart, Don Tapscott, Dr, Jose Claudio Terra, David Ticoll, Dr. Etienne Wenger, and Dr. Karl Weiss, thank you for your vision for making the world a better place. There are many more who are constantly making a difference, but the thoughtfulness of these leaders in their research and practical contributions have laid a strong foundation to understand the impact of digital media, collaboration, and the increasing reality of business going virtual. Cindy would also like to thank her coauthors, John Girard for his leadership in driving results to complete this project and to JoAnn for her editing brilliance. Without you both focused on deadlines, we may still be talking versus celebrating. So thank you for your inspiration, persistence, and virtual leadership! Together, our work can help other leaders understand the importance of the future of work as business goes virtual in its richest tapestry.

PART I

The Convergence

CHAPTER 1

Virtual Business

Real or Imaginary?

All glory comes from daring to begin.

—Eugene Ware

Welcome to the Future

Welcome to *Business Goes Virtual*. We are delighted that you have decided to embark on this journey of discovery. We hope that you enjoy reading this book as much as we enjoyed writing it.

As business leaders look to the future, especially in troubling economic times, many are considering how to remain competitive in an era of scant resources. For most, it seems likely that capital projects will be scarce and the idea of growing the workforce will be a distant dream. So what can business leaders do about this? Some savvy leaders are recognizing the potential of virtual business and the value of implementing a strategy to build a distinctive competitive advantage. *Business Goes Virtual* combines academic theory with real-world practitioner success stories to provide leaders with leading practices and lessons learned to help their organizations innovate and grow more rapidly.

Despite several false starts, the concept of virtual business is finally coming to fruition. Four critical enablers drive this new reality: social technology, visionary leadership, a culture of collaboration, plus an understanding of the virtual word. These four enablers—the so-called TLC+V of virtual business—have combined to create exciting and uncharted business opportunities waiting to be harnessed. Fortunately, many pioneering leaders have blazed the new cow path and demonstrated its untapped potential.

Today our world is a highly diverse and fluid economy where small companies or individual employees reconfigure themselves to quickly solve rapidly changing problems. Companies and individuals will have permanent and nonerasable reputations on the web that can be used to ensure trust and partnerships. Organizations that can think quickly will prevail. The socially connected network economy moves in real time and will continue to tear down and outrank establishment thinking. There is less value in branding when potential consumers rely on live feeds of customer satisfaction data showing how other people like themselves feel about the alternative offerings.

Imagine bringing a mobile Internet-connected device when you go to the supermarket: As you reach for a package of laundry detergent, it warns you that 70% of 10,000 people like yourself who tried the product did not like what it did to their laundry. Walking down the sidewalk in your new Nike running shoes, you are alerted by your watch that there is a sale on running shoes two blocks away, and your GPS guides your shoes where to turn. It sounds farfetched, but it is not really as increasingly the world goes virtual. Increased communication (and automated processing of judgment data) means increased transparency and more power to the customers. The World Wide Web is increasingly intelligent and social. Having strategies that allow you to innovate and embrace the new world of work will be key to your organization's evolution and sustainability.

This book examines four virtual business strategies that are showing unprecedented growth and opportunity. The "any place, any time" strategy focuses on providing high-quality service 24/7 by ignoring traditional geographic challenges. The "people know best" strategy harnesses the power of everyday people to create value. The "everyone has a stake" strategy considers the stakeholder view of the organization and guides leaders in tapping this vast store of wisdom. Finally, the "real in the virtual world" strategy offers incredible opportunity for real businesses to sell their wares in the virtual world.

As with all innovative strategies, some potential pitfalls will demand the attention of virtual business leaders, the first of which is developing a social media policy that creates a collaborative culture while protecting corporate intellectual capital; this is often a difficult balancing act. Equally important and just as challenging is the issue of not succumbing to the forces we plan to tap. Social technology is a double-edged sword and an angry consumer group can quickly become a network army with incredible power: Witness the Twitter Moms who took on a large corporation and won.

Throughout the book, we present a collection of best practices derived from our case studies of *real* virtual business successes. We include a healthy dose of not-so-successful stories to remind us that these strategies are not a quick fix but rather the product of sound strategic planning. Finally, we gaze into a crystal ball and consider what is on the horizon. This uncharted territory will be of great interest to early adopters who are looking for the next *big thing* and to leaders that need reenergizing and a vision to create the future of work to attract the best and the brightest and reinvigorate what they feel has been lost.

The Convergence

As the first decade of the 21st century drew to a close, many observers reflected on the *revolution* that had transformed the way people connect, communicate, and collaborate. Although there is some question as to whether we witnessed a true revolution, there is no question that a convergence of ubiquitous communication networks, low-cost appliances, exponential web-based content growth, and a cultural shift toward sharing know-how has created an always-on, always-connected, always-sharing environment. Today many of us assume that no matter where we are we should be able to connect immediately to our cyber security blanket. In fact, while one of us (John) was writing in Molokai, he was surprised and disappointed that the free Wi-Fi connection in his vacation condo blocked most social media websites, including Facebook, YouTube, and LinkedIn. As a result, he could not boast about the beautiful December weather to his snowbound friends in North Dakota. Ironically, only a couple of years ago he was ecstatic to find a hotel with free Wi-Fi—funny how our expectations change so quickly. No worries though, as both his BlackBerry and his Kindle allowed ease of connection to his needed social media sites . . . and so the boasting still got through.

This convergence has revolutionized how we connect with friends, family, and businesses. Today, executives, students, and soccer moms are equally connected virtually everywhere they go. But why is this of concern to us? The new reality is that all these people are able to use this omnipresent connection to perform business functions that once required a physical presence. Take, for example, the act of browsing for, selecting, and ultimately purchasing a book. Armed with a Kindle (Amazon's electronic book reader), a customer can browse for a bestselling book, preview the first chapter at no cost, and if so inclined, purchase the book electronically in 100 countries around the world—all from the handheld book reader. The book arrives in about a minute, so the purchaser can begin reading the book instantly.

The Kindle is certainly having an impact on the way some consumers purchase books. According to an Amazon.com press release, on Christmas Day 2009, consumers purchased more Kindle books than physical books—the start of a revolution in the book industry.[1] The early success of the Kindle was seen by some to be a fad, though early adopters were convinced this was not a fad but in fact a shift change in consumer behavior. The advent of the Kindle changed the business model for the entire book chain. Other e-book readers followed, and in 2010, Apple launched their tablet, the iPad, which is a book reader on steroids. In 2010, Apple sold approximately 15 million iPads, making it the fastest-selling consumer electronic product ever.[2] Some see this as tremendous progress, while others worry that the physical book may become a relic of the past. From an environmental point of view, it seems that the purchase of an e-book should reduce one's carbon footprint, as no printing or shipping is involved, nor did the purchaser have to drive to a local bookstore or large box store.

Of course, to the companies that print, bind, and ship the book, this might not seem to be the desired way of the future. Nevertheless, the wise printers, binders, and shippers of the world are acutely aware of the transformation. Our point is that this virtual business model provides a new way for customers to purchase books and therefore has the potential to change substantially the industry. Similar transformations have occurred in the gaming and music industries.

Two recent viral videos captured the attention of the online community as they described in graphic detail the impact of the convergence. The first of these million-plus viewed videos is titled "Did You Know? 4.0." As the suffix suggests, this is the fourth in a series of short videos that present interesting *facts* about the new world order. Some of the so-called facts have been disputed; however, for the most part the video series has accurately portrayed the tremendous change in the 21st century online environment.

The genesis of the "Did You Know?" video was a PowerPoint developed for a high school faculty meeting in 2007. The "Did You Know?" architects recognized the U.S.-centric bias in their education system and hoped to create an environment that would help American students "learn and grow so that they may become successful digital, global citizens."[3] Designed to inform local educators, the original version of "Did You Know?" quickly gained popularity and has since been viewed by more than 5 million viewers, while the entire series has a total of more than 20 million viewers.[4] Each version of the video, along with a series of national adaptations and language translations, is available on the Shift Happens wiki—we highly recommend that you visit the wiki at http://shifthappens.wikispaces.com.

The current version of "Did You Know?" was specifically mastered to promote *The Economist* magazine's Media Convergence Forum. Unlike the previous versions, the 4.0 version does not have an education theme but rather focuses on media convergence. We recommend the 3.0 version, which highlights some amazing facts and has been viewed by more than 12 million people:[5]

1. Did you know if you're one in a million in China . . . there are 1300 people just like you?
2. China will soon become the Number One English speaking country in the world.
3. The 25% of India's population with the highest IQs . . . is GREATER than the total population of the United States. Translation: India has more honor kids than America has kids.
4. Did you know the top in-demand jobs in 2010 . . . did not exist in 2004?
5. We are currently preparing students for jobs that don't yet exist . . . using technologies that haven't been invented . . . in order to solve problems we don't even know are problems yet.

Take the time to watch the entire version at http://www.youtube.com/watch?v=6ILQrUrEWe8.

The second of the far-reaching videos is titled "Socialnomics," the namesake of the book it was designed to promote. Like "Did You Know?"

the "Socialnomics" video includes a series of facts and figures about the new world: It begins with the question, "Is social media a fad? Or is it the biggest shift since the industrial revolution?"[6] and continues with statements including the following:

1. By 2010, Gen Y will outnumber Baby Boomers; 96% of them have joined a social network.
2. Social media has overtaken porn as the #1 activity on the web.
3. One out of eight couples married in the United States last year met via social media.
4. A 2009 U.S. Department of Education study revealed that on average, online students out performed those receiving face-to-face instruction.
5. The percentage of companies using LinkedIn as a primary tool to find employees is 80%.[7]

The author provides a list of sources for the various statistics;[8] however, the context of several facts has been disputed. For example, Josh Bernoff, the coauthor of the highly acclaimed book *Groundswell*, posted the following comment on the "Socialnomics" blog:

> This video and blog post are a fascinating example of a social phenomenon—how statistics, shorn of context and eventually of sources, can spread like a meme.
>
> Let's just take as one example, statistic #2, that social media has overtaken porn as the top activity on the Web.
>
> Your source is Huffington Post, but when you click on the Huffington Post link you find the actual article is on Reuters. Going there you find out that the actual research was done by Hitwise (http://www.reuters.com/article/technologyNews/idUSSP31943720080916) and that the actual fact is that social networks have overtaken porn in *Web Searches*, which is not the same as activity. And even Reuters doesn't tell us what region this is in—is the US, or worldwide?
>
> It's not that I don't believe it, it's that in the absence of context these statistics lose much of their meaning.[9]

So what is the lesson? We agree with Josh Bernoff and others who suggest that some of the "Socialnomics" statistics were presented without context, which really is nothing new, as statistics are regularly misrepresented. Of course, we must challenge what we read whether it is on the web, on the television, in print, or in any other media. That said, the ideas presented in both "Did You Know?" and "Socialnomics" videos have awoken millions to the potential of social media, digitization, and the globalization—all that is good. The question for you and your organization is, how are you capitalizing on this convergence?

Interesting enough, in the time it took us to develop this manuscript, December 2009 to December 2010, a new version of "Socialnomics" appeared (see http://www.youtube.com/watch?v=lFZ0z5Fm-Ng) with the questionable statistic removed.[10] This in itself illustrates the power and self-correcting nature of social media.

Virtual Business Defined (Sort Of)

The notion of a virtual business is a relatively new phenomenon and therefore many of the ideas presented in *Business Goes Virtual* are emerging concepts that are uncharted and await ratification. This certainly does not imply that there is not huge potential, nor does it suggest that the ideas do not build on a solid foundation; rather, it suggests that the ideas are new. In many cases, the ideas have been discussed for decades; however, the infrastructure simply did not exist to support the revolutionary ideas. The convergence we discussed earlier in this chapter has changed all that—the time is right to consider the merits of the virtual business.

So far, in this chapter we have penned the term "virtual business" more than a dozen times, we have discussed enablers and challenges, and yet we have not defined the term. As with many emerging domains, there is no consensus of how the term should be defined. Wikipedia defines the term as follows: "A virtual business employs electronic means to transact business as opposed to a traditional brick and mortar business that relies on face-to-face transactions with physical documents and physical currency or credit."[11]

Our use of the Wikipedia definition is very deliberate. We are very aware that some readers will cringe as they read the word "Wikipedia" and immediately challenge the validity of the definition. However, we believe that Wikipedia is an excellent source of material, especially given the subject of the book. Throughout *Business Goes Virtual*, we will use a variety of high-quality online references including blogs, wikis, social media, and corporate web presences as well as more traditional academic sources such as peer-reviewed journal articles, books, and conference proceedings. We will select the sources carefully; however, we will not differentiate based on whether the source is from electronic or paper media.

Wikipedia continues the virtual business article with the following example: "Amazon.com was a virtual business pioneer. As an online bookstore, it delivered and brokered bookstore services without a physical retail store presence; efficiently connecting buyers and sellers without the overhead of a brick-and-mortar location."[12] The Wikipedia article on virtual business includes several subcategories of virtual business, as shown in Table 1.1.

Throughout *Business Goes Virtual* we will consider organizations in each of the categories shown in Table 1.1. Many other definitions exist for the term "virtual business" and although we do not want to engage in a lengthy discussion of which is best, we do believe we should explain what we mean by the term. From our study of businesses in the domain, we define the term as follows: A virtual business provides innovative solutions to new and traditional business challenges by exploiting social technology, leadership, and collaboration in both the real and virtual words.

What's Ahead

The aim of this book is to consider the theory and practice of virtual business with a view to helping executives chart a course toward a winning strategy based on social media. Unlike other books in the domain, this is not a book about the present; rather, it is a guide for the future. To be sure, we will spend some time reviewing what is working and not working today; however, the clear emphasis is building a strategy that will create value in the future.

We have worked diligently to provide a concise, no-nonsense view of virtual business. We have carefully selected the material we included to ensure it will be valuable for you. For those who desire more knowledge, we have included a comprehensive list of more than 100 references.

Table 1.1. Wikipedia's Virtual Business Definitions

Category	Wikipedia definition
Virtual business	"A virtual business employs electronic means to transact business as opposed to a traditional brick and mortar business that relies on face-to-face transactions with physical documents and physical currency or credit."
Virtual services	"Along with connecting customers with physical products, virtual businesses are starting to provide important services as well. Recently, the online delivery of professional services such as administration, design, and marketing services have risen in popularity. Such companies have refined their offerings to include services such as a Virtual Assistant, in which the person providing the service works out of his/her own office and provides services via the Internet or other technology."
Virtual worlds	"Some virtual businesses operate solely in a virtual world. Environments such as Second Life have enough economical activity to be viable for commerce and one can make a living from sales of virtual property, products and services to virtual customers in these virtual worlds."
Virtual corporations	"Groups of people can assemble online and enter into an agreement to work together toward a for-profit goal, with or without having to formally incorporate or form a traditional company. In 2008, Vermont amended its laws governing corporations to accept electronic forms of legally required meetings, operating agreements, documents, signatures, and record keeping. A Vermont corporation (S-corp or LLC), while required to maintain a registered agent with a physical address in the state, can be started, operated and terminated without any of the principals ever being in each other's physical presence."
Virtual enterprise	"A virtual enterprise is a network of independent companies—suppliers, customers, competitors, linked by information technology to share skills, costs, and access to one another's markets. Such organizations are usually formed on the basis of a cooperative agreement with little or no hierarchy or vertical integration. This flexible structure minimizes the impact of the agreement on the participants' individual organizations and facilitates adding new participants with new skills and resources. Such arrangements are usually temporary and dissolve once a common goal is achieved. A virtual enterprise is rarely associated with an independent legal corporation or brick and mortar identity of its own."

Source: Virtual business (2009).

We have also highlighted what we consider the *must-read* sources in the domain. If we mention a book by title or include a web page's URL, that is our recommendation for you to add it to your reading list.

The text that follows examines a number of key concepts in the domain. We hope to present these ideas in a user-friendly style that combines academic theory, real-world best practices, and some personal observations. Each of the styles provides a different view of the same subject; however, together we hope this blend provides a précis of the current state of knowledge management as well as a very exciting glimpse of the future. Each chapter will end with a very brief list of the main takeaways in the "Now You Know" section.

Now You Know

- Virtual business is driven by a melding of three critical enablers: social technology, visionary leadership, and a culture of collaboration.
- The "any place, any time" strategy focuses on providing high-quality service 24/7 by ignoring traditional geographic challenges.
- The "people know best" strategy harnesses power of the everyday people to create value.
- The "everyone has a stake" strategy considers the stakeholder view of the organization and guides leaders in tapping this vast store of wisdom.
- The "real in the virtual world" strategy offers incredible opportunity for real businesses to sell their wares in the virtual world.
- A convergence of ubiquitous communication networks, low-cost appliances, exponential web-based content growth, and a cultural shift toward sharing has created an always-on, always-connected, always-sharing environment.

CHAPTER 2

The New Face(book) of Organizations

It's when a technology becomes normal, then ubiquitous, and finally so pervasive as to be invisible, that the really profound changes happen.

—Clay Shirky, *Here Comes Everybody*, 2008[1]

Enabler 1: Social Technology

In our book *The Leader's Guide to Knowledge Management*,[2] we suggested that the single largest cultural-technological innovation of the 21st century was the social networking website. In *Winning at Collaboration Commerce: The Next Competitive Advantage*,[3] we stated that there is a rapidly emerging dominant voice in business strategy, organizational theory, information technology, and economics that traditional business models are rapidly evolving where the dominant voice is networks of collaboration leveraging adaptive and agile business models to create new growth ecosystems. Nearly 4 years later, we believe that the participatory approach to business that leverages social capital built on trust, reciprocity, and networks is the fundamental growth engine for economic survival.

We stand by this proposition and in fact, we are seeing more evidence to support our belief. Social networking sites help people connect with other people to collaborate in an online environment. Some are designed for connecting friends and family, while others facilitate professional connections. Here we are, just a few years into the new millennium, and it is hard to remember what the world was like before Facebook (http://www.facebook.com), which was founded in 2004. What is clear is what is popular today may not be popular in 10 years, the social networking highways are being rapidly paved, but the eyeballs can rapidly shift to alternative playing grounds, as evidenced in the erosion of MySpace as Facebook has continually eaten their lunch. What will lie beyond Facebook? There will be another play, and it will be smarter and more powerful. New beginnings are shaped virally with the learning tentacles deeply entrenched as business models intelligently iterate.

In this chapter, we will highlight how social technology is changing the business environment and enabling the power of virtual business. The technologies that we highlight are representative of the current tools (circa 2011). Clearly, there will be changes and some of the tools and techniques will become obsolete over time; however, the underlying power of connecting people will remain.

A specific aim of this chapter is to highlight the types of people, companies, and brands that are using various social connecting tools. Most of the brands and companies are early innovators who are experimenting with how to best connect with their stakeholders. The consumers of the various content are now mainstream—as we will see, literally millions of content consumers are using these tools every day. Your challenge is to discover how you can attract these content hungry hoards to your space. In this chapter, we highlight many examples of the state of the technology as of early 2011—make sure to take the time to visit the various social presences to learn from these early innovators.

Social Networking

Face•book
n. 1: A service that "gives people the power to share and make the world more open and connected."—Facebook 2: A "cyberland of rampant narcissism and wasted time."

—Andy Ostroy, *The Huffington Post*[4]

We begin our exploration of social networking with the site that has become synonymous with the term—Facebook. Valued at over $50 billion, with more than 500 million active users, if Facebook was a sovereign nation it would be the third largest country in the world. The number of Facebook users is roughly the same as the population of the continent of North America! According to Alexa.com, a web traffic–ranking site, Facebook was the second most popular site on the planet with a daily reach of nearly 38% of global web users (based on December 2010 data).[5] This is more than 150% increase from January 2009 when Facebook's reach was about 15%.

Perhaps more impressive than the actual number of Facebook users is their level of engagement. The quoted 500 million users are those who are considered active, which Facebook defines as those users who have returned to the site in the last 30 days. Equally notable is the fact that 50% of the citizens of the Facebook nation log on to the site on any given day—more than 250 million unique users log on to Facebook each day. Combined, Facebook users spend more than 700 billion minutes on Facebook each month—yes that was billion with a "b."[6]

So what do these Facebook users do while they are on the site? Well, mostly they share with their friends; an average user has about 130 friends. According to Facebook,

- there are over 900 million objects that people interact with (pages, groups, events, and community pages);
- the average user is connected to 80 community pages, groups, and events;
- the average user creates 90 pieces of content each month;
- more than 30 billion pieces of content (web links, news stories, blog posts, notes, photo albums, etc.) are shared each month.[7]

Although the average user has 130 friends, some brands and companies have amassed huge followings. According to InsideFacebook (http://www .insidefacebook.com),[8] by December 2010 five companies or brands had a fan base of more than 18 million, including the following:

1. Facebook—30,372,142
2. Texas Hold'em Poker—30,229,024
3. YouTube—24,913,379
4. Coca-Cola—20,801,751
5. Starbucks—18,856,485

The numbers alone do not tell the whole story as the growth of some of these companies and brands is almost unbelievable. Consider that in December 2009 when we started researching the material for this book, Facebook had a following of 5,824,049 and today the number is 30,372,142—that is an increase of almost 25 million in just 1 year. Similarly, YouTube saw a 1-year increase of 21 million, Coca-Cola witnessed a growth of 16 million, and Starbucks increased by more than 13 million.[9]

The focus of our book is virtual business at the organizational level. However, in the interest of full transparency, in addition to the companies and brands listed earlier, there are many celebrities and television shows that have a following of more than 15 million, including Michael Jackson (25 million), Lady Gaga (24 million), Emimem (23 million), *Family Guy* (22 million), Megan Fox (19 million), Vin Diesel (19 million), South Park (19 million), Rihanna (19 million), Linkin Park (19 million), and the *Twilight* saga (18 million). Only one political figure is high on the leaderboard; President Obama has a following of more than 17 million.[10]

In November 2009, *The Big Money* (http://www.thebigmoney.com) released *The Big Money* Facebook 50, a ranking of the brands that are currently making the best use of Facebook. *The Big Money* used various metrics—including fan numbers, page growth, frequency of updates, creativity as determined by a panel of judges, and fan engagement—to establish each page's score and ultimate rank on the list. Regrettably, *The Big Money* is no longer in operation; nevertheless, their analysis of the how and why businesses are successful remains very valuable. Table 2.1 is a list of the top 10 companies of *The Big Money* Facebook 50; the entire list is in Appendix 1. We recommend that you visit these Facebook pages to see some very innovative examples of using Facebook to develop a faithful following.

The table includes the number of Facebook fans for each of the pages as reported by *The Big Money* in November 2009. We have also included the number of Facebook users who "like" the page as of late February 2011. The latter was derived by us visiting each of the pages and recording the number of people who like the page. In many cases, the growth has been phenomenal. For example, Coca-Cola increased its following by more than 17 million in 1 year. Equally intriguing is the discovery that one of *The Big Money*'s Top Ten seems to have recorded a decrease, once again highlighting that social media must be cultivated. We should note that in 2010 Facebook moved from a system of "fans" to a system of "likes." Although there is a difference between the two systems, for our purposes the system in place is not as important as the number of Facebook users who made a conscious effort to connect with the page.

Table 2.1. The Big Money *Facebook 10*

Company	The Big Money rationale
Coca-Cola	A Coca-Cola fan created this page last year without much of a strategy. "I sat back and watched it grow and grow and grow," he says. Thanks to the power of the brand, the page eventually became a top page on Facebook. Coca-Cola (KO) has since made the page "official," created some sophisticated apps, and smartly kept the creator and his buddy onboard. The result: An organic fan-centric page without a corporate feel. Fans as of November 15, 2009: 3,996,163 Likes as of February 2, 2011: 22,226,541
Starbucks	Starbucks (SBUX) took over the top spot this summer as the brand with the most fans on Facebook. The coffee company won almost 200,000 new fans in a single week in late July, thanks in part to a free pastry promotion. Fans as of November 15, 2009: 5,034,578 Likes as of February 2, 2011: 19,473,226
Disney	Disney (DIS) fans have uploaded more than 3,400 of their own photos onto the media and entertainment company's page. Fans as of November 15, 2009: 2,119,773 Likes as of February 2, 2011: 16,677,141
Victoria's Secret	Two Victoria's Secret fan pages—the standard page and a separate page devoted to its Pink! line of underwear—are the top-ranked "Fashion" pages in terms of fans. The Limited Brands–owned (LTD) retailer posts lots of photos and videos starring its models. Fans as of November 15, 2009: 2,151,895 Likes as of February 2, 2011: 11,365,267
iTunes	Within a week of launching this page in May, Apple's (AAPL) digital downloading service iTunes already had more than 1 million fans. Fans as of November 15, 2009: 2,236,306 Likes as of February 2, 2011: 10,344,719
Vitaminwater	The "flavorcreator" doubles as a fun app and a market research tool. Users voted on Coca-Cola (KO)-owned Vitaminwater's next drink flavor and submitted designs for the label. Fans have more than doubled since the promotion launched in September. Fans as of November 15, 2009: 1,087,153 Likes as of February 2, 2011: 2,152,039
YouTube	In July, Google's (GOOG) YouTube publicly set out to get more Facebook fans than celebrities Adam Sandler, Lady Gaga, Will Smith, Megan Fox, and Vin Diesel by the end of September. While the video-sharing website didn't end up meeting the challenge, it still gained 600,000 new fans in what it called a "friendly celebrity tussle." Fans as of November 15, 2009: 3,733,242 Likes as of February 2, 2011: 26,658,021

Table 2.1. The Big Money *Facebook 10 (continued)*

Company	The Big Money rationale
Chick-fil-A	Chick-fil-A was the first restaurant page with 1 million fans on Facebook, reaching this milestone in August. Fans as of November 15, 2009: 1,221,064 Likes as of February 2, 2011: 3,740,011
Red Bull	An appropriately energetic page. Red Bull's latest app, called Red Bull Stash, maps out a real-life scavenger hunt for fans of the drink company. Fans as of November 15, 2009: 1,623,102 Likes as of February 2, 2011: 15,055,143
T.G.I. Friday's	T.G.I. Friday's ran a television ad this fall with an enticing premise: Become a fan of this guy and you get a free burger, but only if the page reaches half a million fans before October. The restaurant chain reached its goal by Sept. 13. Fans as of November 15, 2009: 974,192 Likes as of February 2, 2011: 515,392

Source: *The Big Money* Facebook 50 (2009).

LinkedIn (http://www.linkedin.com) is sometimes thought of as Facebook for grown-ups, but in fact it is much more than that. LinkedIn has established itself as the most substantive social space dedicated to connecting professions. According to LinkedIn, "over 85 million professionals use LinkedIn to exchange information, ideas and opportunities" and suggests that users can "stay informed about your contacts and industry, find the people & knowledge you need to achieve your goals, and control your professional identity online."[11] The LinkedIn website suggests that through their network, professionals can perform a number of tasks, including the following:[12]

- Managing the information that's publicly available about one's professional life
- Finding and being introduced to potential clients, service providers, and subject experts who come recommended
- Creating and collaborating on projects, gathering data, sharing files, and solving problems
- Finding business opportunities and potential partners
- Gaining new insights from discussions with likeminded professionals in private group settings

- Discovering inside connections that can help land jobs and close deals
- Posting and distributing job listings to find the best talent for one's company

Blogs

Blogs are a quick and easy way for individuals or organizations to chronicle their existence and share knowledge in an online environment. The word "blog" is actually a contraction of "web" and "log," so it is not surprising that blogs tend to be written in a reverse-chronological order so the most current blog entry will be at the top of the blog. As with many words in our modern vocabulary, the noun "blog" has morphed into a verb: for example, "David blogs on knowledge management."[13]

Matt Mullenweg, the cofounder of WordPress, the largest self-hosted blogging tool in the world, suggested there were more than 100 million blogs in the world.[14] The *Technorati's State of the Blogosphere 2010 Report* categorized American bloggers and suggested that

- two-thirds of bloggers are male;
- 65% are age 18–44;
- bloggers are more affluent and educated than the general population;
- 79% have college degrees and 43% have graduate degrees;
- one-third have a household income of $75,000 or more;
- one-quarter have a household income of $100,000 or more;
- 81% have been blogging more than 2 years;
- professionals have an average of 3.5 blogs;
- professionals blog 10+ hours/week;
- 11% say blogging is their primary income source.[15]

Given the enormous variety of blogs that exist and the maturity of this tool, it is very difficult to select the best blogs to view or the organizations that use the blogs most effectively. Table 2.2 is a list of several web pages that rate blogs.

Table 2.2. Recommended Blogs

Blog title/theme	Blog location
Technorati—Top 100 Blogs (updated daily)	http://technorati.com/blogs/top100
Time Magazine—Best Blogs of 2010	http://www.time.com/time/specials/packages/completelist/0,29569,1999770,00.html
Strategist News—Best Business Blogs 2009	http://www.strategistnews.com/best-business-blogs.php
Smashing Magazine—Corporate Blog Design: Trends and Examples	http://www.smashingmagazine.com/2009/08/20/corporate-blog-design-trends-and-examples

Microblogs

Twit•ter

n. 1: "A real-time short-messaging service that works over multiple networks and devices."—Twitter 2: "A playground for imbeciles, skeevy marketers, D-list celebrity half-wits, and pathetic attention seekers."

—Daniel Lyons, *Newsweek*[16]

One of the newest arrivals in the world of online communication is the microblog, which forces users to keep their updates very concise. The most well-known microblog is Twitter (http://www.twitter.com), which suggests "simplicity has played an important role in Twitter's success. People are eager to connect with other people and Twitter makes that simple. Twitter asks one question, 'What are you doing?' Answers must be under 140 characters in length and can be sent via mobile texting, instant message, or the web."[17]

A Pew Internet and American Life Project Survey conducted in October 2010 determined the following:

Eight percent of the American adults who use the internet are Twitter users. Some of the groups who are notable for their relatively high levels of Twitter use include:

- Young adults—Internet users ages 18–29 are significantly more likely to use Twitter than older adults.
- African Americans and Latinos—Minority Internet users are more than twice as likely to use Twitter as are White Internet users.

- Urbanites—Urban residents are roughly twice as likely to use Twitter as rural dwellers.
- Women and the college-educated are also slightly more likely than average to use the service.[18]

Like many other social networking tools, Twitter is a 21st century development. In the last couple of years, Twitter has experienced extraordinary growth. According to the website ranking company Alexa.com, Twitter is now the 10th most popular global Internet site.[19] Compete.com suggests this translates to about 26 million unique users every month—an increase of more than 1,000% in the last 2 years.[20] One of the best resources to learn the business value of Twitter is *Twitter for Business* (http://business .twitter.com). The site includes an overview of Twitter, a series of case studies highlighting how businesses are using Twitter to create value, a getting-started guide, and much more, including a list of resources for those interested in learning more.

Wikis

Wikis are the epitome of what many people think of Web 2.0—a collaborative web page that is quick and easy to edit. In fact, "wiki" is a Hawaiian word meaning "fast." By far the best known example of a wiki is the infamous Wikipedia (http://www.wikipedia.org), the self-proclaimed free encyclopedia. Wikipedia commands an impressive online following with about 13% of global Internet users visiting the site every day.[21] At present, the English-language version includes more than 3.5 million articles totaling almost 23 million pages. The wiki has been edited more than 433 million times, there have been more than 850,000 uploaded files, and there are about 13 million registered users. If we consider all language versions of Wikipedia, then the total number of articles raises to about 17 million.[22] All total, about 78 million unique users visit Wikipedia each month.[23]

During a recent fundraising campaign, Wikipedia founder Jimmy Wales wrote,

Wikipedia isn't a commercial website. It's a community creation, entirely written and funded by people like you. More than 340 million people use Wikipedia every month—almost a third of the Internet-connected world. You are part of our community.

I believe in us. I believe that Wikipedia keeps getting better. That's the whole idea. One person writes something, somebody improves it a little, and it keeps getting better, over time. If you find it useful today, imagine how much we can achieve together in 5, 10, 20 years.

Wikipedia is about the power of people like us to do extraordinary things. People like us write Wikipedia, one word at a time. People like us fund it. It's proof of our collective potential to change the world.

We need to protect the space where this important work happens. We need to protect Wikipedia. We want to keep it free of charge and free of advertising. We want to keep it open—you can use the information in Wikipedia any way you want. We want to keep it growing—spreading knowledge everywhere, and inviting participation from everyone.

The Wikimedia Foundation is the non-profit organization I created in 2003 to operate, grow, nurture, and protect Wikipedia. For ten million US dollars a year and with a staff of fewer than 35 people, it runs the fifth most-read website in the entire world. I'm asking for your help so we can continue our work.

Imagine a world in which every single person on the planet has free access to the sum of all human knowledge. That's where we're headed. And with your help, we will get there.[24]

Consider the impact of Wales's second-to-last sentence at the micro level; imagine how this might work in your organization. Perhaps your vision might be "Imagine an organization in which every single person on the team is given free access to the sum of all organizational knowledge." A wiki might be a very low-cost, high-return tool for collaboration and knowledge sharing in your organization.

Groundswell

By far the most watched phenomenon of the 21st century surrounds the power of everyday people. Executives across the board seem surprised by the sudden, and sometimes unwanted, knowledge and resultant power of the people. In their book *Groundswell: Winning in a World Transformed by Social Technologies*, Forrester analysts Charlene Li and Josh Bernoff describe part of this phenomenon as a groundswell, which they define as "a social trend in which people use technologies to get the things they need from each other, rather than from traditional institutions like corporations."[25]

The power behind the groundswell concept is that suddenly everyday people have unparalleled power, especially people that gather together and create communities (see http://www.forrester.com/groundswell). But what has changed to empower these communities with such power? Surely groups of passionate people have long yearned for the opportunity to influence or perhaps even hijack issues. Of course, there have been many times in history when large groups congregated to spark change. However, the logistics with massing large groups can be very cumbersome, expensive, and difficult to communicate.

Enter Web 2.0—a World Wide Web based on collaboration rather than content—and suddenly all these obstacles evaporate, at least for virtual groups. In their book *Wikinomics: How Mass Collaboration Changes Everything*, authors Dan Tapscott and Anthony Williams describe how a low-cost collaborative infrastructure is empowering the many—they term these "the weapons of mass collaboration."[26] Tapscott and Williams warn that these weapons support a new level of collaboration that will turn the economy upside down and may well facilitate the destruction of organizations who fail to adjust.

Li and Bernoff developed a model they titled Forrester's Social Technographics to categorize consumers based on their social computing habits. They use a ladder analogy with six rungs,[27] which correlates to the six levels of social computing:[28]

- *Creators* make social content go. They write or upload video, music, or text.
- *Critics* respond to content from others. They post reviews, comment on blogs, participate in forums, and edit wiki articles.
- *Collectors* organize content for themselves or others using RSS feeds, tags, and voting sites like Digg.com.
- *Joiners* connect in social networks like MySpace and Facebook.

- *Spectators* consume social content including blogs, user-generated video, podcasts, forums, or reviews.
- *Inactives* neither create nor consume social content of any kind.

The task facing organization leaders is to find a way to capture the imagination of those in the groundswell, hopefully in a positive way. To achieve this goal, leaders should promote opportunities to engage their end users, a task that is easy to write about but often difficult to implement. In the chapters ahead, we offer some examples of organizations that have achieved this near herculean feat.

What a Difference an Accelerometer Can Make

Many smart phones, portable media players, and book readers are equipped with an accelerometer, which is simply a device that measures angles. The accelerometer was cleverly added to these small appliances because many people like screens that rotate from landscape to portrait mode depending on the task at hand. For example, when watching a You-Tube video, many people prefer the landscape mode but most prefer the portrait mode when reading an e-book.

Some savvy engineers have found some other rather entertaining uses for the accelerometer. For example, games use it to enhance the gaming experience by allowing users to shake dice, drive cars, and navigate through mazes.

At InfoVision 2009 in Bangalore, India, we were amazed to learn how some innovative engineers envisage the future and how the accelerometer will play a big role. These engineers have determined that based on the various angles the accelerometer is reporting they can deduce with pretty high accuracy what the individual holding (or wearing) the accelerometer equipped device is doing. For example, imagine you have your smart phone in a holster on your belt. If the accelerometer is reporting a series of steady, even, and paced angles then perhaps the owner is walking. If the rhythm increases then perhaps they are running. If there is some walking followed by a series of very different, almost erratic angles, then perhaps the owner is golfing.

Based on the cell tower that the phone is using, the likely activity can be further refined. For example, if there is some walking followed by a series of very different, almost erratic angles, and the phone is pinging off a cell tower that is close to a golf course then almost certainly the owner is golfing. Knowing that someone is golfing can be very valuable to some organizations. Imagine you are on the golf course and about 1 minute after you tee off, your phone starts to vibrate, indicating a new message. When you look at the phone, you see a message saying that Tiger Woods (or your favorite golfer) just won (or lost) a PGA tournament. Many people would enjoy receiving a context-specific message related to their activity at that precise moment. You might not want to be bothered by such trivia if you were in an important meeting, but on the golf course, it might be nice to be the first of your foursome to receive the breaking news.

Clearly there are many issues with privacy and the like with such technologies. We are not endorsing such pushed messages, just making an observation of how it could be done. The most interesting thing about this story is how engineers are piggybacking on a technology that was provided for one thing (rotating screens) and have cleverly found another way to use the technology. We expect to see much more of this in the future. Are you ready for the future?

Twentieth-Century Technology

Often when we look to the future, we forget about the past. From a management point of view, forgetting the past and ignoring the lessons learned is both bad form and nonsensical. Although most of this book is about the future, we must not forget there are many leaders who blazed the trail to where we are today. From a technology point of view, today we are very fortunate to have many mature, time-tested technologies that we may employ to create value. But that was not always the case and it is worth revisiting some of the challenges that faced the pioneers of yesteryear.

The story that follows is an adaptation of the case we featured in *A Leader's Guide to Knowledge Management.*[29] Buckman Laboratories is a chemical manufacturer and distributor headquartered in Memphis, Tennessee. They sell more than 1,000 different specialist chemical products around the world while employing over 1,200 people. However, they have become more renowned for their innovative corporate knowledge management network. Today, business leaders from some of the highest technology sectors visit Buckman Laboratories to learn about knowledge management.

In 1992, CEO Bob Buckman decided that his company required a cultural revolution. He decided to develop a system that would create a strategic advantage in the very competitive market in which his corporation operated. The corporate culture he envisaged was one where all employees shared knowledge to help the company rather than guarding the knowledge to use for personal gain. He realized that such a radical change would be difficult for his competitive, sales-oriented employees, but he knew it was the right thing to do for the corporation and its long-term success.

Bob Buckman desired a system where individual salespeople could rapidly exchange knowledge in a collaborative manner to effectively engage the customer. His vision was a system where these individuals would all add to and draw from the knowledge base. The individuals would work as a team and together they would be more powerful and more effective than the sum of the individuals. Having clearly articulated the end state of his proposal, the initial challenge was to determine how to put this revolutionary system into place. To implement his novel knowledge management system, Buckman and his team had to overcome two significant obstacles: technology and culture.

Buckman's major obstacle was a technical one in that the communication infrastructure of the early 1990s was immature. To address this unacceptable situation, Buckman established a virtual Intranet on CompuServe, a public online system. Next, he leased laptop computers with modems for his entire sales force.[30] This early example of a virtual private network was extremely innovative. Although this was a significant challenge for Buckman, we are fortunate that this impediment no longer exists. The lesson is that technological barriers require creative solutions. Organizations must not permit immature technology to stifle sound business practices.

Now You Know

- Facebook popularity and impact continues to grow. By the end of 2010, Facebook had more than 500 million active users; about 50% of their users access the site every day.
- LinkedIn, the social networking site for professionals, now boasts more than 85 million users.
- Eight percent of the American adults who use the Internet are Twitter users. Many companies now have more than one million Twitter follows.
- There are more than 100 million blogs in the world.
- Wikipedia commands an impressive online following with about 13% of global Internet users visiting the site every day.[31] At present, the English-language version includes more than 3.5 million articles totaling almost 23 million pages. The wiki has been edited more than 433 million times, and there have been more than 850,000 upload files.
- The groundswell movements reminds us that we should cater to different categories of social computing users, including the following:
  - *Creators* make social content go.
  - *Critics* respond to content from others.
  - *Collectors* organize content for themselves or others using RSS feeds, tags, and voting sites like Digg.com.
  - *Joiners* connect in social networks like MySpace and Facebook.
  - *Spectators* consume social content including blogs, user-generated video, podcasts, forums, or reviews.
  - *Inactives* neither create nor consume social content of any kind.
- Leaders must not allow technical obstacles to thwart great business ideas and recognize that the world's growth promise is one of abundance versus scarcity and that sharing versus hoarding is the difference between light and darkness or hope versus death.

CHAPTER 3

Real Leadership in the Virtual World

Do, or do not. There is no "try."

—Yoda, *The Empire Strikes Back*

Enabler 2: Leadership

As we began researching material for this book and especially as we developed the case studies for the strategies section, we quickly deduced a common theme that was weaved into the fabric of virtual businesses. The theme was uncompromising leadership. Now the fact that leadership plays such a key role is really not surprising. Many business books include at least a chapter about leadership and it seems every few months a book is published introducing a new style of leadership that will solve all problems of modern organizations.

Our discovery was quite different. We discovered that each of the organizations we studied was led (or had been led) by truly amazing leaders. However, as we analyzed the leaders we found that in many cases they were very different leaders. For example, using Eric Berne's seminal work *Transactional Analysis* as a basis, we found some of the people we studied could be classified as transformational leaders while others would more likely be transactional leaders.[1] Transformational leaders are those who believe motivating their people is the secret to success. In 1978, Eric Berne first coined the term transformational leader, which may be described as follows:

> The transformational leader motivates its team to be effective and efficient. Communications is the base for goal achievement focusing the group on the final desired outcome or goal attainment. Their leader is highly visible and uses chain of command to get

the job done. Transformational leaders focus on the big picture, needing to be surrounded by people who take care of the details. The leader is always looking for ideas that move the organization to reach the company's vision.[2]

Other leaders we studied would be what Berne described as transactional leaders. Transactional leaders are those who subscribe to the management practice that combines the triad of power, reward, and punishment. Berne's concept of transactional leaders may be defined in this way:

> The transactional leader is given power to perform certain tasks and reward or punish for the team's performance. It gives the opportunity to the manager to lead the group and the group agrees to follow his lead to accomplish a predetermined goal in exchange for something else. Power is given to the leader to evaluate, correct, and train subordinates when productivity is not up to the desired level and reward effectiveness when expected outcomes is reached.[3]

In short, what we found was that there was no magic recipe for being a successful leader in the virtual domain. It quickly became clear that leadership was essential; however, the type and style of leaders we encountered on our journey was as varied as the type of organization they were leading.

In Their Own Words

In our previous book, *A Leader's Guide to Knowledge Management: Drawing on the Past to Enhance Future Performance*, we included a chapter on storytelling and how organizational leaders can use written narrative to lead their organization into the future.[4] We highlighted the work of Dave Snowden, storyteller extraordinaire, who suggests,

> I can speak in five minutes what it will otherwise take me two weeks to get round to spending a couple of hours writing it down. The process of writing something down is reflective knowledge; it involves both adding and taking away from the actual experience

or original thought. Reflective knowledge has high value, but is time consuming and involves loss of control over its subsequent use.[5]

Given that we did not want to turn this into a project that focused on leadership alone, we decided to put this idea into action and to invite some virtual business leaders to tell their story. We wanted you to hear, in their own words, about the successes and failures these leaders had celebrated and tackled along the way. We asked them to write their stories in the first person to help personalize the story, which would hopefully enable you, the reader, to better connect with them. We did remind them that although they should be proud of their organization and their successes, this piece should not be an advertisement. Finally, we asked them to be as candid as possible and to avoid sugarcoating the challenges as we believe some the best lessons come from leaders who overcame the many obstacles to success. Other than those guiding principles, we gave them free reign to tell their story in their way.

What follows is a series of stories written by a diverse group of virtual business leaders who very generously shared their story. The style of the stories varies, much as the type or organization, the leaders' generations, their background, their location, and many other factors. We will introduce each of the stories and then present the work as written by the leaders.

A Global African Villa

In chapter 2, we discussed how Web 2.0—a World Wide Web based on collaboration rather than content—was changing the way that many organizations and industries have changed. Recall our brief discussion of Dan Tapscott and Anthony Williams's book *Wikinomics: How Mass Collaboration Changes Everything* and how a low-cost collaborative infrastructure is empowering the many. Tapscott and Williams term these tools "the weapons of mass collaboration" and warn that these weapons support a new level of collaboration that will turn the economy upside down and may well facilitate the destruction of organizations who fail to adjust.

To understand the power of these new collaborative tools, consider the transformation of the travel industry. For many years, JoAnn worked in the travel business. JoAnn's business was all about knowledge and access to information, much of which she paid to access. Over time, she developed a clientele who knew JoAnn and trusted her judgment. They knew that she had incredible knowledge of many destinations and she had access to information, like wholesale prices, that was only available to the industry insiders. Today that has changed as most mere mortals now have more access to higher fidelity information, usually at no cost, than the professionals of just a couple of years ago. Through sites such as TripAdvisor, SeatGuru, Wikitravel, and Orbitz, to name just a few, we are now able to gain the valuable knowledge we need to make travel decisions.

Consider the following example from our recent trip to speak at a conference in Cape Town, South Africa. Whenever we travel to a new destination for business, we try to build in a little time to learn about the host country. We decided to arrive in Cape Town a few days early to tour the city and surrounding area. Our first real question was where to stay. A quick search on TripAdvisor revealed one particular guesthouse, An African Villa, received rave reviews from many people. In fact, virtually everyone who had stayed there rated the hotel as five stars, resulting in An African Villa being rated as the best hotel in Cape Town. In addition to the high quantitative scores the qualitative comments were glowing—most reviewers took the time to describe in detail just how happy they were with the property and the staff. Finally, we reviewed the photos provided by the many happy visitors. We thought this would be a great place to stay and decided to book. We made this decision because we trusted the 100 or so people who had provided feedback to TripAdvisor.

Our next challenge was to decide what to do before the conference. We only had a couple of days to see the sights so we decided it would be best to hire a guide for our visit. We searched several travel sites but did not find any guides that seemed to meet our needs. We decided to contact An African Villa and ask their advice. Suddenly we were treating An African Villa as a trusted authority as we assumed that they would not recommend anyone who might negatively influence our experience and ultimately our rating of the hotel. Within a day, we had an e-mail recommending a couple who were certified guides. We sent one more e-mail and we were set. As it turns out, we could not have been happier with either the property or our guide. This is an example of the power of collaboration and knowledge sharing. Through the collective knowledge of many TripAdvisor contributors, none of whom is paid for their services, we gained invaluable insight to make our decision. Frankly, it would be virtually impossible for a professional travel consultant in our home city to be able to provide this service.

The following is the story of An African Villa, in the proprietor's own words.

An African Villa is a small hospitality business in Cape Town, South Africa, which grew from an even smaller business in the same field: Liberty Lodge Bed and Breakfast. In the early 1990s I resigned from an academic job at 40 years of age. I felt myself ill-equipped to branch out into the daunting world of the "self-employed." I invested all the pension that I was paid out from the university where I had been employed for 24 years and invested it in a small derelict property that had been repossessed by the bank. The original plan was to renovate and sell on, but the renovations made it, by sheer luck, suited to the purpose of letting as rooms with attached ablution facilities.

How to become known in the industry and thus attract business clients was an immediate challenge. I resorted to the "overflow" method. I befriended some competitors in the area and was fortunate enough to be offered some of their "overflow" business. With a very limited marketing budget I was forced to choose the post, a well regarded medium available at a time before widespread acceptance of the Internet as a marketing tool. This proved to be a well researched and well regarded travel handbook called "The Portfolio Collection of B&Bs."

For 12 years this small business grew mainly through word of mouth and with help of the portfolio guide and the next step was to buy a second house nearby that would be suitable to absorb my own "overflow." This second B&B was an attempt to "Africanize" the travelers' experience in contrast to the many Victorian-styled houses in the city (Liberty Lodge included).

Within a few years, Internet marketing sites began springing up, which offered a new and untried marketing strategy full of promise. Many, including myself, were skeptical since the question "How will anyone find you on the Internet?" could never be convincingly answered. Nonetheless, I decided to set up a basic website. I was able to register an excellent domain address (http://www.capetowncity.co .za) and embarked into the "brave new world" of Internet marketing.

The answer to the question "How to be FOUND?" remained elusive although much of our business was still by word of mouth and gradually our past guests began to point their computer-literate friends in the direction of our site. Approximately 5 years ago one of our guests mentioned that they had found An African Villa on a site called Tripadvisor.com. We were then ranked around 45th after many of the larger hotels in the city. We began to try to understand how the ranking was calculated by the webmasters of this site. It seemed that the answer to improving one's ranking lay in encouraging positive comment by departing guests. Gradually we climbed in the ranking and finally ended up (in 2006–7) as the #1 hotel choice in Africa.

Conversely, it became clear that it was equally easy to be slated on this site that could do incalculable harm to one's image. I watched as some of my competitors were give bad reviews and examined their responses, which were invariably retaliatory and highly defensive. When, finally, we received a less-than-perfect review, I decided to react with empathy, trying to understand the client's concerns and set about growing from the criticism. I wrote a positive "owner's response" to TripAdvisor, acknowledging that the client had assisted us in improving our service. We actually gained bookings as a result.

The "People Know Best" theory has become the foundation of our business. One of the best aspects of this kind of marketing is that it is free of charge. At An African Villa, we are acutely aware that it is a two-edged sword that can be wielded by a fickle foe. It is not possible to please everybody all the time but as far as is possible, the hotel owner must attempt to satisfy even the most fastidious of critics. When not possible, then a gracious apology and the promise of a "try harder" attitude goes a long way.

Recently the so-called social media Internet sites have been gradually trickling into everyone's consciousness. Just as the Internet was 10 years ago, they are an unknown entity, breaking new ground. I have recently been bombarded with options of adding widgets to my websites. These will reportedly encourage visitors to link their friends to my web pages and so spread knowledge of An African Villa further afield, in a potentially limitless way in which a static website cannot do. This form of information distribution is still in its infancy in our country and is often regarded with suspicion as possibly just another cunning way to coax money from the unwary. The consoling factor is that it costs very little to set up. I sense that it is going to be worth taking the plunge and I hope that it could be of huge benefit although this requires a conscious change of mind-set on my part.

I am of an older generation: we are not as in tune with the culture of sharing of one's life with anyone who wishes to read about or watch it as younger people are. My jaw often gapes at the extent of the intimacy that reality television reveals to strangers. Clearly, however, both reality TV and Facebook and its clones are here to stay. I may not personally wish to air my own daily doings to the world but it makes good business sense to allow those who do wish to pass information that they consider interesting to as wide a community as possible, especially when this may benefit my product. At present I have 20 "friends" on Facebook, but my younger friends and family have in excess of 200 each. If only a small percentage of these share their interest in An African Villa with their friends, the results could be significant.

There are still nagging questions: Is this the market I am aiming for? Would those who would be interested to stay at my hotel perhaps be alienated by being bombarded with requests to be my friend on Facebook? I prefer to concentrate on the positive. Perhaps we may attract an entirely new market.

For more information about An African Villa, please visit http://www.capetowncity.co.za/villa.

A Virtual MoJo

We first heard about our next pioneer from a colleague whose students had recently visited the physical site of this very virtual business. As you will discover, this is a story of a coffee roaster located in North Dakota. As amateur coffee aficionados, we were intrigued by the how and the why of establishing a coffee roaster in a state where winter temperatures of 0°F (–18°C) are commonplace. Do not get us wrong. North Dakota is a beautiful state; however, we when we think of coffee we tend to think of Kona, Hawaii, or Seattle, Washington—maybe even Brazil or Costa Rica, but not North Dakota.

The more we learned about MoJo Roast, the more we realized how its innovative proprietor's story would be an excellent one to profile. The future and growth of MoJo Roast are tied to three key components: quality, location, and a virtual-based business plan. The quality issue is likely outside the scope of this book—we do not know much about coffee roasting; however, the latter two are of great interest. Like many small business owners, they are keen to live in a certain part of the country or world. The reasons for these geographical ties are many: family, cost, quality of life, schools, and so on. Often successful entrepreneurs "outgrow" the local market and must consider the global business environment. Such is the case with MoJo Roast where the concepts embedded in virtual business bring the global market to North Dakota.

In many ways, there could not be more differences between the previous story and this one. The two businesses are located in very different locations; one is very close to the geographical center of North America while the other is on the very southern tip of Africa. One is a very established business that literally stumbled upon the power of social media while the other was built to exploit the power of social media. On the other hand, these two businesses are very similar because the future is based on maintaining and growing the virtual portion of the business.

In the proprietor's own words, here is the story of MoJo Roast Inc.:

I have always had the entrepreneurial spirit within me and had dabbled in several different arenas of business and business ownership, pre-Internet back in the 1980s. As an entrepreneur, I have never looked at adversity as a loss or failure; it's just a temporary hurdle to get through. In knowing this, I have had my best growth through those times. If I knew in my younger years what I know now, I would have taken all the risks, and just went for it. I've learned valuable lessons from road blocks and have always moved forward.

In the first 6 months of being in business, I was in a roast-off with 250 roasters from around the globe. My team came in third place; that was a defining moment in my life. Word of mouth combined with virtualization is powerful and has been instrumental in growing my business. The toughest part for me in starting this business was finding my niche, in a very dense market. The days of personal service, in my opinion, have been long gone and I thought what if anyone could have and afford "their very own" personal coffee roaster? My niche was filled; I am a personal coffee roaster and a virtual assistant. I know my venue well and present it with passion and knowledge, and the thing that sets me apart from this vast industry is my personal touch. What this means to my customer is a company that is transparent, offers education and a knowledge that helps them to become savvy consumers, provides a top-quality product, and personalized roasting for each and every one, both wholesale and retail.

Now add the virtual picture to a business, and where do I go from there? I have just made a choice to take my business global. How do I attract the consumer and potential customer to my business with such a saturated industry; how do I personalize the virtual end of my business? With that goal in mind, I found a web developer that could take me to where I needed to be in order to set myself apart from the rest of the virtual businesses. I knew there was great financial concern with the market place, and I had experienced a down-turn in drive through revenue, but noticed an upturn in my grocery and specialty store sales. This was an indication that people weren't necessarily going for that morning coffee, they were brewing at home more. I created a "Be Your Own Barista" section to my website, where the consumer can purchase the same items as they would at a coffee shop and create their favorite drinks at home at a fraction of the cost. Along with this program, I will be incorporating a blog and video section soon to educate the consumer face to face, which will in turn gear them to various sections of my website to purchase products. In order for any business to stand out from the crowd and stay on top, they need to be virtual and find a way to be personal with their customers and interact with them. Taking a look at the invention of the telephone and telegraph to now, with computers and cell phones, our need to communicate is overwhelming. How are you going to connect and communicate with your customer, consumer, and client? As this technology grows, it will be essential for me to stay on the cutting edge of technology that will forever be evolving, to continue to connect with my existing and potential customer base. For me, it's about keeping it personal and making sure my customer knows how valued they are to my business.

I look back to the short time that I have been roasting coffee and see the power that word of mouth and virtualization truly has; I was invited to present President Obama with an inaugural coffee basket, my coffee is served in restaurants, coffees bars, and specialty shops across the country. Because of my presence on the Internet, a member of the show *CSI* found my company and I was able to contribute to the show's story line on a coffee-related issue. Fort Abraham Lincoln in Mandan, North Dakota, asked me if I knew about the coffee and the roast that Custer and his 7th Calvary would have been drinking during the late 1800s and if I could recreate that for them. I knew exactly what they were looking for, and now they offer an authentic era-specific coffee to the tourists that travel through.

I know that I have been given a great gift; and with that gift it is my obligation to give back. My passion is fueled by the coffee growers and their stories. Their stories are stories of poverty, hunger, anguish, and abuse. I'm involved in the Café Femenino Foundation that helps with education and domestic abuse in several coffee-producing countries; the women that grow the coffee for me are paid at least their countries minimum wage. Some of the monies from this foundation are also donated to a local domestic abuse center. I'm also involved in cancer foundations and their causes.

Consumer education has been very important to my business because so many people do not understand the world of coffee and helping them to understand has tremendously helped my business grow. With every business endeavor that I pursue I have two questions in mind: who will it help and who will it benefit? My future goals are to help unite people throughout the coffee world.

My secrets to success include the following:

- Virtualization
- Passion
- Values
- Can-do attitude
- Determination
- Education
- Willingness to share and mentor
- Concentrating on following your dreams and not chasing others
- Believing in yourself
- Having a gift and giving back
- Joining groups and organizations that pertain to your field
- Always being the best that you can be

For more information, see

- http://www.mojoroast.com
- http://www.linkedIn.com (Jo Khalifa)
- http://www.facebook.com (MoJo Roast, INC)
- http://www.whohub.com (MoJo Roast)
- http://www.twitter.com (MoJoRoaster)

Virtual Education in Action

Our first stories chronicle how two virtual business pioneers have applied the concepts we discuss in this book to transform their existing businesses. It almost sounds too easy: take an existing business, apply some emerging tools and techniques, and magically everything turns to gold. If only it was as easy as MoJo Roast and An African Villa make it sound. The story that follows highlights the complicated nature of the virtual world. Sometimes pioneers are ahead of their time, as was almost certainly the case of our next pioneer.

In the interest of full transparency, a colleague of John's who is a very good friend of his penned the story that follows. Dr. Lori Willoughby is the chair of the business information technology department at Minot State University (where John works). In fact, a key reason John joined the university was because of the forward-thinking, innovative leaders who develop an undergraduate degree in virtual business. Although today the concepts of virtual business are becoming commonplace, in 2004 when this degree received State Board of Higher Education approval it was the only degree like it in the country. Remember, 2004 was the same year as Facebook came to fruition, so much has changed in such a short time.

Here is Dr. Willoughby's story, in her own words:

The days of doing business solely in a brick and mortar environment are gone. They have been enhanced with the virtual environment. This requires a change in the skill set of students graduating with a bachelor's degree in business. The business students of tomorrow will need to function in a virtual environment necessitating the need for a tool kit that includes how to function as a virtual employee, manage a virtual employee or team, and communicate with virtual customers.

In a rural, sparsely populated state, such as North Dakota, the idea of virtual business is an exciting opportunity. With this new opportunity comes the challenge of creating a new business degree that will prepare the students to manage a virtual business. The questions that need addressing include what types of businesses would benefit from a virtual business degree, what types of courses must be included in the degree, what types of technology would need to be included, and what learning outcomes would be required of students seeking to become managers of a virtual business.

In 2004, the business information technology department at Minot State University began the research to develop this new degree. A panel of experts representing several managers and employees of virtual business was formed to participate in a Delphi study to help answer the following questions:

1. How would you define a virtual business?
2. How would you define a virtual organization?
3. How would you define a virtual employee?
4. What type of business will this degree benefit?
5. What does a graduate of the virtual business degree look like?

6. What are the assessment criteria and learning outcomes that would measure the success of the program?

7. What should the curriculum for this degree look like?

The answers to those questions were used to develop the criteria and the curriculum for the new bachelor of science virtual business degree as well as a minor in virtual business. Although the degree is in the business information technology department, it truly is an interdepartmental degree with an emphasis on virtual technology and management skills. The degree is offered on campus and online.

One would think that creating the degree would be the difficult part, but actually it was the easy part. It was easy to gather the panel, pose the questions, and come to a consensus on the answers. The difficult part has been attracting students to the degree. This seems to be a twofold problem; understanding what a degree in virtual business would mean and getting students to declare the major.

During the creation of the degree there was substantial support from the managers of several virtual businesses; however, that support didn't transcend out to the business community. This made it very difficult for the promotion of the degree. I truly believe that the business community didn't and still doesn't fully understand the differences between e-commerce and virtual business. In fact, there are many educators who don't understand the difference. I have presented the creation and need for the degree at two national conferences where the same difficulty existed. Although the methodology used to create the degree has been complemented, much of the discussion time has focused on the definition of a virtual business. The panel of experts, used in the original research study, defined a virtual business as a business that integrates the services of many organizations by replacing proximity with communication technology and has technology and people that drive a successful business model independent of geography. E-commerce consists of conducting business over the Internet or through a network. The major difference is that a virtual business isn't constrained to a traditional brick and mortal business with employees and customers in one physical location. The virtual business may be geographically separate from the customers and employees are typically separated geographically.

The lack of a clear understanding of the difference between e-commerce and virtual business has many faculty teaching in information systems degrees confused and wondering if there really is a need for a specific major. In 2004 when the degree was developed, there seemed to be a clear separation between the types of businesses conducting business virtually and electronically. Then most of the virtual businesses were those providing service such as technology support, medical assistance, insurance, and hotel or vacation reservations, while e-commerce businesses focused on selling a product. Today the list of virtual businesses includes a wider segment of business and now includes the typical e-commerce business.

As the business information technology department contemplates the future of the virtual business degree, there is clearly a need to consider blending the courses into the current management information systems degree or stay the course and continue developing and marketing the virtual business degree.

For more information, see http://www.minotstateu.edu/business.

A Virtual CEO

A true pioneer in the field penned the following story. Chris C. Ducker set out a plan to become a virtual CEO, a goal that many people contemplate, but that few actually work toward, and even fewer ever achieve. Well, Chris is very unique because by the end of 2010 he had achieved his goal of being a virtual CEO—this is the epitome of virtual business in action.

The story that follows is an adaptation of a blog post by Chris. We highly recommend a visit to Chris' website (see http://www .virtualbusinesslifestyle.com), where you can track his progress. The following short story highlights the dynamic and quickly changing nature of the virtual world; it also reminds us of the incredible possibilities of the new world.

In his own words, here is Chris's story:

Everybody wants the 4-hour workweek dream of being able to make money while they sleep or travel around the world, myself included, if the truth be told. But let's face it—it's pretty hard to do. The fact is, however, it used to be a hell of a lot harder than it is today, and I believe that as time continues to go by, it will actually become a lot easier than it is today, even. Here's why . . .

The new-age entrepreneur is a totally different breed of entrepreneur than we had 10 or 20 years ago. We are now a lot more tech savvy in general. We are also hungrier, I believe, than ever before to make money. And we have this remarkable business partner just ready and waiting to get into bed with us and help us to start making money—perhaps not overnight, but nonetheless. That partner is called "The Internet."

If you have an idea for a product or a service that you feel can genuinely help solve a problem for someone, get them to the next level in their career, or just make their life easier, then you can, utilizing the Internet and all that goes with it (such as social media), start making money while you sleep.

How I Am Now Making Money While I Sleep

A couple of months ago I set up a new consultancy service, Virtual Staff Finder (see http://www.virtualstafffinder.com). Since then, I have done very little search engine optimization (SEO) on the website and absolutely no traditional marketing at all for the service. All I've done is focus on the community that I have been lucky enough to build online and to utilize the power of incoming leads from the website of my outsourcing company, the Live2Sell Group.

I set up the Virtual Staff Finder (VSF) service because every day we get a lot of inquiries from entrepreneurs all around the world wanting to hire virtual assistants and other types of virtual staff (telemarketers, bookkeepers, and so on) but want them to be based at home, for the cost saving benefits, obviously.

Although as a company, this is something that we didn't used to do, the businessman inside of me finally came around to thinking that it was a real waste to a) not be able to help these entrepreneurs and b) not make some money from doing so.

The Process of Building My Online Consultancy Business

I did my research and found out that there was nobody else out there, with the experience and reputation in the outsourcing industry that I have, that was doing anything similar. So I got going with it. Here's what I did to get this "idea" to market in less than 4 weeks:

1. Brainstormed and eventually registered virtualstafffinder.com domain name.
2. Plotted out how the process of the service would work, fine-tuning it to death to make it as simple as possible for both the entrepreneurs using the service and us, too!
3. Sat with my web developer (who works for me full time, in house) to come up with a concept for the website and a minimum of three different designs. I also decided that I didn't want the site to be a blog style but rather a static website that required very little attention, to save my time.
4. Put together the written content, and shot the "welcome" video clip.
5. Set up several different avenues, locally, within the Philippines to be able to find the talent needed from the virtual staff side of things (which is actually still ongoing all the time, although it is now done by my VSF project manager).
6. Got going with an e-Junkie account (see http://www.e-junkie .com) and linked it up via PayPal to be able to accept online payments.
7. Tweaked and tweaked the website until we were happy with it (we will, however, be making some changes soon).
8. Went live!

And that is it. Not a lot required, and to be very honest, if my web development guy wasn't working on several projects at once, the chances are we could have got this entire thing up and running in perhaps half the time.

Since the launch, we've had 25 people sign up for the service (average of 3 per week) at a rate of $350 a pop. That's $8,750 in around

8 weeks, or $4,375 a month—almost $220 per business day. And here's the clincher, above and beyond everything else. I've made the majority of those sales while I was sleeping. Seriously.

Because I live here in the Philippines, when you guys are up and about in the United States, I'm hitting the sack—usually by your lunch time. So when I wake up in the morning (around midnight EST most days), I check my e-mail and start the day with a smile.

Here are a couple of instances where sales have come in at odd times just recently. I've had two sales come through while at my son's playgroup (on separate occasions). I had two come in within the space of a 3-hour meeting with a client when I was in the United States last month, one at BlogWorld and just yesterday I had three sales come through while working out and then having lunch with my wife.

Why I Wrote This Story

I wrote this story because I get so many e-mails every month from people that are interested in starting some kind of "make money" venture online but either (a) are not sure how to get started, (b) don't have a solid idea, or (c) can't believe that it's really possible and therefore never really go for it.

The main point here more than anything else is that I had an idea, I realized that there was a hole in the market and that the idea was going to be solving a problem for people (in this case, saving people valuable time more than everything else) and used the resources and people around me to make it happen—quickly. Can you do the same—YES!

Fact: Everyone has the chance to make money while they sleep or get beaten up by toddlers at their son's playgroup. You just have to simply plan and execute. Stop procrastinating and get going with it. Start it up. Promote it. Sell it. And make money from it.

For more information, visit http://www.virtualbusinesslifestyle .com.

A Crowdsourcer Extraordinaire

This next story is from Alex Blom, a serial entrepreneur, born and raised in Australia, who has founded and successfully exited multiple companies. Alex is currently recognized as one of the top digital entrepreneurs in North America and Australia. What most people do not know is that Alex is 22 and founded his first business at the age of 16. He was going to school, successfully growing and selling businesses, and most recently completed his business degree from the University of Wollongong in Australia. I (Cindy Gordon) met Alex when he was looking for a mentor and to be employed in Canada for 2 years so he could start a business in North America. His story follows and reflects three qualities of leadership to be cherished: (a) encourage entrepreneurship at earlier ages in life; (b) consider the value of crowdsourcing: how to successfully build trust with online relationships to grow a business; and (c) do it once and do it again with more confidence!

I grew up in a smaller town on the eastern coast of New South Wales, Australia. Around 10 years ago the "Internet thing" was happening in my area. Yes, many other towns had already noted the benefits but some towns adopt slower than others. I knew I had the technical and sales ability to bring these businesses online and promote their presences, and more importantly was one of the few who could, but I faced several challenges:

1. With little money in the bank, I needed to establish a strong technical infrastructure and team to complete client projects.
2. I needed the ability to offer a "full" solution to clients and a way to cover my technical knowledge gaps,
3. And the biggest challenge: I was in my early years of high school. Attending meetings in a 9–5 capacity was impractical and being so young, it was difficult to inspire confidence in clients.

Today outsourcing, and perhaps even crowdsourcing, are known terms, commonly accepted practices, and are easy to access. Filling gaps is not a question of where and how but instead who and for how much. Sadly this was not the case back then.

I turned to online forums, a popular communication channel at the time, to communicate with other vendors and gain business by overflow. More importantly, I needed to generate a list of contractors who were available on call, with no cash outlay, to fill my knowledge gaps. The challenge was that those with the technical ability from Western countries were seeing they could capitalize on their own skills and were unwilling to participate. In turn, I focused on forging relationships with individuals in emerging countries to be available in an elastic, on-demand capacity. With no cash in the bank, all these relationships were forged over the Internet.

Within a few years, early pioneers tried to capitalize on the concept of crowdsourcing with hosted forum contests. Most failed, partly because they lacked sophisticated websites and partly because the contractors lacked quality. There was a burning desire, especially in the outsourced technology community, on how to effectively leverage the combined talents and sell to our local communities.

By this point I expanded my business to offering technology services and support (i.e., website hosting). Again, locating customers was never a question. In many ways the Internet had not been settled, demand was exceeding supply, and leaving online forum posts kept business consistent. Excluding more capital outlay, I faced a larger knowledge gap than I had faced before. Not only did I need to manage an existing service-based business but I lacked any knowledge on how to properly maintain servers or establish such a clustered technical infrastructure.

It is around this time that emerging market firms were created by locals, leveraging offices of 10–15 engineers across hundreds of companies at once. They would monitor technical questions from customers and infrastructure in return for micropayments (generally $1–$3) per issue solved. This is perhaps one of the earliest illustrations of modern-day crowdsourcing techniques.

It is only now, nearly 8 years later, that crowdsourcing is reaching general popularity. Looking back into the technology services industry new models are being innovated to answer the shortfalls of crowdsourcing. The reality is that virtual businesses, by necessity, are far ahead in their business models.

Since selling these companies, I have gone on to be awarded Young Citizen of the Year, create other companies, and manage sales and marketing organizations. In each of these roles, I have seen continued crowdsourcing as a key way to handle elastic projects and manage knowledge effectively.

I've also been watching the rise of social media quite closely. The entire success of social media can be attributed to a flipped crowdsourcing model and I attribute much of my popularity to my knowledge here.

I have now joined Helix Commerce International Inc. (Helix) as their chief technical officer and Social and Innovation Practice Leader. Growth is also about mentorship and trusting friendships. As I look forward to what the future offers, I am actively cultivating networks for my next big thing and ensuring that I am surrounded by experienced leaders. For example, I have now cultivated a Social Media following of over 40,000 people, and I respond to each individual personally.

A Millennial Entrepreneur

The next story is about Spencer Thompson, who like Alex Blom, had a young start as an entreprenuer. The idea for Sokanu came to him in high school. Sokanu (http://www.sokanu.com) is a place to discover your passion in life. Spencer recognized that it was very evident that the majority of his graduating class didn't have any idea as to what they wanted to do with the rest of their lives. In high school, guidance is typically given from parents, friends, and career counselors about what path to take into post-secondary education and beyond. However, what about guidance from an online source? With the majority of people using Facebook, e-mail, and Twitter as methods of communication, online networks are changing the way that we communicate and share information. The story that follows is about Spencer's roots and insights on how he plans to take advantage of the incredible opportunity online by building a brand new platform aimed at helping each individual find their true purpose in life. His vision is, "We at Sokanu believe that every single person put on this planet is able to do something amazing. We help you find that something amazing, online."

Sokanu is a new web platform with the mission of helping individuals find their passion in life, which has grown from a single neuron fire into a fully featured product today. But the intermittent steps are the most interesting, as every single journey is unique. And while I am still young and still early into the journey, there are so many things that I have learned. Going through any business, small or large, is an amazing process that only a few people ever get to experience.

I graduated from high school in 2009, seeing a huge market opportunity among my classmates and decided to pair that with the explosive growth and virality of the social web. When I was younger, for some background, I was enamored of becoming a particle physicist. I wanted to work at CERN, discover the Theory of Everything, and become like Einstein. I then started reading about entrepreneurship, got hooked, and read some more. But despite the amount of reading, real-life business was totally different. That was my first lesson.

When we first started to develop Sokanu from a kernel of an idea into a product, we knew nothing. (The "we" includes my mom; she is my cofounder.) Nobody in my family has a business background, let alone knew anything about the tech industry. But after reading about entrepreneurship, I was in a state of mind that I didn't care what it took, I was going to become an entrepreneur, period. Some of the books that really helped me get started were *Think and Grow Rich* and *The Magic of Thinking Big*. These are always the first two books I recommend to any person, regardless of what he or she is doing. I still reread them time to time. But these books were my mentors and my starting point. And so the journey began.

As I started to research some things related to the web, I thought I understood how it worked. You build a website, and then you got someone to market it. By doing that, millions of people flood onto your site, generating millions of dollars that allow you to live a life of opulence and wealth. Right? We began working with a business advisor, who was my best friend and badminton partner's dad. His job was to help small businesses start and grow to become real businesses. Knowing nothing, it seemed as if this person was the supreme ruler of the business world. And so we began to work with him on a weekly basis. His first recommendation was to a web designer he knew (i.e., the person to build the easy "website").

We began to work with this designer (and keep that word in mind) as we learned about the design process. We brainstormed, wrote down some ideas, sketched out some wireframes (awful ones looking back) and built a plan for the future. The only problem was that the design shop wanted to stop what they were doing and join Sokanu full time. And of course, they wanted to keep their salaries too. Keep in mind that we were a couple of months into the learning process, and now we were looking at paying $90,000+ for salaries to people we barely knew. Needless to say, we walked away quickly.

Lesson learned: Always know what you are getting upfront. You write the contracts, you set the timeline. When other people are in control, it is bad for your business.

The next step, we figured, was to go to some professionals. No more working with these local guys I said. At the time, at a conference near us, a marketing firm from Vancouver had sent a social media expert to speak. I had done some research on the firm and had decided we would like to work with them and made an appointment with the speaker. One introduction led to another, and soon we had both a marketing and development firm working for us in Vancouver. This time, however, the dealings were much more professional. We worked with both firms for an entire summer, coming up with a marketing strategy document, wireframes, slide decks, sitemaps, rollout strategies, and ultimately a list of costs. The amount of money these two firms would have wanted to be paid (remember this is a third party, not an internalized team) would have destroyed us from day one. Once again, a very simple solution presented itself: Move on. But again, the development team saw a way to riches and fun and wanted to close up shop and become our internalized development team. Sounds great, right? Well, personalities didn't mix, and of course, they wanted to be paid first.

Lesson learned: Never outsource your core competencies.

After these great lessons (I try not to call them mistakes, as we knew very little) we were in a position where we were learning to become more and more careful. I had read a quote that Donald Trump had written that said, "Hire the best and then don't trust them." While you may not have to be that extreme, the lesson in business is that it is all about people, people, and then people again. Speaking of people, we had finally connected with some great ones. We had previously had a chat with a fabulous PR firm down in San Francisco and set up a meeting to meet with them. When we flew down, they set up a couple of meetings in Silicon Valley for us. These meetings were unbelievably helpful, as they give us an indication of how little we knew. After the meetings, we had a new realization as to what we had to do, and the level of intelligence that we were competing with. It was time to get back to business.

Lesson learned: Always remember, the most intelligent people always realize how little they actually know.

We hired a fourth-year university student late in the year to help us develop the alpha product. We had moved from a "launch a website" model to a "product development" model. In product development, your path develops in stages, first with an alpha product (usually private), testing, followed by a public beta, more testing, and finally a fully featured product launch. Some of the best examples in recent years of product development execution are Mint.com and Xobni.com. And so we started developing, month after month. The product was really coming together, and we were beginning to develop a relationship. The product was three-quarters of the way to launch when the developer had both his fourth-year exams and was getting married. We completely understood these events, as they are monumental in any person's life. We went to his wedding, met the family, and had a good time. But when he came back, I noticed that all lines of communication had been broken off. He ignored all calls, didn't respond to e-mails, and basically left us high and dry. It was just a bit of bad luck, but one that another great lesson was learned.

Lesson learned: you can never predict dates, even when things seem to be going well. From an outsider's perspective, they don't care about your developer problems; they just want to see a product. Get back on the horse and get a product out.

An iRetail Virtual CEO

This next leadership story is from David McDougall, the CEO of Vision Max Solutions, based in Toronto, Ontario, Canada, whose pioneering intelligent and immersive retail leadership efforts have allowed him to rethink the retail shopping experiences using virtual avatars and 3D immersive experiences. They have partnered with global leaders like Alcatel-Lucent, Arrow, Bloomingdale's, and *Elle* magazine to bring virtualization, immersive, and intelligent technology experiences to the retail industry. A case summarizing their recent successes at the Consumer Electronics Show in January 2011 follows. Now scaling Vision Max's iRetail solution gives us a vision of how everything will change around us as increasingly immersive and social experiences will integrate into all core business processes. Business in retail goes virtual.

What will the future of retail be like in going virtual? Recently, I had the pleasure of seeing firsthand the reactions of scores of people at the Consumer Electronics Show (CES) as they strolled through our Alcatel-Lucent booth in Las Vegas in early January 2011. What caught their attention? Well, was it a 6-foot-tall blonde Swedish model from *Elle* magazine? Yes, but not what you might expect. She was a virtual avatar on an 82" LCD flat panel projected off the screen in new patented 3D technology. She could move to easily stand in front of you and just with the click of a button on a wireless tablet, she was wearing a new outfit, while twirling around to give a 360-degree vantage point. Samantha, the actual 6-foot-tall *Elle* magazine model, was controlling her own avatar and virtual wardrobe. She was able to stand in a new white light "shadow scanning" technology that in 12 seconds takes over 300 measurements in a complete body scan from head to toe. These measurements are stored in a virtual Software as a Service (SaaS) cloud and the avatar software takes over generating an exact wireframe that allows your new avatar ready to try on your virtual wardrobe. During the experience, Samantha talked to a Virtual Personal Stylist (VPS), over 1,000 miles away in Dallas using a high-definition video conference session and telepresence. By starting the video conference, Samantha has allowed the VPS to have access to her avatar and learn about her preferences, measurements, and style choices. The stylist now helps Samantha by showing her video fashion advice recommended by *Elle* magazine on the latest trends and styles. She can also watch the videos and see the images of outfits that she can like or dislike and give feedback to Samantha's style preferences. The stylist provides some of her own advice and guides Samantha to her virtual wardrobe with a new set of outfits that the VPS has recommended to her. In a matter of less than 5 minutes, Samantha has gone through 20 outfits and has added 3 of them to her shopping cart using her measurements to get the perfect size.

The integrated point of sale (POS) solution in the store retrieves all the items in Samantha's shopping cart and the mobile salesperson checks current inventory for that store knowing which items are in stock. As the salesperson consults her mobile POS tablet, they gather the items for Samantha from the store. They use the store layout planogram to guide newer sales people to the merchandise and check it off the list—it decides the most efficient route to pick up the items in store. If Samantha also happens to see something she likes while walking around the store she can quickly add that to the mobile POS tablet by scanning the bar code. However, upon scanning the bar code the tablet POS provides a warning that according to Samantha's measurements, it would recommend a smaller size as this item of clothing tends to fit a little larger. The salesperson finishes collecting the in-store items and notes that there is one item missing in-store and offers to have the item directly shipped to Samantha's home or office address free of charge with overnight shipping, or she can come back to the store tomorrow and the item would be put aside for her. Samantha works right next to the mall and says she will be back tomorrow to pick up the item. The salesperson takes Samantha's credit card and processes the transaction right there on their mobile POS tablet.

Another loyal shopper, Amanda, enters the store with her mobile smartphone running the store's mobile app. Amanda has already spent time doing her research with her own personal avatar, and using her TV and Wii game console at home has gone shopping virtually. She has tried on many new outfits on her avatar and added the ones she likes the most to her virtual wardrobe. For a few outfits that she liked but was not 100% sure about, Amanda clicked to post the outfit to her Facebook page to ask for feedback from her social network. Within a few minutes, she had the feedback she was looking for to make her decision to buy the outfit. Amanda had the choice to order the outfits with the click of a button but decided she wanted to see and feel the fabric—this was important to her before purchasing. Now in the store, Amanda is greeted by a salesperson and lets her know she has items in her virtual wardrobe for purchasing. The salesperson presses a button on her tablet to receive information and Amanda presses a button on her smartphone application and the information is instantly transmitted to the salesperson's mobile POS tablet via Bluetooth. (If Amanda did not have a smartphone, she could have signed on to the mobile POS tablet with her e-mail and PIN and the information for that store only would have been transmitted.)

All outfits, correct sizes, location in the store, and pricing information along with any electronic coupons for in-store pickup are transferred in less than a second. The salesperson is also provided some suggestions entered by the head office into the application for other items that go well with the outfits chosen and can show Amanda other recommendations chosen by the retailer's fashion experts. Some of the recommended items may not be in-store, so the salesperson will be notified and can easily take over and show the item on one of several digital signage displays around the store for a larger view by directing the picture and information to an unused display.

The salesperson collects all the items and when Amanda elects to pay cash the salesperson brings all items to the front, puts them in a bag and transfers Amanda to the electronic queue management digital signage. She is fourth in "line" to pay cash. When it is almost Amanda's turn, her smartphone vibrates asking her to come to the cash. She can see her position in the queue on her smartphone store application and the integrated in-store digital signage, and if she doesn't arrive in time for her turn, the POS application can send a gentle automated page via the store's PA system. If Amanda has picked up something else in the store while she is waiting, she can simply add it to her order before paying. All items that were purchased at the POS are now permanently stored in Amanda's Virtual Wardrobe to be able to mix and match with other outfits that she owns or would like to own. Amanda can now access images and avatars of her purchases any time in the future to show friends or match up later. She is also able to share view access to her close friends that may request a trade of outfits the next time they meet.

As a CEO of Vision Max, I have been immersed in innovative SaaS solutions in the cloud and only recently have evolved our company's future business model to focus on iRetail to create the world's most innovative virtual shopping software to take advantage of business going virtual.

The future is incredible as one can imagine easily how stores world-wide can help to create these cloud-stored Fashion Virtual Wardrobes. They can target market the best outfits to their customers by creating a personal advertising campaign. By using cloud SaaS browser tools, they can run a campaign to build a blind list of customers that they feel would appreciate a particular outfit. They can choose from their 100,000 customer list, to only choose customers that have shopped in-store or online in the last 3 months (list goes down to 75,000), then woman aged 35–50 (list goes down to 25,000), who like blue as one of their top three colors and have spent more than $100 on a blouse and finally are a size 10–14 (the list is culled down to 5,000). With that blind list, the store can send them a recommendation of an outfit with this new $120 blue blouse being worn by their own avatar and where they can click to buy it.

The possibilities are endless once people have the ability to create their fashion profile, have their avatars, measurements, and preferences in one central cloud hosted place. The key will be to give the customer the ability to use this information in many of the places they shop (not having to create an avatar for each retailer).

The future of retail is changing and the problem of guesswork in online shopping is being solved through better visualization and sizing capabilities. Recognizing that many still love the retail store experience, we think that that too is dramatically enhanced using a fully integrated cloud solution.

This new business model for our company is requiring us to tap into new skills in design, virtual and immersive technologies, supply chain innovation by bringing the fashion influencers with the stores and technology solution providers to create a compelling and high value iRetail virtual immersive experience that can be experienced online or in real life.

This type of stretch puts tremendous pressure on my CEO leadership style to be more agile and to think in all directions all at once but also ensure a conviction of clarity and focus as the learning is in real-time. Each new experience helps us to identify patterns for driving scale with our new offerings. At the same time, we often feel like we are walking potentially on hot coals as the markets are unconditioned and most customers cannot express their needs in this area as they have not experienced virtual worlds of this nature. So every day I wake up I tell myself and my team that we need to be role model listeners as the journey of leadership is in series of conversations versus the transactional sale.[6]

Now You Know

In this chapter, we had the opportunity to hear firsthand from some virtual business pioneers. Although it is difficult to distill the most important advice they provided, we think the following lessons learned and tips are especially worthy of your consideration:

- One of the best aspects of social media marketing through sites like TripAdvisor is that it is free of charge. However, leaders must be aware that it is a two-edged sword that can be wielded by a fickle foe. It is not possible to please everybody all the time but as far as is possible, leaders must attempt to satisfy even the most fastidious of critics. When not possible, then a gracious apology and the promise of a "try harder" attitude goes a long way.
- Everyone has the chance to make money while they sleep. You just have to simply plan and execute. Stop procrastinating and get going with it. Start it up. Promote it. Sell it. And make money from it.

- The top tip from one of our pioneers: crowdsourcing is a key way to handle elastic projects and manage knowledge effectively.
- Always know what you are getting upfront. You write the contracts, you set the timeline. When other people are in control, it is bad for your business.
- Never outsource your core competencies
- Always remember, the most intelligent people always realize how little they actually know.
- Even with detailed planning and creative marketing, some innovative virtual business ideas will not succeed, likely because they were before their time.
- One of our pioneers suggested her secrets to success included the following:
  - Virtualization
  - Passion
  - Values
  - Can-do attitude
  - Determination
  - Education
  - Willingness to share and mentor
  - Concentrating on following your dreams and not chasing others
  - Believing in yourself
  - Having a gift and giving back
  - Joining groups and organizations that pertain to your field
  - Always being the best that you can be

CHAPTER 4

The Power of Sharing

Any company trying to compete . . . must figure out a way to engage the mind of nearly every employee.[1]

—Jack Welch, former CEO of GE

Enabler 3: A Culture of Sharing and Collaboration

In the abstract, we suggested that as the first decade of the 21st century drew to a close, many observers reflected on the *revolution* that had transformed the way people connect, communicate, and collaborate. Although there is some question as to whether we witnessed a true revolution, there is no question that a convergence of ubiquitous communication networks, low-cost appliances, exponential web-based content growth, and a cultural shift toward sharing has created an always-on, always-connected, always-sharing environment. Today many of us assume that no matter where we are, we should be able to connect immediately to our cyber security blanket.

We continued by suggesting that this convergence has revolutionized how we connect with friends, family, and businesses. Today, executives, students, and soccer moms are equally connected virtually everywhere they go. But why is this of concern to us? The new reality is that all these people are able to use this omnipresent connection to perform business functions that once required a physical presence. The separation between work, family, and life is simply one endless stream of "connectedness."

In chapter 2, as we discussed social technology, we suggested that the single largest cultural-technological innovation of the 21st century was social networking. We argued that social networking sites help people connect with other people to collaborate in an online environment. Some are designed for connecting friends and family, while others facilitate professional connections. Chapter 2 highlighted how social technology is changing the business environment and enabling the power of virtual business. We also reminded you that there will be changes and some of the tools and techniques will become obsolete over time; however, the underlying power of connecting people will remain.

As you read these chapters and practitioner stories, you may have believed that technology alone was creating this new world; however, we are not convinced. Clearly, technology, as we pointed out, is a key enabler, but technology alone is not enough to sustain the revolution. Technology certainly fueled the growth and provided some heretofore unimaginable opportunities, but it is only part of the puzzle. Perhaps the most important sentence in our abstract was the following: there is no question that a convergence of ubiquitous communication networks, low-cost appliances, exponential web-based content growth, and a cultural shift toward 24/7 sharing has created an always-on, and always-connected environment. We believe the emphasized text; the idea of a cultural shift is absolutely key to the success of virtual business.

A Generation (or Two) of Hoarders

During World War II, the United States launched a very successful campaigned titled "loose lips sink ships." The premise of the campaign was to remind U.S. servicemen and women, especially those serving in England awaiting the D-day invasion, that they must not share anything that might allow the enemy to learn of the Allies' war plans. Well, it seems that 60 years later this culture of "need to know" is alive and well in many organizations. Perhaps the adage of today should be "tight lips, business slips" because we believe that failure to share frequently results in lost opportunities.

To illustrate the point, here is a short story that we included in *A Leader's Guide to Knowledge Management*. The story is loosely based on a real company, but given we embellished a few parts to make our point, we must declare it is a fictional company. Let us call them IQ.

IQ is a well-known brand that for many years operated with a divisional organization structure. Once a year, each of the divisional vice presidents was afforded the opportunity to brief the board of directors on their plans for the future. This rare occasion was seen to be a time when senior executives could describe the next big thing that would provide IQ with a competitive advantage.

One year, the printer division's vice president was extremely excited about his time with the board. He was sure the directors would agree that his new idea, a printer that could also scan, would be a history-making innovative product, a must-have for many small businesses. The R&D arm of the printer division had been working secretly on the project for some time. After investing considerable resources, their prototype was ready to be showcased to the board. They were very proud of their clandestine operation; it was quite a coup that none of the technology press had picked up on their work.

Finally, the big day arrived. The vice president was waiting patiently in the anteroom reviewing his presentation. Suddenly, an unprecedented level of applause from inside the boardroom interrupted his thoughts. Shortly afterward the vice president of the scanner division emerged, smiling, and clearly happy with her performance in the room. The printer executive politely asked his colleague why the board erupted into applause. After a short pause, she replied, "I just showed the board our prototype for the next big thing . . . a scanner that can also print." Needless to say, the printer executive was no longer excited about briefing the board.

The moral of the story is that a "need to know" culture, which is commonplace in many technology companies, does not facilitate knowledge sharing. Here is a case where senior executives did not share, let alone collaborate on the project. Imagine if the two divisions shared resources and knowledge to design the printer scanner. Regrettably, many organizations fall victim to the organizational malady because they do not foster a collaborative environment with a need to share philosophy.

Of course we are not recommending that organizational leaders haphazardly tell the competition everything, nor are we encouraging employees to deliberately sabotage companies by releasing critical information. However, somewhere between "need to know" and "give everything to WikiLeaks," there is an organizational culture that encourages and rewards responsible sharing.

Hoarders Meet the Sharers

Many people would agree that the "need to know" philosophy is a common trait of the so-called Baby Boomer Generation, those born between about 1946 and 1964. Well, if the Baby Boomers are the need to know generation, then it might be said that the Millennial Generation, those born between about 1980 and 2000, might be the need to share generation. This is the generation that grew up digital, hardwired to everything; in other words, they are the group of children who had access to technology at a very young age. We are not generally huge fans of the labels that are attached to various age groups; these labels are loaded with assumptions. For example, when we generalize by saying the millennials grew up digital, that ignores the fact that many millennials grew up in homes where technology was considered a luxury and not universally available—often referred to as the digital divide.

Understanding that we must be careful not to generalize, it is true to say that many of the millennials did grow up digital and many have adopted a culture where they openly share. Frequently, we hear educators, parents, and other stakeholders comment that the youth of today share too much and that they will regret their openness in the future. We have all heard stories of high school students sharing pictures or stories on social media sites that are inappropriate and have career implications downstream or moments of embarrassment that cannot be erased from the permanent web. We are not necessarily convinced this inappropriate sharing is unique to the millennials, as we have often read of much more "mature" people falling into the same trap. The difference might be that for the millennials sharing is a natural trait, whereas for the others it might be a learned trait.

There is research that supports that different age groups share at different levels. Returning to the Forrester research that resulted in groundswell, we can see some compelling evidence. For example, using the creator category of the Social Technographic ladder as an example, we see a distinct difference by age. Based on Forrester's most recent research that was conducted in early 2010 and included 26,913 respondents, we learned that different age groups of creators share more frequently. Recall that creators are those adult Internet users who write or upload video, music, or text, in other words share what they know. The following is a breakdown by age group and the percentage of each age group that create content (share):

- 46% of 18–24 year olds create and share content
- 32% of 25–34 year olds create and share content
- 23% of 35–44 year olds create and share content
- 19% of 45–54 year olds create and share content
- 12% of those 55 or older create and share content[2]

Perhaps the time is right to stop the debate on the merits of sharing and instead harness the power of the desire to share. Is there a way that your organization can benefit from the desire of the younger people to share what they know? Is there a way that you can develop cross-generational teams that combine the sharing talents of the 18–24-year-olds with the vast organizational knowledge of the 55 and older group? Explore how to infuse the uniqueness of each generation into a corporate culture that embraces collaboration and knowledge sharing leveraging as the preferred working styles, as not everyone will want to use solutions like Yammer for microblogging or wikis for shared document cocreation.

Let's also not forget the importance of real authentic voice-to-voice conversations and the art of effective discourse or dialogue. Dialogue is essential online or offline to solve the large problems of a multicultural or global society. Finding a way that allows humans to talk, think, and act together makes it possible to talk across our differences and invent new directions. To have successful collaboration outcomes, dialogue is a key competency that cannot be overlooked.

Dr. William Isaacs is the pioneer in this area. "Effective dialogue is often the missing link that frees people to take a quantum leap in vision and action," he says. "If everybody got the idea that there's a different way to talk and think together, the seed of a very new kind of inter-action could begin to sprout." Isaacs, who in 1990 cofounded MIT's Organizational Learning Center, is now a lecturer at the Sloan School of Management and is director of the Institute's Dialogue Project.[3] People who think and talk together effectively possess the following qualities:

- *Listening.* We must listen not only to others but to ourselves, dropping our assumptions, resistance and reactions.
- *Respecting.* We must allow rather than try to change people with a different viewpoint.

- *Suspending.* We must suspend our opinions, step back, change direction, and see with new eyes.
- *Voicing.* We must speak our own voice. Find our own authority, giving up the need to dominate.[4]

One of the key factors we need to ensure we appreciate as we undergo this social 24/7 connected transition is to understand that the Internet may also be an attempt of our isolated culture to somehow return to community values. People seem to imagine that if we are digitally connected, then we would all be in touch, and the great malaise of the age—the isolation and disconnection many of us feel—would be allayed. But so far, the digital revolution is giving us connection but not necessarily human contact with its richest senses of touch. As the future unfolds and simulated touch and smell is integrated into the networks and web experiences, it will be more difficult for us to tell what is real or artificial.

We can send more information to each other via social networking solutions, but we are not necessarily any more capable of sharing understanding, insight, wisdom, or our hearts. Learning to talk and think together in honest and effective ways is an essential element to true human connectedness. Let's ensure as the communication means evolve, we also not forget what it is to be uniquely human.

Why Is Collaboration Important?

Collaboration is the act of people working together to reach a common goal. It also involves getting the right information to the right people at the right time to make the right decision. This sounds so simple—but collaboration is so much more than well-informed and speedy decisions to help organizations get work done.

Collaboration is the fundamental DNA or essence in the way that people in an organization function together to achieve a mutually desired outcome. This chapter defines collaboration and provides leading practices to demonstrate the value of collaboration in supporting an organization's growth. Collaboration, value networks, social networks, and open-source innovation (often called crowdsourcing) approaches to business virtualization are priorities with global leaders who understand that a new world order is rapidly evolving.

This new collaborative and more connected world is more adaptive, more agile, more fluid, more virtual, and finally, more collaborative and quite frankly more refreshing, fun, and inspiring. Just look at the energy of Gen X and Y in how they approach their day-to-day work practices. This precious energy needs to be harnessed to unleash further our human potential and also prepare for the Generation Virtuals growing up with 3D virtual avatars and animated worlds to make way for the entertainment social experiences overlaying all business processes. Just think of how much more enjoyable working in an SAP order entry system would be if the employees were connected to each other and able to enjoy peer-to-peer problem-solving support, creating conversations in real time. We spend more time at work in our lives than any other place—at least we can leave as boomers as a legacy is advocating for more inspiring virtual workplaces.

There is no question that collaborative business models are reaching deep into business model design logic and challenging our assumptions related to governance, strategy, organizational design, leadership, people practices, process, culture (core values and rituals), technology, and our performance measurement systems.

In order to understand the significance of collaboration, it is helpful to go back to the beginning. The first generation of business collaboration tools began with a focus on documents that were created and shared by individuals who used one device: primarily the personal computer. Information resided safely within the walls of the enterprise, and personal productivity over time improved. Collaboration shifted the focus from documents and personal computers to a more mobile and virtual model where people collaborated in social web-based sessions, defining the new fundamental unit of collaborative work, in which groups of individuals interact across company and geographic boundaries.

The goal of virtual collaboration is to create the experience of presence with the absence of being face to face, hence creating a virtualized experience. This new collaborative experience helps us cope with information overload by delivering only what we need, just when we need it. We can find experts in an instant and participate in social online conversation, using diverse social and virtual toolkits from a variety of devices, like blogs, videos, wikis, social networks, team spaces, and conferences. Fortunately, due to advanced security and policy management, we can also engage diverse stakeholders, including partners, customers, and suppliers in our one-to-many communications.

Collaborative conversations on the web form a new fundamental unit of collaborative work. The goal of a virtual collaborative conversation is to create the effect of presence within the absence of face-to-face (live) connections.

When we first wrote the book *Collaboration Commerce: The Next Competitive Advantage*,[5] it was very clear that collaboration is a participatory process leveraging social capital know-how that is also built upon strong cultural value foundations based on trust, reciprocity, networks, and risk-taking models. With global market dynamics stressing customer solutions that are real-time, agile, adaptive, and Internet accessible, the customer experience value chain is under a collaborative design rethink. Already attracting, developing, and retaining Gen X and Gen Y talent pools is a challenge; creating virtual businesses is a key success factor to drive a sustaining growth future.

For the first time in the history of academics and business leaders at the top of their game, we are seeing more aligned wisdom that collaboration is a fundamentally higher order of leading, thinking, and behaving; it is challenging old rigid views as we emerge to a more human organizational experience leveraging networked, virtual, social collaboration, and modernized design experiences that connect the mind, heart, and spirit to achieve higher productivity performance levels.

Effective collaboration can improve many aspects of an organization's performance, whether it is an increase in innovation capacity, increased time to market by streamlining the product-development process, taking time out of the sales cycle, reducing customer wait time in call centers, using instant messaging (IM) to find the person who can respond to an opportunity immediately, or avoiding travel costs due to unified and ubiquitous telepresence capabilities. There is sufficient evidence that hardwiring your organization to achieve collaboration and virtualization practices is critical for long-term growth and survivability.

When you implement more efficient processes, achieve faster time to market, and reduce cycle times, you extract more value from your collaboration investment. If you can identify opportunities to shorten the time needed to make critical decisions, there is no better place to invest than in investing in smarter, more collaborative, and more virtualized capabilities.

Where Is the Beef?

These good points all aside, the practical reality is that many executives still say, we get that this collaboration stuff is important, but how do we infuse it in our day-to-day management and operational practices so it really sticks? In other words, where is the evidence (where is the beef) that investing in collaborative practices and next generation technology solutions really makes a difference to the bottom line?

There are many types of collaboration reports of value in terms of strategic customer growth due to ensuring employee engagement practices are more collaborative and when there are more investments in human and social capital practices. Simply speaking, happier people interact more positively with customers, yielding stronger customer loyalty outcomes.

Perhaps the real beef is recognizing that we are human beings, and once our basic needs for safety and shelter are satisfied, humans thrive on having a sense of belonging. They develop a sense of connectedness and know their ideas are valued and respected. They are motivated to achieve higher levels of productivity, and hence they are more open to collaborate and work together to develop and deliver stronger products and services to their customers or stakeholders.

This sounds logical, and intuitively we know that this is right; however, we still like to overlay productivity return on investment (ROI) efficiency evidence to ensure for all the "tough nuts" that demand this rigor. We thought it prudent to enclose some recent research from credible sources, plus our own research with doing global e-collaboration and social virtual programs for many global organizations striving to get the business goes virtual formula right. These stories would be helpful for our readers.

Productivity ROI: Focus on Efficiency

Raising the productivity of knowledge talent whose jobs can't be automated is the next great human performance challenge—and the stakes are high.[6]

Cost savings is one traditional ROI predictor that executives still like to see in validating business value. ROI has long frustrated collaboration solution providers because of the difficulty in quantifying "soft" benefits such as corporate or brand reputation or employee satisfaction. Yet the corollary evidence is that investments in human capital (talent), creating a more balanced and fulfilling work environment increases customer satisfaction and also impacts growth levels. Simply happier people give more and execute more effectively. Studies such as Frederick Reichheld's *The Loyalty Effect* (1996) and James Heskett, W. Early Sasser, and Leonard Schlesinger's *The Service Profit Chain* (1997) produced the first sets of hard data quantifying these links. These collective studies conclude that there are direct and quantifiable links between customer service variables (such as satisfaction and loyalty), employee variables (such as satisfaction, enthusiasm, loyalty, commitment, capability, and internal service quality), and financial results. A Watson Wyatt Worldwide[7] study also found that the practice of maintaining a collegial, flexible workplace is associated with the second-largest increase in shareholder value (9%), suggesting that employee satisfaction is directly related to financial gain. One of the most well-researched studies was a 2001 study published in *Personnel Psychology* that examined whether positive employee behaviors and attitudes influence business outcomes or if the opposite, that positive business outcomes influence employee behavior, is true. Study findings include the following:

- The study broke down employee attitudes and satisfaction into five measurable employee behaviors: conscientiousness, altruism, civic virtue, sportsmanship, and courtesy.
- The study measured participants in the five categories, reviewed turnover rates within the participant population, and compared this data with the organizations' financial performance for the following year.
- Findings also supported the idea that employee satisfaction, behavior, and turnover predict the following year's profitability, and that these aspects have an even stronger correlation with customer satisfaction.[8]

As former CEO of GE, Jack Welsh has said, "Companies measure links between employee satisfaction and customer satisfaction and productivity by conducting employee surveys. Any company trying to compete . . . must figure out a way to engage the mind of nearly every employee."[9]

Return on Collaboration

The following section summarizes a recent Cisco report titled "The Return on Collaboration: Assessing the Value of Today's Collaboration Solution."[10] The report includes compelling arguments from a variety of experts for measuring collaboration and demonstrates the business value achieved through improved productivity.

Fortunately, there is increasing quality research that is rapidly putting the facts on the line, and in time, we will be able to move past the questions of if there is value in investing in collaboration and social business practices. The recent research, conducted by Frost and Sullivan, identifies a new model for measuring what it calls return on collaboration (ROC).[11] ROC measures the impact of collaboration on key functional areas. These include research and development, human resources, sales, marketing, investor relations, and public relations. Traditional ROI measures money gained or lost on an investment. In contrast, ROC tracks the amount of "improvement" derived from a financial investment in collaboration. The study identified research and development and sales and marketing as the functional areas with the highest ROC.

The study called *Meetings Around the World 2: Charting the Course of Advanced Collaboration*[12] is based on questionnaires completed by 3,662 information technology and line-of-business decision makers in 10 countries. Respondents represented enterprises plus small- and medium-sized businesses. Nearly half the organizations are using unified communications and collaboration tools ranging from enterprise instant messaging to Cisco TelePresence. Among the study's key findings is that collaboration is more than twice as important as strategic orientation and six times more important than market factors in determining business performance.

Frost and Sullivan observed the network effect at work in companies that collaborate. As more people interact, the organization enjoys more of the benefits of collaboration.[13] For example, engineers improved product development and lowered costs associated with innovation. Sales and marketing professionals saw improvements across sales performance, customer retention, and their ability to respond to competitive threats. Investor relations and public relations staff reported that collaboration helped them increase shareholder value and shape corporate reputations. Human resources teams found collaboration tools useful in recruitment, retention, and training activities.

To summarize, researchers also observed that the most profound effect was in the areas of the business where the largest numbers of people interact in many-to-many relationships that accelerate productivity and create value. The study revealed some other interesting findings:

- *Collaboration technologies can help reduce stress.* More than half of respondents say collaboration tools allow for greater balance between work and personal life and help them gain more control over their busy lives.
- *Confidence in virtual meetings is growing.* More than half think conferencing tools are a good alternative to visiting business contacts face to face.
- *Telecommuting is becoming more popular.* Almost half (47%) of respondents report having a formal telecommuting policy in place. However, less than a third (27%) telecommute at least once a week, and 22% telecommute on a daily basis. This tallies with the numbers in a Forrester study, which reported that one-third of workers telecommute at least some of the time.
- *The environment is a priority.* More than half (53%) say reducing an organization's carbon footprint and other environmental concerns are important factors in determining collaborative technology requirements.

In another research study conducted in early 2010, Salire Partners published a report on the operational ROI of collaboration.[14] Over a period of 3 years, they conducted hundreds of ROI analyses for companies of different sizes and in different industries around the globe that had deployed diverse collaboration technology solutions including unified communications, IP telephony, and collaboration and social media solutions. Researchers asked companies to report on the net benefit of their technology investment, the total expected cost to implement their solution, and the length of the payback period.

The report concluded that most companies—nearly 80%—see a positive return on their investment in collaboration technologies. Numerous important industries showed a 5-year ROI of more than 100% and payback periods of 21 to 40 months. And the positive results apply to companies large and small: Those with between 1,000 and 25,000 employees posted returns of more than 170%.

Collaboration enablement is a result of many factors, but to connect in real time, organizations must invest in collaborative technology to enable a broad array of business functions to make contact successfully. One conclusion is that a $1 million investment in collaboration tools and technologies will deliver a $4 million dollar "improvement."[15] However, this result fails to recognize the importance of adopting a collaborative culture. So while the study does highlight the role of culture and structure, more work is necessary in integrating these elements into measuring ROC.

Organizations find the most significant value in technology's ability to support complex and distributed teams, improve business activities like customer service and new product development, and provide greater reuse and manageability of documents and other content artifacts. It is important to also recognize that the technology enablement or virtualization of business is only one key success indicator and a foundational one; however, if the organizational culture and leadership behaviors are not aligned to collaboration outcomes, or employees are not motivated to engage to solve issues and challenges using the toolkits invested in— organizations will simply waste precious resources (budget, time, etc.) and achieve lackluster results.

What is important to understand is that organizations that invest more in collaboration business models and operating practices and integrate tools that support developing and fostering a stronger collaborative culture will enjoy greater benefits than those that concentrate on the basics.

Now You Know

- A convergence of ubiquitous communication networks, low-cost appliances, exponential web-based content growth, and a cultural shift toward sharing has created an always-on, always-connected, always-sharing environment. (We mentioned this in chapter 1, but it is important enough to repeat.)

- When you implement more efficient processes, achieve faster time to market, and reduce cycle times, you extract more value from your collaboration investment.
- Collaboration technologies can help reduce stress. More than half of respondents say collaboration tools allow for greater balance between work and personal life and help them gain more control over their busy lives.
- Confidence in virtual meetings is growing. More than half of the survey respondents think conferencing tools are a good alternative to visiting business contacts face to face.
- Telecommuting is becoming more popular. Almost half (47%) of respondents report having a formal telecommuting policy in place. However, less than a third (27%) telecommute at least once a week, and 22% telecommute on a daily basis. This tallies with the numbers in a Forrester study, which reported that one-third of workers telecommute at least some of the time.
- The environment is a priority. More than half (53%) of the survey respondents say reducing an organization's carbon footprint and other environmental concerns are important factors in determining collaborative technology requirements.

CHAPTER 5

Making Sense of
Virtual Worlds

As pioneers, we are obligated to pursue the development of virtual interface technologies in a systematic way and leave a technology base and tools as a legacy for others to build upon.

—Thomas A. Furness III, *Creating Better Virtual Worlds*

Enabler 4: Virtual Words

Globalization continues to place intense demands on business leaders. Our world as we know it is far more distributed; business is faster paced and highly competitive. As organizations continue to expand and experiment with 3D virtual environments to reach specific customer needs, business leaders will need to ensure that they understand how these new and richer immersive experiences will impact their organization's future.

Today's residents of the simulated universe are not just socializing, but they are also doing big business. The market value for virtual worlds is currently estimated at $6 billion.[1] This is a woeful underestimate since one part of Facebook, FarmVille, may soon be worth a billion and it is already capitalized at more than $4 billion. In the future, too, the mobile phone is likely to be a major incubator of virtual products.

In a recent study, Gartner predicted that by 2011 up to 80% of active Internet users, or 250 million people, will participate online in virtual worlds.[2] There is clearly a growing demographic preference shift to mixing online commerce with media and entertainment attributes.

In 2009, a man bought a space station for $330,000 in virtual world Entropia, while in 2010 all Planet Foods, a subsidiary of General Foods, introduced a new brand of organic blueberries. What have these two products got in common? Neither actually exists. Well, not except as pixels in the virtual worlds where they are traded. Only the money is real.[3]

We are in the midst of a virtual revolution that might one day be considered more important than the industrial revolution. Nic Mitham, founder of KZero, a Cambridge-based consultancy, says that there are over 175 virtual worlds that are live or in live beta and that the number of registered users has risen from 880 million in the fourth quarter of 2009 to 1.1 billion today, a 25% increase within 6 months, in the middle of a recession.[4] The registered population of virtual worlds (even if this is not the same as active users) is greater than the populations of the United States and Europe combined.

Our virtualization business outlook is simple, B2C and B2B organizations will need to plan effectively for virtual worlds into their business model customer and employee engagement experience strategies, and the time to start this competency development is now! In less than 5 years, an entire new type of work force is entering the market: they will not only demand social, collaboration experiences; they will also demand 3D virtual and immersive experiences. This is the first generation in the history of mankind that will strongly seek out and desire 3D immersive purchasing experiences, and most organizations, like leading financial institutions, are still debating the business case and value of social and Web 2.0 access to their employees, let alone being ready for virtual world and rich immersive experiences.

What Are Virtual Worlds?

A virtual world (VW) is a computer-based simulated environment. There are currently numerous VWs in existence and they vary from one another in terms of design and technology. Based on extensive global research by Helix, VWs can be distinguished from each other in five key ways: by perspective, content engagement, user interaction, geography, and community dynamics. Each of these distinguishing qualities is summarized briefly here:[5]

- *Perspective.* VWs can be 2 dimensional, 2.5 dimensional, or 3 dimensional. The first VWs were 2 dimensional; however, the majority of current VWs are either 2.5D (e.g., vSide) or full immersion 3D (e.g., Second Life). While simple-perspective VWs have the advantage of easy user access, the immersive experience of 3D is quickly becoming the norm. The disadvantages with these are that with more advanced visual experiences comes a heavier reliance on expensive, dedicated graphic cards. There is also a cost impact to organizations in ensuring heavy graphics are downloaded rapidly for effective end-user experiences.

- *Content engagement.* The content within a VW must be created by someone—a developer, a user, or both—who is responsible for content and shapes its existence. In Second Life, for example, the dominance of user-generated content is arguably one of the VW's most popular features.

- *User interaction.* The majority of VWs allow for multiple users. The method with which users communicate varies from VW to VW. Communication can occur in the form of live local text chat, instant messaging, e-mail, avatar customization, and real-time voice interaction using Voice over Internet Protocol (VoIP). Within VWs, users interact using a combination of these forms of communication.

- *Geography.* Virtual landscapes often appear similar to the real world with real world rules such as gravity, topography, locomotion, real-time actions and communication. Such environments, however, range from realistic to arbitrary and creative.

- *Community dynamics.* How do users spend their time? Some VWs such as Second Life and There.com are free-form and contain no real goals or quests. Other VWs and massively multiplayer online (MMO) worlds come with a certain amount of built-in direction. In the World of Warcraft, for example, users spend most of their time taking on specific quests with other players.

Current popular VWs are Blue Mars, Second Life, Entropia Universe, and Kaneva. While VWs share similar aspects to massively multiplayer online role playing games (MMORPGs), it would be more correct to label MMORPGs and massively multiplayer online games (MMOGs) as subcategories. "True" VWs do not have gamelike rules: In other words, they do not have goals, quests, prizes, or players.

A Brief History

Virtual worlds (VWs) can be traced back to the early 1970s. Pinpointing the first VW is debatable, as it depends on how one defines a "virtual world." However, according to Wikipedia, the credit for the first VW tends to go to Habitat, developed in 1987 by LucasArts.[6] Habitat first introduced the concept of visual avatars. The world ran on the Commodore 64 system and was made available by QuantamLink, the service that would become America Online. Habitat was the first MMORPG with a graphical interface; it was the first attempt at a graphically based large-scale virtual community ("Habitat"). Habitat's large user base of consumer-orientated users contributed to the lasting influence of the VW.

Before Habitat, there were a number of multiuser environments. The inclusion of these depends on how one defines a "virtual world." Bruce Damer, author of the book *Avatars*, cites Maze War as the great-grandfather of modern-day VWs. While Maze War was a game rather than a social environment, it had many of the features of today's VW.[7] Updated versions could be played over ARPAnet and had users appearing as eyeballs. Essentially the goal was to solve the maze while gaining points by shooting other players. For Damer, this can be considered the first VW because it was the first graphical user environment wherein multiple users interacted.

In the late 1970s and early 1980s, text-based multi-user dungeons (MUDs) were developed. The very first was developed in 1979 by Richard Bartle and Roy Trubshaw at Essex University. MUDs were entirely text-based worlds, yet they belong on the VW timeline because of the primarily social, role-playing aspects.[8] Between 1987 and 2000, many of the multiuser environments that appeared could be considered virtual worlds. A thorough timeline can be found at http://www.raphkoster.com/gaming/mudtimeline.shtml.

In 1992, the novel *Snow Crash*, by Neal Stephenson, was published. Part of the "Cyberpunk" literary movement, *Snow Crash* tells a story set in the near future when the "metaverse," a mainstream VW, is a major part of everyday life. Most VWs are now in some way or another modeled on Stephenson's vision. Online social virtual environments that were released in the 1990s include Meridian 59, The Palace, Worlds Away, and Traveler.[9]

Market Dynamics and Segmentation

Understanding how the market dynamics and segmentation is unfolding is complex as interactive 3D technology represents an emerging innovative market that is at the crossroads of several different growth areas. When you look at the market landscape, there are four segments rapidly evolving. Each of these is summarized briefly here:[10]

- 3D customer interaction management
- Interactive 3D virtual meeting
- Simulation-based learning
- Immersive 3D solutions

3D customer interaction management has a larger potential number of end users than the traditional design-oriented computer assisted design (CAD) market as there are significantly more people in sales and training, marketing and operations, and support versus design. Still, the 3D Customer Interaction Management market segment is an emerging market and the adoption rate will take some time. The total 3D CAD market is estimated to reach $8.2 billion and is estimated to grow 10% by 2012, approximately $800 million in growth.[11]

Interactive 3D virtual meeting is a subset to the traditional online meeting market. According to Wainhouse Researcher's project, the online web presentation sessions and various video meetings in North America alone, revenue from audio, video, and web collaboration services will reach $4.4 billion by 2011.[12] This technology is currently in high demand, as no other solution merges video, voice, VW, interactive 3D functionality, and meeting management into one single environment. Just imagine what functionality would rapidly evolve if Cisco acquired Second Life and evolved Second Life's capabilities further.

Simulation-based learning. As an extension of e-learning solutions and changing learning environments, the market is rapidly expanding in education for more advanced, simulation-based 3D learning experiences. Simulation-based learning (SBL) environments allow learners to be actively engaged in the learning experience moving them from isolated, high-end yet static tech centers to engaging, scalable, Internet-connected networks. The video game industry is fueling and setting the expectations for SBL with interactive experiences through new technologies like Nintendo Wii, PlayStation 3, and Xbox 360. If we look at the market for both corporate and education, another term often used when referencing SBL is serious games. The serious games market is estimated to be $1.5 billion by 2012.[13]

Immersive 3D solutions. This area includes portable tablet PCs and glass-free stereo displays to curved-screen and immersive rooms consisting of multichannel projection walls. These new technologies are allowing people to move away from purely physical communication to "augmented/mixed" reality communication and interaction. Enhanced visualization will become ubiquitous, as it will provide added contextual information to functions like communication, product development and R&D, and medical imaging. Augmented telepresence is one of these technologies, where real-time display of 3D information and images assists and enhances collaboration and interaction. Companies like Cisco are betting their future growth on their telepresence offerings.

Mobile immersion market. In the longer term, the mobile immersion market will rise significantly. New ultramobile devices with virtual glass displays overlaying and augmenting the real world are also providing real time guidance and explanation. Augmented reality is the capability to link the VW with the physical world through, for example, a "superman vision" where a video image is superimposed with a 3D model of the same environment and adding hidden information accessible from sensors like Radio Frequency Identification (RFID). Target uses include the following:

- Assisting difficult tasks
- Installation and support
- Medical visualizations
- Education/tourism, location-based information, and cultural heritage
- Construction and infrastructure

The adoption of ultramobile devices may take some time, but it will likely be a multimillion market in the next 5 years.

The Virtual Tween Market

Twenty million strong nationwide, tweens—kids ages 8 to 14, often called "Generation Z" or "digital natives"—flex $43 billion worth of annual spending power. The young consumers receive an average weekly allowance of $12 each, up from only $5 in 2009.[14] So despite family belt-tightening these days, parents still aren't scrimping on their kids. This is big business for businesses looking to grow with new products or expand into new markets. Predictably, the biggest slice of the tween money pie goes to VWs and video games (31%), with apparel/footwear and impulse buys, like snacks, tying for second (20% each). Consumer electronics and music/books vie for third (10% each), followed closely by toys/crafts (9%).[15]

Tweens offer the highest market growth segment for VWs, driving another reason for leaders to recognize an entire generation of virtual and immersive experience: Tweens will enter the work force in less than 5 years. We should not be debating the value of these tools but rather seeking to understand how to sell our products and services to create virtual social purchasing experiences.

A VW is more than an online game. It is a place where tweens can build anything from a complete empire to a farm or even a universe. It is a chance for a tween to use his or her imagination to design and customize his very own bedroom, create a business, or even create a castle with a dragon and a moat. Of course, VWs, like World of Warcraft, offer tweens plenty of game power to play solely or compete with other online members.

Some current examples include the following:

- *Woozworld.* Woozworld is a VW where kids ages 6 to 14 can create a person (a Woozen), land a dream job for a Woozen, and socialize with other Woozers. A tween creates a Unitz (similar to an apartment) for her person and decorates it by earning Wooz or Beex (similar to coins), which are given for playing games on the site, voting for the best Unitz, plus other ways to earn Wooz and Beex. The site offers parents to manage their child's subscription and read blogs related to the site,

which can answer many questions parents have before allowing
a tween to join.

- *Poptropica.* Tweens create a character (a cartoon-style person)
  upon entering the Poptropica VW. Once inside, tweens play
  games, use problem-solving skills in quests, and interact with
  stories and comics. Poptropica is an educational game as it
  allows tweens to learn about historical facts in a fun way.
  Designed by FunBrain, Poptropica is a very safe virtual environment for tweens.

- *SecretBuilders.* SecretBuilders is a VW that includes taking care
  of a pet, building and maintaining a place to live, and going
  on quests in different lands. It all starts by creating a character to interact with and allows tweens to design, create, and
  publish videos, artwork, or stories. This game also allows other
  friends and family to comment on published works. This site
  stimulates tweens' imaginations and entrepreneurship and is a
  real motivator for tweens to build on their creativity skills in
  this VW.

- *Innerstar University.* Other growth trends for tweens included
  the recent launch of Innerstar University, created by a U.S. toy
  company, where preteens can create doll avatars to navigate the
  campus of a virtual university, earning stars by competing in
  cheerleading or horse-riding games that can then be redeemed
  for pets or a haircut.

- Other popular VWs for tweens include Runescape and Club
  Penguin.

In addition to the platform and subscription models, there is a lot of
innovation using VWs to create targeted communities. For example, the
Canadian Edmonton Oilers have recently launched a VW for young fans
called Rinksters, in conjunction with developer Visimonde. The VW is
aimed at children aged 6 to 12 and features customizable avatars, chat
rooms, virtual currency, mini games, and virtual collectible trading cards.
Rinksters is also partially educational in nature, designed to help teach
kids about hockey.

The Oilers will participate in certain contests involving the VW, such
as letting kids spend virtual currency to enter raffles for tickets to Oilers

games. The Oilers and Visimonde plan to launch Rinksters in 2011. Currently it's available in closed beta. Interested parties can apply to join the beta at the Rinksters website. The VW will feature some branded content, like vintage Oilers costumes for avatars. The game will be available for all users to play for free but will also offer an optional subscription-based service. Rinksters is being designed and built to help grow enthusiasm for the Oilers and the sport of hockey at a grassroots level.[16]

Other innovations in research on tweens' usage of VWs can be found at the UK institution at the University of Sunderland to use VWs in a cultural study called eCUTE (Education in Cultural Understanding, Technology Enhanced) that will use VWs to help study, over 3 years, how children and young people respond to culturally different behavior in a VW. The study's VW will use "intelligent characters" that display various types of different cultural behaviors. The eCUTE research program will involve leading experts in emotional and cultural psychology, artificial intelligence, virtual reality, human-computer interaction, and cultural computing. Eight research partners and institutions from Portugal, Germany, the Netherlands, and Japan will take part in eCUTE.

The VWs will use characters that display behaviors associated with different cultural, ethnic, and social backgrounds. The characters will be incorporated into a variety of scenarios that will be tested on children aged 9 to 11 and young adults aged 18 to 25. The eCUTE research program is scheduled to last 3 years. This will be a major study to learn from in terms of diverse cultural stimuli and unique differences, if any, in using VWs to understand cultural behavior with tweens and young adults.[17]

Business Implications of Tweens in Virtual Worlds and Business

What is clear is this is going to be one of the most significant consumer groups in the history of business, as this is the first generation growing up socialized in 3D VW experiences, from being coddled in Webkinz with plush virtual and real dogs, cats, or other cuddly toys; to migrating to Club Penguin; to Habbo Hotel; to joining other VWs as a young adult, this generation will have higher expectations of having virtual business experiences bringing their avatars to work with them. So with this insight, what can business learn to engage with tweens and build more confidence in using VWs. The following are a few pointers:

- *First, offer experiences, not transactions.* Businesses need to champion the tween and resist to be the adult or authority figure.
- *Tweens want to be entertained.* They want interactive adventures, whether that involves in-store contests; product testing seminars; or product promotion fairs at schools, sports leagues, or other events.
- *Tweens are not that complex.* They watch TV ads, desire anything their older sibling has, and are highly influenced by what their friends and peers are into.

Thinking Outside the Box

- *If you are a global bank,* why not develop a learning simulation game on managing your bank account and teaching basic financial concepts in a VW and partner with a leading VW gaming company to offer a unique interactive experience. As the participants learn, they also gain valuable money to play their favorite VW game. Be the first bank to help them set up their first banking account online in a safe behind the wall VW experience.
- *If you are in the government in the justice department,* think about developing an educational internet safety simulation using a VW online learning game. Once completed, offer it not only to all the justice departments worldwide but also freely to all social gaming companies so they can also easily integrate it into their software offers. There is nothing more priceless than the safety of our children on the web.
- *If you are in education,* develop training programs to teach children how to design VWs and work with businesses to set up experiences that help promote and sell their products and services. Let the children partner with local businesses on what ideas can be generated that would motivate them.

- *If you are a media and entertainment company*, develop more videos using avatars integrated into the life of in-world and out-of-world characters to simulate the future experiences where human and avatar are one, work with university students studying film, and virtual tweens who fit your demographic specs.
- *If you are an insurance company*, think of how you can use media and advertising more creatively using VW characters.
- *If you are in a not-for-profit organization*, think of developing a branded avatar personality that is one of your spokespersons to communicate your advocacy needs.
- *If you are running a major sporting event*, like the Olympics, think of how you can engage the crowd with your brand creating 3D immersive experiences to learn about your products and service offers.
- *If you are a major retailer* like Nike selling running shoes, perhaps have an avatar personality explain in a VW the product features in an online simulation but also purchase a unique avatar wearing the online customized runners purchased on your very own avatar.

Whatever business model you are in, nonprofit or profit, the reality is a VW 3D experience can easily be translated to any business model that has a tween value proposition but also extending the reality check that these tweens are rapidly growing up, and 3D experiences will be as commonplace to them as having a beer at a local pub. We believe that the time to experiment and learn is now.

Taking a Deeper VW Plunge: Meet the Business Gorilla, Second Life

Second Life (SL) is a persistent online VW that is globally accessible via the Internet. It simulates the physical world in some respects, making it readily navigable and accessible by users who appear, communicate, and transact within the world as highly detailed "avatars" (simulated characters). Users of SL (called "residents") are equipped with tools that enable them to create structures, clothing, vehicles, equipment, and applications within the world and to optionally integrate these artifacts with assets from the 2D web.

Launched in 2003, it now claims to be approaching over 15 million registered.[18] For some it's been a rocky road: Its San Diego–born creator Philip Rosedale stepped down as CEO in 2008 but is now back in charge as the company recently laid off 30% of their staff in June 2010. In turnaround mode currently, the company was reportedly valued between $658 million and $700 million a year ago.[19]

The latest published figures claim that virtual transactions (sales of land, clothes, and artifacts) in SL came to $500 million last year and that the volume of user-to-user transactions (selling each other clothes, furniture, and land) rose between April and May 2010 from $49.9 million to $52.6 million.[20] However, it would be surprising if this growth were maintained in view of SL's managerial problems and a sharp decline in the value of land within the VW. Casual visitors are arriving in fewer numbers and long-term residents seem focused on educational projects, virtual business meetings, dating experiences, or art.

In terms of the getting started experience, users have to set up an account and download the appropriate software, then they enter SL with a choice of several default avatars. An "avatar" is a third-person simulated character that users control while in the virtual space. Users begin SL in an orientation area where they can customize their avatars to assume a more personal appearance. From there, users learn to buy and develop land, socialize, and essentially do whatever they like.

Technically, SL presents the illusion of a VW. In fact, the land is a stitching together of 256 x 256 "meter" regions, each running on a separate server. Each region is referred to as a "Sim" (from the word "simulator"). In real life, SL comprises over 2,000 Intel and Advanced Micro Systems servers in two colocation facilities in San Francisco and Dallas.[21] According to Philip Rosedale, the landmass of SL requires nearly 100 terabytes of space and is equivalent to 390 square miles. In an interview with *Forbes*, Rosedale compared SL to the MMORPG World of Warcraft and estimated SL is roughly 100,000 times as large.[22] When users "buy" land from Linden Labs, they are leasing server space and paying (in U.S. dollars) according to the amount of server space they use. Almost everything in SL is user created: "Virtually every object, terrain and animation is the creative work of its membership."[23]

Second Life has its own in-world economy. What distinguishes SL is the fact that its dollar can be traded on the open market. There is extensive discussion in the mainstream media about the economic potentials of this virtual world. Second Life dollars are referred to as Linden dollars (L$) and are relatively stable at around L$270 to every one U.S. dollar. Virtual dollars can be traded for U.S. dollars, and users are making real money from their SL lives. Real world companies already have brand presence, while new companies are daily going live with their own "builds" or setting up an office.

Since its inception, hundreds, even thousands of companies and nonprofits have been created in SL. The goals behind a corporate presence in SL vary. Organizations seek to establish or enhance their brand, participate in a global community (ideally resulting in lead generation and sales), conduct research and development, and test markets. Second Life also provides inexpensive immersive facilities for corporate training, quarterly and annual meetings, employee communication sessions, conferences, and offers persistent conference and exhibit facilities. Second Life also provides companies with the opportunity to "meet" in world with international clients, to demonstrate products, provide training, and give presentations.

Second Life is in the early stages of development for enterprise business applications. Second Life–based, "indigenous" businesses have earned small revenues (< $1 million) in fields ranging from virtual real estate investment to virtual goods and services. Lack of hard earnings by businesses, however, reflects more on the absence of long-term operational business plans than on any intrinsic failing of SL technology, audience, or business opportunity.

Simply put, few companies are selling real world goods in SL at this time because, thus far, SL development has been carried out by marketing and communications personnel, often in a maverick or experimental manner. To date, SL assets have been created primarily for public relations, branding, education, generalized customer engagement, and employee engagement (recruiting, training, products, or technical learning labs) rather than for sales or virtual commerce. There are some exceptions. Major consumer packed goods firms and automotive firms experimenting with avatars use their VW products to mirror real-life products as a new source of lead generation. Hard measurements of success are difficult to glean, however, since companies hold the intelligence close to their vests during these early stages of VW adoption.

In summary, revenue can, and will, be generated by businesses through a comprehensive approach to virtual environments. The multi-faceted approach and ultimate rise in sales need to include the following:

- Advertising and marketing programs across the company that provide portals to SL. Investment in graphic cards and effective processing power is also critical to ensure the experience is an enjoyable one.
- Adoption of an integrated approach to sales that incorporates online, event, and SL assets.
- Second Life training and usage orientation programs are needed to ensure the initial experience is a positive one, and the end users are not frustrated with their VW navigation experiences.
- Second Life sales facilities provide
  - knowledgeable sales people that can respond to a global audience;
  - 24/7 staffing of the sales and product offices if there are plans to expand or increase sales on an international basis;
  - in-world links to existing websites;
  - programmed event and event management to increase traffic that results in a viral branding on a global scale;
  - in-world point-of-sales (POS) systems that accept debit and credit cards and PayPal.

Other Virtual World Perspectives

As mentioned earlier, in 2009, a man bought a space station for $330,000 in VW Entropia. The space station was sold in the VW Entropia Universe, which has its own economy and currency. The buyer, who converted his $300,000 into 3.3 million PED (Project Entropia dollars), is convinced that virtual shops on his virtual space station will produce virtual profits that can be converted back into real dollars.

General Foods is experimenting with virtual blueberries to represent a "brand extension" of a product that exists in the real world as they are aiming to establish a presence in FarmVille, a game that exists as an application on Facebook and that at its peak has had nearly 80 million players. It is a classic example of a new genre.

Farmers in FarmVille buy cartoon-like virtual farm animals, which have to be regularly fed, or crops that require fertilizer (virtual, of course) to help them grow, in order to be more successful than their friends. The real-time game has its own virtual currency that makes it easier for members to trade and for the game's makers to profit.

FarmVille may one day be seen as a milestone in acclimating non-geeks to the idea of online currencies and virtual products. Virtual products have a particular attraction to businesses because beyond the cost infrastructure already in place, overheads are few and manufacturing costs zero. Carbon footprints become less of a concern, too. And in a recession, VWs offer their colonists the chance of a cheap escape from everyday reality. Parent company Zynga has revenues of more than $600 million a year, which come mainly from FarmVille, despite competition from half a dozen other farm games on Facebook. Zynga is reckoned to be worth between $4 billion and $5 billion, based on the value of investment stakes that have been taken in it.

Habbo Hotel, another major VW where teenagers trade goods and clothes, has increased the number of its registered residents to 175 million from 160 million a year ago. The London-based Moshi Monsters, a tweenie world where kids meet and trade virtual goods with each other, now has 20 million members compared with 12 million at the end of last year.[24]

Other market leaders experimenting include SceneCaster, which creates virtual 3D experiences and cards. It is little wonder that Mark Zohar, CEO of SceneCaster, believes "there will be a time in the future when kids spend more money in certain areas on virtual goods than they do in the real world."[25]

Other VWs now competing with SL are several similar online communities, including OpenLife, Blue Mars, and Inworldz.

OpenLife is an open-source alternative grid for SL, set up in Australia in 2007, to create a user content created VW orientated toward users, affordable ownership, and community.

Blue Mars is more restrictive than SL in terms of allowing its users to make their own content, but this 3D VW platform developed in Hawaii by Avatar Reality has let more than 200 developers—mostly individuals or indie game designers—loose on creating cities, games, and 3D environments on a replica of Mars. Opened to the public in September 2009, and still in beta testing, it promises users better graphics and a more streamlined experience as a result. Blue Mars further differs from SL in that avatars cannot be fully customized and the emphasis is on shopping and gaming rather than social interaction.

Increasingly, VW educational companies are developing. Reaction-Grid, based in Florida, was founded by three SL programmers in January 2009.[26] They build VWs for business clients (including Microsoft and a number of universities), usually as a "fun" way to facilitate business learning experiences, such as an interactive arcade version of a PowerPoint–like presentation. Virtual world experiences created include classrooms, campuses, and bar lounges.

Another interesting trend is developing 3D reproductions of actual places in the real world in the hope of attracting people to buy goods and entertain themselves without an irksome journey to town. There is, for example, a virtual London in SL with a 40,000-strong community that now boasts a small profit mainly from renting out shops and clubs. This has spiraled at least five other virtual city versions of London being built by other companies like Microsoft, Twinity, NearGlobal, and University College of London. Visitors to Twinity can also enjoy VW replicas of Berlin, Singapore, and Miami.

Perhaps the most intriguing project is Project X, the brainchild of Mike Fotoohi from Egham, Surrey, England, who intends to reproduce the entire planet as a VW in which members will be able to build replicas of their homes on the same street as in real life.[27] Project X is still in beta and they have just recently finished building central New York and a few other places, but after merging the open source Openstreetmap—a free and open source editable map of the world—with publicly available satellite image mapping from the U.S. government to produce a 3D skeleton of practically every road on the planet, users will be invited to take over the planet. Just wait until Google Maps is fully integrated and strikes on this acquisition play.

It is clear that Project X is reinforcing the inevitable reality that VWs and social media will integrate with a three dimensional web. As bandwidth increases and technologies like ray tracing, simulating 3D effects, and video delivery become more realistic, we will start to have VW experiences that will look very real in the future.

One feature being developed in Project X will also be using mobile technology aims to sync the virtual and the real worlds so that your avatar in a VW will follow you in real life wherever you go. Shopkeepers will be able to advertise their products and will be able to see customers attracted to their store as a result of that advertisement. This is something that has never been done before and for the first time you can measure accurately the dollars that you spend. The person who uses this system will also get a revenue share, which is great for the consumer and advertiser.

One of the most creative spots in SL is the Nemo trilogy, consisting of three distinct VW locations inspired by the three natural elements of water, earth, and air. Designed by Sextan Shephard, this Sim takes inspiration from the author Jules Verne and inventor Nikola Tesla. The designer loved the "mix of science, mystery and imaginary" style when he was a child with movies like *Steamboy* and *The Illusionist*. In terms of the Nemo experiences there is a mechanical manta ray, shrimp, horseshoe crab, and as the inspiration continues, tunnels and entrances; unique Nemo experiences are born.[28]

Success Laws for Virtual Worlds

Law #1: *Virtual Worlds Are Not Games*

The first assumption that businesses often make is that VWs are games. This is a wrong assumption. The right answer is that VWs are a *new, rich media communication channel*. While the market for nongame VWs is still relatively emergent compared to MMOGs, VWs are a rapidly growing new market segment. Based on our research preparing for this book, businesses need to start planning an online presence in VWs in order to create interactive community experiences so that they can learn how to exploit new ways of communicating with customers, suppliers, and employees in rich, virtually immersive environments.

Virtual worlds are powerful as they have tremendous online reach and can easily bring together large groups of simultaneous players in a fast-paced online environment; they can provide an interesting capability for the future of organizations. MMORPGs represent a growing business that, according to the Tower Group, will reach 40 million people and generated over $9 billion in revenue by 2010.[29]

Virtual worlds present the next frontier for customer and employee interactions. Organizations need to start preparing now for these new methods of communication, or they will lose talent and customer segments who desire this form of customer interaction experience. In North America, companies like Dell, Coke, IBM, and Nike are actively experimenting with new consumer purchasing experiences using virtual avatars.

Law #2: Experience Must Be Relevant to Solve a Business Need and Create Value

Developing an effective and profitable online channel in VWs requires an acute focus on creating online experiences that have the following traits:

- *Highly interactive.* Leveraging multiple forms of communication—instant messaging, VoIP, community forums, regularly scheduled events, special events with featured speakers, social mediated forms of creating connections, linkages to Facebook, Google groups, and other Web 2.0 applications—are all possible in a VW. Ensuring activities are diverse, interactive, and frequently changing will determine the success of a VW.
- *Sales supported customer experiences.* Having live customer sales agents actively interacting with visitors' in-store experiences is critical for developing relationships in VWs. Customers, in avatar persona, do not like going into a shopping store to interact with a voice-activated system or with an e-mail system—they want to have a real conversation like in real life. The companies that miss understanding this will not create any unique branding value; rather, they will only aggravate their customers by creating disappointing VW experiences. Like in real life, customers will tell their friends of their poor shopping experiences, thereby impacting a brand's reputation.
- *Learning labs.* Companies that create VWs need to also understand this is a learning opportunity for creating a new channel experience; hence, expectations need to be realistic. Generating

significant sources of new revenue will be slow for at least 2–3 years. Yet as market demands increase, the early investors will benefit from their early VW learning.

Law #3: Each Avatar Is a Real Person

One important reality of VW conversations is that behind every avatar is a real person. There is a unique culture in a VW, and expectations for behavior need to be acknowledged. In time, VW reputations will be more visible and transparent than other face-to-face conversations. Therefore, if an organization is going to engage in VW customer experiences for buying and selling goods and services, recruiting talent, or holding a convention, it is critical that effective codes of conduct and behavior are followed. Some of the guidelines are summarized here:

- Concept of personal space is as relevant in the VW as in the real world; hence, establishing space boundaries for VWs interaction is important.
- Taking responsibility for communicating implies socially acceptable behaviors in a VW, much like in the real world. Unacceptable interactions are those that we would not tolerate in a business environment—abuse, harassment, stalking, threatening, misrepresentation, violating obligations of confidentiality, violating the privacy of others, and so on. All these social communication skills practiced in real life still apply in the VW.
- Nothing should be said online that would not be said in person. When we believe someone is unfairly attacking another, we take action.

Law #4: A Virtual World Experience Is a New Branding Opportunity

Virtual world experiences provide a new way of interacting with customers to create a unique branding experience. VWs like SL and Entropia Universe provide opportunities to interact and communicate with users in ways not achievable through traditional mediums. It is critical to make the VW experience an extension of your current marketing and communication strategies. Always be mindful of your brand—when trying out new VW "real-estate" and marketing techniques, you do not want conflicting messages or images. Creating VW experiences or events that are complimentary to existing marketing branding and communication strategies is critical for successful VW branding success. It is becoming increasingly important to collaborate with brands that exist solely in the VW. The brands that become most successful in the VW are those that can satisfy a purely virtual need.

Now You Know

- These approaches are relatively low cost and can interrelate easily between real-life and SL experiences.
- The technology is rapidly evolving: it won't be long before all customer experiences will have an optional engagement experience to use 3D for their online experiences.
- With the tweens growing up rapidly and arriving in the workforce in less than 5 years, their quest to experience 3D will continue to alter everything we know about immersion.
- From a business perspective, it is also important to understand that VWs are changing from levying monthly subscriptions to charging small amounts for virtual goods, a practice made popular by FarmVille. Brands are now creating their own VWs to sell their products.
- Virtual goods that carry real-life brands have 10 times the buying power of virtual brands. Brands like SL may not continue to dominate the business experience landscape, as new VWs like Blue Mars and Project X evolve their footprint.
- We can also be assured that Google is following this market space very closely as the interplay between Google Maps, VWs, social and geolocal/spatial mobile devices is a powerful overlay that will change even further the world we interact in.
- One thing we can count on is that it will be incredibly rich, immersive, and the long-awaited entertainment economy will be embedded in the virtualization of business.

- In chapter 9, we provide deeper case study experiences from Helix Commerce's extensive research into VWs, with a primary focus on SL experiences. We have included this as a foundation to learn from. Some of these experiences have been retired but the application scenarios hold a great deal of relevance to businesses striving to envision what is possible.

PART II
The Strategies

CHAPTER 6

Any Place, Any Time

A place for everything, everything in its place.

—Benjamin Franklin

Strategy 1: Place

Most introductory management textbooks remind students to consider the four "Ps" of marketing: product, price, promotion, and place. The place component of the marketing mix usually refers to the location where the end consumer may purchase the good or service. In virtual business, the term "place" takes on a much more important role. First, we are able to use many of the tools, techniques, and technologies that we examined early in the book to make the product available to the consumer. For example, we might sell our widget to consumers through a blog, wiki, or some form of social media. However, there is much more to place in the virtual business context.

In the virtual business world, we widen the scope of place by considering the best physical place to house each of the components of our goods or services. Often this physical place will not be geographically collocated with the remaining components. In short, we find the best locations for each link in the chain and then join the links using technology. For example, if the best people for a particular task are in one part of the country, a part very distant from the end consumer, then we locate the people there and find some innovative technology to allow us to serve our customers. Likewise, if the cost of physical space is too expensive where our traditional brick and mortar competition is operating, then we set up shop somewhere less expensive and use technology to connect with our customers. Technology truly is an enabler of virtual business.

In this chapter, we examine a number of real-world examples of place creating value in ways heretofore not in the realm of possible. As you read the cases, consider how your organization could benefit from similar implementation.

Remote Customer Ordering

Our first case study features an innovative way to tackle a major challenge facing leaders in the restaurant industry. Although this challenge is not unique to the restaurateurs, it often creates a management nightmare in the fast food segment, especially for urban-based stores. The specific challenge is how can managers recruit and retain high-quality people in an industry that is not renowned for high compensation. In essence, the management challenge is to find bright, hard-working, polite people that are willing to work long hours and keep smiling throughout their day. The *super employees* should also be capable of multitasking—taking an order from the drive-thru, pouring coffee, flipping burgers, making change (hopefully correctly)—and they should remember to keep smiling as the *customer is always right*. Finally, and often most importantly, we want these employees to speak a particular language, usually English, flawlessly so that the customer is in their comfort zone.

Even in tough economic times, it is difficult to find this type of person in the scale that is necessary. Traditionally, managers have relied on training, both language and customer service, to help improve the situation. However, this is an expensive and time-intensive process that often does not offer a good return on the investment. The ensuing skills are very transferable to other segments, which leads to high employee turnover and unhappy customers.

Enter Verety with an innovative solution.[1] Verety operates a series of customer order centers in rural America where the cost of living is more manageable, a high quality of life is commonplace, and many people speak English. For example, some of their most successful centers are in North Dakota. But how can a center in the Great Plains help a manager with a challenge 2,000 miles away in a southern California fast food operation? That, as they say, is where the innovation comes in. The order centers take over part of the management challenge, specifically the customer interaction at the drive-thru. By eliminating part of the process, the onsite manager is able to focus on the remaining challenges in the restaurant.

So how exactly does this work? Imagine that you would like to purchase your favorite burger, fries, and drink from a local fast food restaurant. You decide to purchase your order using the drive-thru to avoiding the lines inside the store. As you approach the speaker post in your car, an agent many miles from you is alerted that you are approaching. Just as you arrive at the speaker post, you are greeted by a very courteous voice who invites you to place your order. As with many business dealings, the first few seconds of the transaction are vital in establishing the tone of the entire experience. If you are not greeted in a way that you consider acceptable, it is likely that you will not have a good experience and perhaps not return. On the other hand, if your order is taken in a professional, hassle-free manner, you will likely start the process in a good frame of mind.

The success of the Verety system is largely due to the technology that enables this solution. As with many innovative ideas we will review, Verety could not offer this creative solution without technology. In this case, the remote agents connect with the customers at the drive-thru using a Voice Over Internet Protocol (VoIP) connection. Without this technology, the innovation simply would not be possible. The technology is what allows the people—those polite, professional, and prompt remote agents—to do their job. Verety suggests their technological solution provides a robust and reliable platform capable of dealing with more than one million customers per hour. The real-time nature of Verety's solution is key to the success—the system connects the agent to the customer within milliseconds, thus avoiding the delay that is sometimes associated with remote services. Most customers are unaware that the agent is not physically located in the restaurant.

A second element of the technological solution is the real-time and seamless integration with the in-store point of sales system. As an order is being taken, other team members can hear the order on their headsets, in exactly the same way as traditional, on-site ordering systems. Similarly, the order appears in real-time on the in-store displays. For most team members, including the managers, the remote ordering system operates exactly as it would if it were onsite. The system receives constant feedback from the store to ensure the remote agent is aware of the minute-to-minute challenges, such as menus changes and the availability of various specials.

However, technology alone would not have solved this management challenge. A big part of the solution is the great people Verety recruits to work as remote agents. As we mentioned, many of the remote agents are physically located in North Dakota in cities such as Minot, Steele, Rugby, and Hazen. These cities are well-known as down-to-earth, friendly, and safe communities inhabited by some of the nicest people you will ever meet. The result is the people who work as remote agents are polite, hard-working, honest people who love their communities and do not want to leave. Verety taps into this great group of people and provides them an opportunity to stay in their communities and earn a good living—truly a win-win situation.

Although we mentioned the towns in which many Verety remotes agents work, we have not described the physical attributes of the actual customer order centers. In fact, there is no physical location per se as all the agents work from their homes. Verety works with local telecommunication companies to ensure an acceptable broadband infrastructure exists in these small communities and provides the necessary equipment for the home agents. This unique virtual order center concept ensures that high-quality people are ready and able to assist drive-thru customers miles away.

Geographically Relocating

A real challenge for many hospitals, especially small rural facilities, is to recruit and retain high-quality radiologists who are willing to provide around the clock coverage. The competition for radiologists is tough enough without demanding that these highly trained professionals work the graveyard shift from midnight to 7 a.m. Regrettably, though very predictably, few of these professionals are keen to relocate to remote parts of the country, especially to be on standby each and every night.

In other cases, the medical facilities simply cannot substantiate the expense of having radiologists "on call" waiting for a rare night event that necessitates an X-ray being read. Of course, when the need arises, it is difficult to put a price on the missing expert. Some would argue that the on call practice is not desirable because who wants to have a tired physician reviewing critical medical images? Even in larger cities where there is a clear demand, it is sometime difficult to convince these professionals to agree to work the nightshift.

But what if there was a way to have the radiologists only work during the day? And what if that location was close to one of world's most beautiful beaches? Would that make it easier to recruit and retain such sought after professionals? Well it turns out the answer is a resounding "yes." There is a way to improve patient care while simultaneously providing a high quality of life for the radiologists, a true win-win situation.

In 2001, NightHawk Radiology Services (http://www.nighthawkrad .net) started offering what they term *off-hours emergent radiology interpretation*.[2] Their unique solution to this difficult challenge was to locate U.S. board-certified physicians in Sydney, Australia, to provide preliminary interpretations to U.S. hospitals. As it turns out, when it is night in America, it is daytime in Australia, so well-rested experts are able to review and interpret images. The results of a 2007 survey indicate that U.S. doctors had "a high level of comfort with images being read by U.S. board-certified physicians located in a foreign country (89% reported no concern)."[3]

By late 2009, NightHawk Radiology Services reported that foreign-based U.S. board-certified experts were providing radiological readings for more than 1,350 American hospitals. The service they offer is to complement, not replace, the services provided by local experts. When there is a need for an image to be read during the hours of darkness (American time), the image and select patient information is securely forwarded through a virtual private network (VPN) to Sydney or perhaps another foreign facility.[4] Normally within 20 minutes after the arrival of the requisite files, the preliminary interpretation is completed and returned to the U.S. facility. This facilitates the immediate patient care; however, the process does not stop there. The next morning, the local expert will review the patient's file, including the images, and decide the next steps as necessary.

This is a case of technology, the VPN, facilitating a sound business process. This particular implementation is slightly more complicated than some solutions as the process must be Health Insurance Portability and Accountability Act–compliant. Of course, all parties demand the highest standards of data security and integrity when patient care is at stake. In many other businesses, the solution may be less demanding. However, this business solution is not as much about technology as it is about place. The key to success was finding a "place" where the experts could do what they needed to do in the conditions they needed to have. In this case, the solution was a place with daylight during U.S. darkness . . . of course, Bondi Beach, the amazing restaurants of Sydney, and a pleasant climate probably did not hurt.

Outsourcing With a Twist

At first glance, our third place case may seem to be a simple example of outsourcing. It is certainly true that outsourcing plays a vital role in the success of the example. It is also true that like many outsourcing adventures of late, this case involves value-added services being completed in India. However, this case is much more than that: this case is about combining cutting-edge technology with innovative business practices to achieve a competitive advantage.

Before examining how we can combine technology, innovation, and place to create value, it may be worth quickly reviewing the history of technology outsourcing. In his book, *The World Is Flat*, Thomas Friedman does a brilliant job of reminding us how technology outsourcing to India began.[5] Friedman suggests that the impending Y2K crisis provided an opportunity for Indian companies to take the tedious, but important, task of searching millions of lines of computer code looking for the offending date fragments. If these fragments were not found and corrected, it was feared that many computer systems would not correctly change from December 31, 1999, to January 1, 2000. Many scaremongers painted pictures of catastrophic failure.

Truth be told, on January 1, 2000, many of us breathed a sigh of relief, largely due to the work we outsourced to India. Fast forward a few years when most of us had forgotten about Y2K and suddenly offshore outsourcing, especially to India, had lost favor. Many people became very critical of overseas outsourcing, largely due to concerns such as loss of domestic jobs, perceived inferior quality, and security.

So given the current situation, is it wise to consider outsourcing service activities to India (or other countries)? Well, one company certainly believes it is wise, perhaps even vital, to augment domestic business processes with targeted and strategic use of outsourcing to countries like India. The company is Xpitax LLC of Braintree, Massachusetts (http://

www.xpitax.com), whose tag line is "innovative outsourcing for CPAs [Certified Public Accountants]."[6]

Xpitax's business model appears simple enough: send U.S. residents' tax returns to India to be completed by Indian accountants. But how many Americans really want their private financial data shipped halfway around the world? Probably none, and hence the need for an innovative solution. Xpitax website suggests,

> To achieve profitability, firms must operate in an organized, systemized and efficient manner. When it comes to processing tax returns, efficiency, accuracy, timeliness and cost-effectiveness are crucial. Xpitax helps CPAs manage the tax preparation process by combining the latest in business process outsourcing (BPO) with state-of-the-art web technologies and extensive accounting experience.[7]

The Xpitax solution is innovative, as it provides a balanced workflow system that allows key steps in the tax preparation process to remain in the United States. To achieve the speed demanded by customers, part of the process is sent to India and completed by highly qualified, India-educated tax preparers. This army of tax preparers in India are experts in U.S. tax laws and are extremely accurate, but perhaps more importantly, they fill the growing shortage of U.S.-based CPAs. The time-zone difference between the United States and India adds great value as the work in India is completed when U.S.-based offices are closed. Often the India portion of the tax return is completed and returned to the U.S. office before it opens in the morning.

The educated workforce and timeliness are attractive; however, the true Xpitax advantages lie in the business process. Three elements are key. First, the U.S. customer interacts with a U.S.-based CPA. This allows the customer and the CPA to develop a relationship. The process starts and ends with the domestic CPA. Second, the customer's sensitive data never leave the United States. Once the necessary customer financial data are collected, they are stored on a U.S.-based server and never leave the country. The India-based accountants access a VPN to retrieve and process the file, but the data are not stored offshore. Third, there is a high level of security in the Indian facilities. For example, all employees sign nondisclosure agreements, there are no printers or Internet access in the Indian facilities, and their facilities are very secure and require fingerprint access.

The Xpitax solution is a good example of how businesses may counter expert domestic workers shortages to create value. Their solution combines technology, the VPN, with an innovative business process that ensures the company caters to its customers' needs and wants. This is not an example of simply sending domestic jobs abroad, but rather it is a creative way to balance cost, time, and security to create an effective and efficient way to serve domestic clients.

The Place for Homemade

Our final example of place in action is quite distinct from the others we have examined. This example considers a virtual gathering place, a space where artisans and handmade aficionados can meet, virtually of course, to exchange goods, services, and learn from each other. This unique web presence is provided by Etsy (http://www.etsy.com), whose stated mission is "to enable people to make a living making things, and to reconnect makers with buyers."[8]

Etsy is different than many other web-based storefronts in that the folks at Etsy have created a community of like-minded people who seek an alternative to mass production. The result is a virtual community that connects consumers with creators and creators with other creators. The Etsy model is filling an important niche, and they are doing very well. By January 2011, Etsy boasted 7.2 million members (almost double the 3.65 million member of December 2009) with over 400,000 sellers (compared with 250,000 in December 2009). They have about 7.7 million items listed, and sales have risen from $166,000 in 2005 to more than $314 million in 2010.[9] In addition to the business value of these connections, Etsy encourages and promotes social responsibility and environmental awareness.

Etsy is an excellent example of how combining a great idea with some Web 2.0 ideas can create value. The Etsy creators carefully designed their virtual gathering place with the needs of the end users in mind. They quickly realized that their users—who must become members—would want more than just another storefront. To ensure that members would return frequently, the designers added a series of engaging features. In fact, this could be a playbook straight from *Groundswell*. Consider how the Etsy leadership teams caters to the consumer at different stages of Forrester's Social Technographics.[10]

In addition to catering to the want of members in the various categories, Etsy has developed some innovative ways to engage their community. The first is called *Alchemy*, which "is a space on Etsy where buyers can

Table 6.1. Etsy's Use of Technographics Categories

Forrester's Social Technographics category[11]	Etsy example
Creators make social content go. They write or upload video, music, or text.	Etsy facilitates content creation within the community in spaces such as the virtual labs, which they describe as follows: "The Virtual Etsy Labs are a multiuser online space with various rooms. We use the Virtual Labs to connect with our community, host events, put on streaming webcam how-to's, invite special shopping guests showing off their picks, host team meetings, demos, and shop critiques!"[12]
Critics respond to content from others. They post reviews, comment on blogs, participate in forums, and edit wiki articles.	The Storque (*Etsy's Homemade Blog*) is a full-featured blog were members may participate in dialogs in areas such as The Homemade Life, Craftivism, How-To, Reviews, and Events. The Forum section includes discussions about a variety of subjects including being an independent business owner, the Consumer Product Safety Improvement Act, critiques about each other's shops, sharing and seeking advice about creating items, and more. In the Voter section members are able to vote on the favorite item in various categories.
Collectors organize content for themselves or others using RSS feeds, tags, and voting sites like Digg.com.	Etsy provides RSS feeds for their blog (The Storque), forums, and also provides the ability for members to add RSS feeds to their individual shops.
Joiners connect in social networks like MySpace and Facebook.	Etsy is all about joiners. To participate in most activities, users must become members. Members can also follow Etsy on Twitter and become a fan on Facebook.
Spectators consume social content including blogs, user-generated video, podcasts, forums, or reviews.	Clearly, Etsy strives to engage their members by convincing spectators to become joiners. Although spectators are able to access content, they are not able to becoming fully engaged without moving up one rung on the ladder to the joiner level.

post requests for custom items. Sellers then bid on the opportunity to make the item and win the sale. It's your opportunity to collaborate with a crafter or artisan to get exactly what you're seeking. Buyers can even make private requests to a specific seller within a shop."[13] The second is the ability for members to shop local, a growing trend for those consumers who are concerned about the environment. The point is the Etsy leadership team added a series of components to engage the members. The result is that members like the virtual gathering place, and of course buy a few things while they are there, hence the 1,000 times revenue increase in 4 years.

The Future of Work

The future of work in going virtual is increasingly pervasive in the new branding messaging by Cisco, a role model virtual and collaboration centric leader. Finally, it seems, everyone wants to reduce the carbon footprint and go green and virtual value is now accelerating as the social good demand and pull to protect our planet.

Fortunately, new virtual solutions like Cisco's telepresence offerings enable collaboration with colleagues, partners, and customers around the globe at a moment's notice. The telepresence application integrates advanced audio, ultra-high-definition video, and interactive collaboration tools with the underlying network to deliver an immersive remote meeting experience. Through this powerful combination of technology and design, local and remote participants feel as if they are in the same room. The immersive experience enables organizations to effectively bring talents and information together from around the globe and elevate creativity and collaboration to a new level.

Virtual leaders like Robert Dixon, senior vice president and chief information officer of Pepsi, echo his organization's experiences by stating, "Cisco TelePresence will reinvent the way we work. It will enable us to travel less, which will allow for greater productivity and a smaller environmental footprint. In this day and age, it's simply a smarter way of going about our business."

At the same time, these solutions acutely enhance the quality of relationships and life balance. In reviewing some of Cisco's recent marketing messaging, the key messages for going virtual are amplified in the list that follows. We have taken statements from Cisco's marketing collaterals on telepresence and reworked the language to reflect statements on the value of virtualization. Many of these statements form benefits to communicate the value proposition of your business going virtual to achieve competitive advantage.[14]

- *The new way of working.* Today you face greater business demands and a more competitive marketplace. You must continually find new ways to be agile and increase speed to market while reducing costs. Effective communication and collaboration are critical. The ability to engage immediately across geographies with employees, suppliers, and customers is a must to sustain competitive advantage.
- *Virtualization for everyone, everywhere.* Business going virtual powers the new way of working, where everyone, everywhere can be more productive through face-to-face collaboration. Virtualization connects coworkers and extends face-to-face collaboration around the world. Virtualization meets your needs from team to personal use, to specific applications for your business, and even via public access. By building your global video community, you can do more with less, transform your organization, drive competitive advantage, and be greener.
- *Do more with less.* Move quickly and gather important stakeholders to improve workflows, new programs, and decision making. By taking your business virtual, it allows you to meet "in person" so you can be more effective, productive, and available than ever before.
- *Transform your organization.* Video and social media are changing the way we communicate and interact. Video stimulates more effective relationships and enhanced engagement. Enabling your business to evolve to new ways of working and allows you to approach processes in ways never before possible. Making faster, better decisions, bringing in expertise immediately and unifying team members are just some ways that video can change the way a business operates.
- *Drive competitive advantage.* As you transform your business, virtualization can deliver new levels of organizational

performance to help you elevate and enhance the customer experience.

- *Be greener and improve quality of life.* By reducing the need for travel and taking your business virtual, you can help boost your company's environmental sustainability efforts: Less travel means a smaller carbon footprint. And reducing travel gives your employees more valuable time, improving their quality of life.
- *Build a collaboration strategy.* By incorporating virtualization capabilities into your collaboration strategy, you can bring the power of increased connectedness in your organization.
- *Powering the new way of working.* Virtualization powers the new way of working. Learn how you can empower teams to collaborate like never before, transforming your organization by leveraging collaboration and social approaches; your world will simply get better.

By further consolidating, these key benefits have core communication messages for leaders to consider in positioning the value of virtualization with their employees. We have filtered these down to these virtual value propositions:

- *Create new ways of working.* Increase your connections with your coworkers and customers and reduce your time to market, increase your agility, and reduce your costs.
- *Accelerate decision making.* You can bring talents, resources, and decision makers dispersed throughout different geographic regions and organizational areas together to synchronize and commit to business objectives and relevant execution blueprints.
- *Innovate across the value chain.* You can see your partners and customers and communicate effectively to transform business processes and enjoy new levels of customer satisfaction and innovation.
- *Scale resources.* No matter where people are available, by going virtual you can use your resources to full advantage. In challenging economic times, your company can continue

to do business at the same level, but more productively and cost-effectively.

- *Support the environment by going green.* Improve the quality of your life and sustain the environment to create a more con-nected, smarter, and healthier planet.
- *Create the foundation for the new world of work.* By going virtual you can power the new world to attract, develop, and retain your talent.

Verety: That Was Then, This Is Now

A few years ago while one of the authors, John, was facilitating a graduate virtual business class, he was looking for local examples of virtual busi-ness in action to share with his students. Verety seemed to be the perfect example for many of the reasons we outlined at the beginning of the chapter. Unfortunately, in 2010, Verety closed the doors on the virtual part of the operation when they closed their remote ordering facilities in four remote North Dakota sites.[15] The decision to close the facilities was apparently due to tough economic times. This is a good reminder that virtual businesses are just as susceptible to external factors as brick and mortar businesses.

Now You Know

A common theme is interwoven in the place cases we highlighted. In each example, innovative leaders discovered a way to use place to their advantage:

- In our first-place case, we witnessed how Midwest virtual order centers help fast food restaurants on the West Coast. By geo-graphically relocating a mission critical step in the drive-thru process, the restaurateurs created real value for the store and home-based agents alike.
- Our second example featured U.S. board-certified radiologists completing off-hour emergent radiology interpretation. In other words, highly qualified doctors living in Australia read X-rays for American medical facilities. The physicians, who

work during Australian daylight, which is American night-time, are well rested, alert, and delighted with their work environment.

- Next we reviewed an innovative way to outsource selective steps in the tax return process. Accounting firms are to protect clients' privacy by ensuring no sensitive financial data leaves the United States. This creative use of VPNs allows the firm to combat the increasing shortage of U.S.-based CPAs.
- The fourth case described how businesses may expand their call center operations without the cost of huge capital projects normally associated with new places. By employing home agents, the companies are able to forego the need for new buildings.
- Finally, we learned how Web 2.0 tools and techniques can be used to create virtual gathering places.

CHAPTER 7

The People Know Best

Better be wise by the misfortunes of others than by your own.

—Aesop

Strategy 2: People

In this chapter, we examine a number of real-world examples of how organizations can harness the power of the people to achieve a competitive advantage. We start our examination by exploring an intriguing concept called *crowdsourcing*, which we view as a brilliant twist on outsourcing. This novel approach to problem solving is creating value in ways that simply were inconceivable only a few years ago. Through a series of *open calls*, organizations can create a competitive atmosphere and choose the ideas, goods, or services that best fit their needs.

Next, we explore the inverse of the crowdsourcing. Rather than attracting many people to compete for our business, the viral option seeks to spread our word to the crowds. The idea is to consider how we can appeal to the masses by examining the impact of viral marketing in a Web 2.0 world. As you read the cases, consider how your organization could benefit from similar implementation.

Finally, we look at an idea that really combines the crowdsourcing and viral marketing. In this case, we seek ways to send out the open call (crowdsource), and rather than selecting one winner, we try to incorporate all the responses to develop a huge database. The desired end state is crowd developed, adds value, and is of interest to the masses: in other words, a viral database.

Strangers in the Night

In a 2006 *Wired* magazine article, Jeff Howe coined the term crowdsourcing to describe "everyday people using their spare cycles to create content, solve problems, even do corporate R & D."[1] In his book, *Crowdsourcing: Why the Power of the Crowd Is Driving the Future of Business*, Howe defined crowdsourcing as "the act of taking a job traditionally performed by a designated agent (usually an employee) and outsourcing it to an undefined, generally large group of people in the form of an open call." Howe wrote, "The amount of knowledge and talent dispersed among the human race has always outstripped our capacity to harness it. Crowdsourcing corrects that—but in doing so, it also unleashes the forces of creative destruction."[2]

Our first example of crowdsourcing in action is 99designs (http://www.99designs.com), whose self-proclaimed role is "to provide a friendly, professional, and secure environment where designers from all walks of life can compete on a level playing field—where they can show off their work, improve their skills, communicate with peers, and win new clients."[3] Their business model is relatively simple: they connect clients needing design work with designers wishing to complete the work. What makes 99designs unique is the way they make the connections. According to 99designs,

> We help you [the client] run a *design contest*, where thousands of designers compete to create the best possible design to meet your needs. All you need is a clear idea of what you want designed and how much you're prepared to pay for it.[4]

The idea for 99designs grew out of a game played by graphic designers. *Photoshop Tennis* is a way designers improve their skills by volleying a project back and forth between players. The game starts by one player making up a design project and serving it to another player. The receiver reviews the design and makes some modifications and then returns the project. During each volley the designer adds to the project and after a predetermined numbers of hits, a judge declares a winner based on the design improvements. As 99designs cofounder Mark Harbottle recalls, "Then a smart entrepreneur came along and suggested that rather than making up the projects why not design his logo and he would pay the winner a cash prize."[5] Today, 99designs includes an army of nearly 55,000 crowdsourcing designers. Together they have submitted more than 3 million designs for clients to review and they have earned over $8 million in prize money.[6]

For many small businesses, the idea of working with a professional design house is a daunting task, one that is often unaffordable. 99designs removes much of the anxiety by providing a simple, stress-free, and inexpensive four-step design process. The process starts with the completion of a design brief in which the client answers a series of questions. Next, the client decides the budget. For example, if you want a logo designed, the budget ranges from about $200 for a budget design to nearly $1,000 for a premium design. A budget design will return about 25 design options compared with a premium design, which will offer 250 designs: essentially the more you offer the more choices you will have. At the budget level, the prize earned by the winning designer is $150 and 99designs fees are $54. At the premium end of the spectrum, the designer earns $795 and 99designs fees are $118. The client may also select from a series of premium options such as fast-tracking, private projects, and featured listing.

Once the budget is established, the crowdsource designers review the project and decide if they wish to compete. Those who opt in will prepare and submit designs for the client's review. The clients provide feedback on the initial designs and ultimately select a winner. The entire process normally takes about a week, and after the contest is complete the client receives the original artwork including the copyright. If the client is not satisfied with any of the designs submitted, then 99designs will refund the total amount.

Our first example of crowdsourcing in action focuses on a many-to-many relationship. In other words, many designers are competing in many different projects. This model offers advantages to both players. The client receives designs from many different designers, each of whom has interpreted the design brief in his or her own creative way. Often the client receives designs from a very diverse group of designers: diversity in age, experience, and nationality is common in many contests. From the client's point of view, all the competition provides many varied choices, certainly more than one would expect to receive from a traditional brick and mortar design house.

The designers also benefit from the many-to-many relationships. First, the overhead for the designers is low. There is no need for a huge marketing budget as the designers may elect to compete in many designs simply by reviewing the open contests. Second, the designer receives feedback from the clients. Even if they do not win a particular prize, they receive very valuable feedback that may make them more competitive in future contests. Finally, the designers may compete on the global scale. They may have one client in Australia, another in the United States, and a third in South Africa. Few freelance designers could sustain a physical presence in several countries around the world.

The result is a win-win situation. Although individual prizes may be relatively small, the cost of participation is very low.

Big Challenge, Big Payoff

Our second group of crowdsourcing examples is very different. Rather than a many-to-many relationship of the previous example, these crowdsourcing examples are a many to one relationship in that many competitors were competing for a single large prize.

Netflix

Netflix, the online movie rental company (http://www.netflix.com), offers their 11 million members a huge database of movies and television shows to rent. At present, the collection includes more than 100,000 titles.[7] If Netflix can better predict what movies a client might want to rent, presumably the consumer will be content and remain a member. However, developing an algorithm that correctly matches a consumer's viewing preferences with the available movies is a very complex and expensive task. Rather than trying to improve their current algorithm in-house they turned to crowdsourcing. They designed the contest in such a way that there would be a winner if there was a significant improvement in performance.

In September 2009, Netflix awarded a single grand prize of $1 million to a crowdsourcing team that "substantially improved the accuracy of predictions about how much someone is going to enjoy a movie based on their movie preferences."[8] The contest, especially the grand prize, attracted participants from around the world. In total, more than 50,000 contestants from 186 countries registered for the event and more than 44,000 valid submissions were received.[9]

Although some may argue this was a very large prize, the point is that Netflix did not have to pay a single dime unless and until a team met their performance standards. As it turns out, they had an army of people (50,000) working on the problem and only once the desired end state was achieved did they pay for the work. Consider the many research and development laboratories around the world that invest millions and do not reap the benefits.

Toyota

In 2010, Toyota announced a similar crowdsourcing project "Ideas for Good," in which they sought ideas for their next generations of cars (see http://www.yourideasforgood.com). Toyota describes their contest in the following way:

> Big ideas are bigger than cars. Toyota has proved this time and time again by sharing our big inventions with the world outside of cars. Everybody has a few good ideas, and Toyota wants to help make some of them a reality. So we're sharing some of our most innovative technologies with you in the hope that you'll share your good ideas to improve the world.[10]

The contest has five categories including safety, solar-powered technology, hybrid technologies, advanced parking, and touch display technologies. The winner in each category will receive a brand new 2011 Toyota vehicle.

Appealing to the Masses

What if you could have millions of people learn about your goods or services at no cost to your organization? For many marketing executives and small business owners, this would be the answer to their dreams. The explosion of media on the Internet, especially on media sharing sites

such as YouTube (http://www.youtube.com), Google Videos (http://www
.video.google.com), iTunes (http://www.apple.com/itunes), and Flickr
(http://www.flickr.com) has presented an interesting opportunity for a
number of businesses to reach millions of potential customers. In most
cases, *going viral* has served the business well; however, the viral nature of
pieces sometimes results in uncomplimentary messages traveling at lightning speed. Three examples follow, two positive and one negative.

The Eruption of Viral Marketing

An early example of a viral video was the web introduction of the now
famous chemical reaction that occurs when a certain candy is dropped
into a certain soda bottle. An amateurish video of the resultant eruption astonished, amazed, and amused millions of Internet users. So much
so that the original video was repeatedly e-mailed to entire contact lists
around the globe, proving the theory that e-mails can reproduce much as
Fibonacci suggested for rabbits.

What is particularly interesting about this pioneering viral marketing example is that neither company featured in the "experiment" was
involved in the design, production, or distribution of the "commercial"
for their product. The popularity of the geyser was the result of two self-
proclaimed mad scientists named Fritz and Stephen who replicated an
experiment that first appeared on a late night talk show in 1999.[11] As the
2006 video grew in popularity and a demand for sequels became appar-
ent, the companies did provide one of the needed ingredients at no cost.
In fact, they have now given Fritz and Stephen 4,000 bottles of Diet
Coke and over 24,000 Mentos.[12] This arm's length support turned out to
be ingenious as the company was not the office sponsor of what could be
seen as a childish prank. The company did, however, reap the benefits of
literally thousands or perhaps millions of copycat "scientists" who felt the
need to replicate the experiment.

Today every fifth grader with access to the Internet knows that
dropping a Mentos candy into a two-liter Diet Coke bottle creates a
volcanic-like eruption. We suspect that every fifth grader's parent is a willing accomplice, having purchased the necessary ingredients and assisted
in the experiment (and probably cleaned up the mess as well).

In this case, two companies, Coca-Cola and Perfetti Van Melle (the maker of Mentos) benefited from a viral video without contributing very much. However, key to the success of this viral was the companies' implicit agreement. Not all companies are as welcoming to this sort of attention. Some organizational leaders would be tempted to try to prevent any unauthorized videos from circulating with their products so prominently displayed. Anchored in the era of media control, 20th-century business thinking would support a notion of cease and desist. However, early in the new millennium some business leaders were rudely awoken to the fact that it is difficult to directly control what happens on the web. Today, savvy leaders will work to influence the web through engagement with stakeholders; however, few CEOs believe they can truly control what is said about their goods and services.

Crasher Squirrel

One the most spontaneous viral-creating events must be the so-called Crasher Squirrel. In 2009, a vacationing couple were enjoying an amazing vista in a particularly picturesque part of western Canada. The moment was so special that the couple wanted it to last for eternity. They decided to take their own picture with a beautiful background of a lake surrounded with near-perfect mountains. To achieve their snapshot of time, the recent groom carefully balanced his camera on a rock and scurried back to be with his beautiful bride as the self-timer counted down. Three, two, one . . . say cheese, and the shutter snapped.

Excited to see if they had captured the moment, they looked at the LCD screen to view the photo. To their surprise, there were three faces, not two, in the picture. The third face belonged to a gray squirrel that scampered into camera view while the groom was taking his place. The photographer submitted it to National Geographic and it was selected as part of their Daily Dozen series. Be sure to look at the photo (http://tinyurl.com/CSquirrel), which includes the following caption:

My husband and I were exploring Lake Minnewanka in Banff National Park, Canada, when we stopped for a timed picture of the two of us. We had our camera set up on some rocks and were getting ready to take the picture when this curious little ground

squirrel appeared, became intrigued with the sound of the focusing camera and popped right into our shot! A once in a lifetime
moment! We were laughing about this little guy for days![13]

Once the Banff/Lake Louise Tourist Office knew about the picture, they
decided to act quickly and decisively. After securing the rights to the
picture, they took the bold decision to make Crasher the focus of the
very successful media campaign.[14] This is another example of an opportunity being presented to an organization, one the bold leaders seized and
reaped the benefits of. Could or would your organization jump on a social
media opportunity? Is your organization agile enough to capture the
moment?

Careful With My Instrument

Our final example of viral media is a rather negative example that most
leaders would wish to avoid. In 2009, Canadian musician David Carroll
launched a music video that chronicled how a major airline treated his
guitar on a flight. Needless to say, the musician was disappointed that
the airline broke his guitar and then would not compensate for his loss.
He took action by creating a music video about the whole incident. The
video was an instant hit with more than 150,000 views on the day of
its launch and almost 9 million more hits in the year after its release.[15]
The video titled "United Breaks Guitar" is worth a look (see http://www
.davecarrollmusic.com/ubg/song1).

According to *The Times* the impact may have been significant as they
reported on their story titled "Revenge is best served cold—on YouTube:
How a broken guitar became a smash hit":

> Meanwhile, within four days of the song going online, the gather-
> ing thunderclouds of bad PR caused United Airlines' stock price
> to suffer a mid-flight stall, and it plunged by 10 per cent, cost-
> ing shareholders $180 million. Which, incidentally, would have
> bought Carroll more than 51,000 replacement guitars.[16]

There is some debate about the impact of negative viral pieces such as the
song we just described. In this particular case, not all observers believe

that United's loss could be attributed to the song. Whatever the actual loss, we are confident that United would have wished to avoid it.

So did any good come from this viral video? Well, for David Carroll it was a life-changing event that swept him from unsigned musician to one with a record deal. The biography on his website sums up the rags to riches story by stating,

> Kudos and credits notwithstanding, it was a broken Taylor guitar that made Dave Carroll an international celebrity. When United Airlines baggage handlers tossed his beloved instrument and refused to accept responsibility, Carroll retaliated with "United Breaks Guitars," the first in a trilogy of songs that were to become immense YouTube hits with over nine million views. The story broke from CNN to The New York Times to Rolling Stone, and culminated with Dave's appearance on The View with Whoopi Goldberg, Joy Behar, Elisabeth Hasselbeck and Sherri Shepherd. "Music is the only thing I've been doing to make a living for years," says Dave. "I've never had a day job, so by that definition I've been successful. But as an indie artist it is tough to make your way—so this is my record deal, my chance of stepping up."[17]

Armies of Volunteers

In chapter 2 we introduced the six levels of social computing as introduced by Li and Bernoff in the *Groundswell*. When introducing the idea, we challenged you to think about how you could apply their ideas to your organization. In the last chapter, we shared one example as we highlighted Etsy. In this segment, we showcase two innovative uses of the Forrester's Social Technographics in action. Recall the six rungs of the ladder:

- *Creators* make social content go. They write or upload video, music, or text.
- *Critics* respond to content from other. They post reviews, comment on blogs, participate in forums, and edit wiki articles.
- *Collectors* organize content for themselves or others using RSS feeds, tags, and voting sites like Digg.com.

- *Joiners* connect in social networks like MySpace and Facebook.
- *Spectators* consume social content including blogs, user-generated video, podcasts, forums, or reviews.
- *Inactives* neither create nor consume social content of any kind.[18]

CNN iReporters

In 2006, CNN, the global news network, launched a project called iReport (http://www.ireport.com). The concept was simple: recruit an army of volunteers to report the news that is happening in their region of the world. This idea really builds on the joiner and creator categories of *Groundswell*. CNN believed that people like to join social spaces and create content: in short, they want to tell their story. The growth of the community grew and added real value to CNN as they witnessed great iReports on subjects such as the Iran elections, President's Obama's inauguration, and the tragedy of the earthquake in Haiti. Most of the iReports remain as unvetted stories on the iReport.com site; however, the very best and newsworthy stories are featured on the company's main site CNN.com. For the iReporters, it is a great honor to be featured on the main site. By the end of 2010, there were more than 700,000 iReporters and at least one story from all 194 countries on the planet.[19]

The iReport project allows CNN to provide much more breadth and depth in their reporting than would otherwise be possible. It would simply not be possible to have 700,000 reporters on staff or even freelancers. The system has matured to the level that CNN now provides *assignments* for iReporters allowing them to augment, complement, or fill gaps on major news events around the world. Of course, we are not suggesting that iReporters provide the same fidelity or accuracy of reporting the news; however, they provide an interesting view of the world and occasionally provide CNN a real scoop on the news.

TripAdvisor

An excellent example of *Groundswell's* critics category is TripAdvisor (http://www.tripadvisor.com). We highlighted TripAdvisor in the leadership chapter where we profiled An African Villa. We first discovered An

African Villa through TripAdvisor, which in turn connected us with our incredible tour guide. We booked our stay at An African Villa based on the wonderful comments by many people who stayed there before us. In other words, we trusted an army of strangers and we were not disappointed. Likewise, because we trusted An African Villa we booked, sight unseen, a guide who we would trust with making our stay in Cape Town safe, enjoyable, and memorable. Again, we were not let down. This brief recap reminds us of the power of critics in a Web 2.0 world. Despite the millions of dollars that are spent to promote various travel wares, more and more people are listening to the laypeople critics rather than professional travel writers and marketers.

TripAdvisor truly has an army of volunteers who rate their travel experiences around the world. Since they launched in 2000, TripAdvisor has witnessed tremendous growth and now boasts a global army of critics including more than 50 million unique monthly users, 20 million members, and over 40 million reviews and opinions. The sites operate in 26 countries worldwide, including China under daodao.com visitors.[20] According to TripAdvisor, they feature the following:

- More than 40 million honest travel reviews and opinions from real travelers around the world
- 1+ million businesses
- 80,000+ cities
- 450,000+ hotels
- 125,000+ attractions
- 650,000+ restaurants
- 6,000,000+ candid traveler photos
- Ninety-eight percent of topics posted in the TripAdvisor forums are replied to within 24 hours[21]

Now You Know

- Crowdsourcing is "the act of taking a job traditionally performed by a designated agent (usually an employee) and outsourcing it to an undefined, generally large group of people in the form of an open call."

- Crowdsourcing may be an excellent alternative for organizations lacking the know-how or resources to solve a difficult problem.
- Viral videos can be positive or negative as they tend to move at lightning speed. Is your organizations ready to exploit the momentum of a positive video? Are you ready to quickly deal with an unwanted viral video? Remember to think about squirrels and guitars!
- By the end of 2010 there were more than 700,000 CNN iReporters and at least one story from all 194 countries on the planet.[22]
- TripAdvisor (a good example of *Groundswell's* critics category) truly has an army of volunteers who rate their travel experiences around the world. Since they launched in 2000, TripAdvisor has witnessed tremendous growth and now boasts a global army of critics including more than 50 million unique monthly users.

CHAPTER 8

Everyone Has a Stake

Collaborate or die.

—Jim Balsille, CEO of Research In Motion[1]

Strategy 3: Collaboration

Collaboration in the workplace is as important to free enterprise as competition in the marketplace. The spirit of win-win cannot survive in an environment of stiff competition. For collaboration to flourish, win-win needs to be a mature operating practice, and the systems have to support it. The recruiting system, the on-boarding system, the training and educational systems system, the strategic and operational planning systems, the communication systems, the budgeting system, the information system, the compensation system—all have to be based on the principle of win-win.

So how many organizations have got this deep collaboration systemic organizational DNA tapestry right? Many do not—but increasingly many do. The next section covers case studies from diverse organizations from leading Fortune 500 companies, government organizations, retail, and small businesses.

Millennials at work are not passive consumers of the technology that information technology departments provide. A 2008 study by Symantec showed that younger workers are many times more likely to access social networks at work, use outside instant messaging services, download software to their business PCs, and other risky behaviors. Sixty-nine percent said they used whatever technology they wanted to at work, and only 45% said they "always adhered to IT policies," compared with 70% of older workers. Employers that take a hard line on enforcing policies can win short-term battles over IT control and management but risk losing the long-term war to recruit and retain next-generation talent that knows the value of social computing, both in their personal lives and at work.[2]

To help millennials reach their full potential, companies need to find ways to support their networked learning styles. This means giving them access to people and data in context, at the moment when they need the knowledge to make a difference in an operational process or customer engagement.

Social Media in Action

Molson Coors, founded in 1786, is the oldest beer brand in North America. The company represents a merger between the Adolph Coors Company (Colorado based) and Molson Inc. (Canada based) to form the Molson Coors Brewing Company in February 2005. The Canadian business unit is headquartered in Toronto, Canada. Molson Coors now has 15,000 employees, and 18 breweries distributes to 30 countries. In 2009, the company's net sales totaled $3.1 billion.[3]

The company culture has maintained the values of both Adolph Coors (1873) and John Molson (1786), who founded both companies. Both men maintained a deep commitment to the community and a passion for innovation, which the company still leverages today for differentiation and brand building. Molson Coors believes that to win in the long term, they must "create and sustain a winning culture . . . by living our values."[4] These values are as follows:

- *Integrity & Respect*: being honest, ethical and open as a basis for building trusting relationships;
- *Quality*: being obsessive about the quality of our products and everything we do to better serve our customers and consumers;
- *Excelling*: committing ourselves to doing things that are key to winning and doing them better than anyone else;
- *Creativity*: supporting the development and execution of fresh ideas that will make us win in the beer business; and
- *Passion*: displaying and evoking extraordinary enthusiasm and commitment to delight customers and consumers.[5]

Molson Coors feels that doing business the right way is part of corporate responsibility, which should be organization-wide and not in one specific department. Molson Coors launched their first website in 1995 with content focused on music and sports. After an internal transformation of philanthropic approaches, the company noticed traditional media were not interested in the story. Even having a website, Molson Coors recognized their reliance on media to propagate information so they established a blog in 2007, in an attempt to promote extra news and break their dependencies.

This blog was largely unsuccessful, in part, because the focus was on internal communication and because the content was not relevant to their audiences. Realizing the original attempt was unsuccessful, Molson Coors realigned their social media strategy and relaunched it in 2008. Their new social portfolios spanned e-mail, Twitter, Facebook, and blogs and promoted Molson Coors in the community message. Instead of focusing on internal communication, the company established a platform for telling the company story. Molson Coors aimed to engage consumers with content they were interested in consuming.

Molson Coors Canada was the first beer brand in Canada on Facebook and, to date, remains the most popular beer brand on Facebook. The Molson Coors blog can be found at http://blog.molson.com/community. Note the frequent updates and Twitter integration, highlighting each tweet with the word Molson. Molson Coors found their social media tipping point during the 2010 Vancouver Olympics by allowing fans to create Canadian Jerseys for their profile pictures. The move went viral and Facebook fans increased from 30,000 to 360,000 in just 6 days.[6]

Another successful campaign was #Brew2.0, where social media influencers were invited to taster sampling parties with Molson Coors. For this campaign, they registered 40+ blog posts from influencers, and over 150 tweets were featured on a podcast that won the 2008 SNCR Blogger relations award at the event. More importantly, Molson Coors was able to form relationships with influential individuals that traditional marketing channels could not.

By September 2010, the Facebook Page grew to over 427,000 Facebook fans.[7] Coors Light remained the company's most popular Facebook product page with over 75,000 fans. The company primarily focuses on blogging and Facebook over Twitter (where it still maintains an active presence) due to the increased personalization and duration of the message in this channel.

Molson Coors view social media as an integrated solution. Like the company's organizational culture, social media is a medium to portray a companywide message. Devins (2009) has explained that social media is about having conversations, a feature that distinguishes it from the core marketing group.

Internally, social media is measured as a part of the marketing communication's mix. Instead of rigid internal policies, social media practitioners are advised to use common sense. The company recognized social media as a way to extend their customer service and customer relevance to the online world and saw this as a natural extension for the company's existing communication projects. As Adam Moffat, manager of marketing and brand public relations, explained, "It helps us get closer to our drinkers, and lets them see the people and personality behind our brands. Stronger relationships lead to increased customer loyalty, which ultimately drives sales."[8]

One example of reaching out is when an individual questioned their Canadian heritage for not drinking Molson Coors. The company reached out over Twitter, jokingly saying he was still Canadian to them, to which he tweeted back, "Oh no, I'm caught."[9] Thus Molson Coors is creating personal relationships with customers and noncustomers alike. Devins explained that out of every 10 negative comments they respond to on Twitter, 9 inevitably turn out positive.

As part of the new social media approach, Molson Coors changed their guiding principle. Ferg Devins, chief public affairs officer, explained that the goal was to build authentic, trusting relationships with Canadians and build relevant communities, not push a marketing message. The company wants to be part of the conversation and listen for relevance. More than just talk, the company manually follows up with all new Twitter followers to introduce themselves.

The company also monitors online conversations about their brand and industry, which allow them to create a targeted pitch to traditional media. By utilizing this tactic, they can ensure that pitches are relevant to the Molson Coors audience and prove traction to traditional media. Molson Coors actively track Twitter sentiment in relation to their communication campaigns. Molson Coors modify their efforts and modify tactics, messaging, and outreach on demand, based on feedback and opinions.

The following are the social media lessons learned from Molson Coors:

- *Early objectives are key, and success should be measured.* Companies should always be stating clear, actionable, and measureable objectives when defining a social strategy to solidify a meaningful success, as was the case with Molson Coors. Different industries and companies can leverage social media for different purposes. Additionally, measuring ongoing success ensures that social media channels can be compared to other mediums.
- *Speak to, not at, an audience.* Another key issue with the earlier iterations of Molson Coors social media strategy was the way in which content delivered. Traditional media and marketing campaigns are accustomed to speaking at audiences, delivering one-way content message. Social media is primarily social network and communication based, where users have the choice to opt in to brands. As such, brands must recognize that successful strategies engage individuals in meaningful dialogue. Later, successful versions of the Molson Coors strategy recognized that speaking with audiences in dialogue was a far more successful strategy.
- *Social media success can be iterative.* As with any new medium, companies do not always get it right the first time. The field of social media is new, quickly growing, and best practices are still being defined. Like many companies, Molson Coors' success on social media was an iterative process, testing many messages and using metrics to define what was successful.

The Idea Factory

MTS Allstream is one of Canada's leading national communication solutions companies and provides innovative communications solutions for the way Canadians want to live and work today. The company has more than 100 years of experience, with 6,000 employees across Canada. MTS Allstream has nearly two million total customer connections spanning business customers across Canada and residential consumers throughout the province of Manitoba.

With offices across Canada, MTS Allstream's 6,000 employees live and work in cities from Halifax to Vancouver, with the highest concentrations of the workforce in Winnipeg and Toronto. MTS Allstream's employee base is diverse. Hundreds of employees work in corporate roles, others are in customer service roles, and several hundred employees are in technical jobs and on the road. The vast majority of internal communication is done by e-mail, online or face to face, through the company's daily e-newsletter, Intranet, an annual All Employee Roadshow, and regular employee calls with executives. In the province of Quebec, most employees speak French at home and in the workplace.

MTS Allstream's CEO and two business unit presidents travel each year to meet with employees face to face as part of the company's All Employee Roadshow. These sessions have traditionally followed a formal business presentation structure where executives discussed the previous year's results and plan for the year ahead. The MTS Allstream corporate communications team modified the program for 2009 by doing the following:

- Eliminating the formality of the events (traditionally included a lectern, formal presentation, PowerPoint Q&A session, audience in theater-style seating) to create a more informal and participatory environment.
- Adding an interactive, idea-sharing "conversation" to the program. Each table was given one of five key questions related to improving the company; employees discussed at their tables and participated in a larger conversation between all participants and the CEO. There was no lectern, no PowerPoint—it was a very open environment with the CEO and presidents in the middle of the room surrounded by employees.[10]

The response from employees was overwhelmingly positive. They had questions. They had ideas. They had solutions. It became clear that a conversation once a year was not enough to sustain the dialogue and momentum generated at the 2009 All Employee Roadshow. The question was how to facilitate an ongoing conversation between the 6,000 geographically dispersed employees and the executives of the company.

Initially, using the existing SharePoint environment and functionality, an internal online discussion forum was established on MTS Allstream's Intranet. Although it met the immediate need, it did not provide the user experience or truly collaborative experience that corporate communications envisioned. Employees asked for a place where they could do the following:

- Offer up their ideas
- Rate and comment on other's ideas
- Volunteer to be part of the solution
- Remain informed about their ideas by being alerted to updates
- Follow along as ideas are put into action

MTS Allstream's corporate communications team conducted significant research on best practices for using online tools. They identified the functionality and user experience that would be required for the tool to be successful. The result of this work was the concept for a site that would later be named Idea Factory: a unique employee engagement tool.

With a concept and strategy in hand, the team engaged external resources and internal stakeholders, including the IT and HR groups, to develop a solution that would meet MTS Allstream's unique needs. After several months of development, Idea Factory was launched. The site is accessible through a large graphic link on the company's Intranet site and automatically recognizes employees when they log on. Employees have the ability to upload a photo to their profile, which appears as a thumbnail beside their ideas and comments. In initial planning sessions, it was determined that transparency would encourage professionalism.

In developing Idea Factory, corporate communications determined there should be several ways for employees to interact on the site. Allowing employees to volunteer to be part of the solution and inviting them to weigh in on ideas by rating them against two different criteria ("good for me" and "good for the company") would encourage ownership, participation in the problem-solving process, and thinking about the greater good. Once posted, ideas are given time to provoke conversation and gather comments and votes. The newest ideas are featured on the site's homepage to draw visitors. Ideas are reviewed and assessed at weekly management meetings and summarized for the company's executive committee.

Many ideas are solved or resolved through employee participation alone—for example, if consensus is built, or if the owner of a process or function steps forward and takes action. These ideas are moved directly to "Success Stories."

Although employees at every level including leaders and management are encouraged to take accountability for their participation on the site, ideas that require subject matter experts or executive-level support or resources are forwarded to the appropriate departmental executive for a decision to action or to provide an explanation of why the idea will not move forward. For ideas that are not actionable—because they have already been considered, because the resources do not exist to support it, or because they have already been done—an explanation is posted and the idea is moved to the Idea Factory archive. No ideas go unanswered.

Ideas that are deemed actionable are moved to the In Action section of the site and a key person is assigned to provide regular updates until the idea is complete. It is then moved to Success Stories when completed.

The following lessons can be learned from the Idea Factory:

- *IT development.* An external vendor was engaged to design and build Idea Factory, integrating an externally built platform (Drupal) with MTS Allstream's secure, internal IT infrastructure.
- *Budget challenges.* When the concept for Idea Factory was conceived, there was no budget available to build a new site. Corporate communications overcame budget challenges by reaching out to other groups within the company who also believed strongly in the project and were willing to put some of their budget toward its development. This cooperation made Idea Factory a reality.
- *Executive support.* Implementing a nonhierarchal means of communicating with employees within an environment that had relied most heavily on one-way communication was challenging. Fortunately, Pierre Blouin, CEO of MTS Allstream, was a huge champion for the project, as were many other members of the company's leadership.
- *User-friendly design.* Developing a platform that would be user friendly and accessible to all staff, regardless of age and

familiarity with social media was a serious consideration during the planning and development of Idea Factory. Corporate communications, with advice from the external vendor, structured the site in a simple and intuitive way.

- *Outcomes*. Evaluation to June 30, 2010, proved that Idea Factory achieved its key objectives of increasing employee engagement and working collaboratively on ideas and solutions:[11]
  - Between February 23 and June 30, 2010, Idea Factory recorded 7,304 visits, an average of 1,826 per month.
  - Between February 23 and June 30, 2010, 2,005 MTS Allstream employees, which represents just over 33% of the workforce, visited Idea Factory.
  - In May 2010, 2 months after the launch of Idea Factory, the company conducted its biannual employee engagement survey. The survey showed that employee engagement increased 4% over 2008 levels. In those 2 years, corporate communications launched Idea Factory and updated the format of its All Employee Roadshow. With a score of 80%, MTS Allstream is now above the global telecommunications benchmark for employee engagement.
  - 981 comments were posted on the site during the initial measurement stage.
  - 274 ideas were posted on Idea Factory in its first 4 months.
  - Of the 274 ideas (or 15%) posted to Idea Factory, 41 were moved to In Action between February and June 30, 2010, demonstrating that an atmosphere was created that welcomed and encouraged valid ideas that could be moved to action.
  - Eight ideas were moved to Success Stories in the first 4 months post launch. Since dozens of ideas are still In Action, with results pending, the number of Success Stories will likely spike in the next 4 months.

MTS Allstream's first major foray into online, social-mediated conversation to engage employees and improve the company through employee idea generation has been a major success. Idea Factory has successfully initiated an ongoing conversation between employees and leaders that has resulted in increased employee engagement. Approximately one-third of MTS Allstream's 6,000 employees currently participate in this conversation passively (by regularly checking the site) or actively by contributing and participating.

Four months postlaunch, site statistics remain strong. Idea Factory was viewed 1,156 times in June. Corporate communications anticipates that Idea Factory will become an important and ongoing part of MTS Allstream's internal communications toolbox and will evolve with the company and technology.

Currently, the corporate communications team is preparing to launch a 6-month Idea Factory renewal campaign to drive new and returning traffic to the site. Idea Factory will improve other areas of employee communication, as corporate communications is exploring ways to integrate Idea Factory into the 2011 All Employee Roadshow.

Leadership Passion for Collaboration

Research In Motion (RIM), headquartered in Waterloo, Ontario, Canada, has revenues approaching $5.5 billion, with nearly 14,000 employees. They provide wireless hardware, software, and services to customers worldwide. Its popular BlackBerry smartphones handle voice, e-mail, and text messaging, as well as Internet access and multimedia applications. RIM also provides software development tools and makes radio-based modems that other manufacturers incorporate into portable devices. In addition to hardware sales, the company generates revenue from network access fees and software licensing fees. RIM sells to corporations, resellers, and wireless carriers.

One of the cofounders of RIM is Jim Basille, and his passion for collaboration and open ecosystems in his Waterloo community is well known and respected. One of his passions has been to connect the manufacturing community into a virtual network called the Manufacturing Innovation Network (MIN). The MIN is the central place for local manufacturers in the Waterloo region. This network developed on the Igloo community platform connects all manufacturing stakeholder groups in an effort to create a more responsive and globally competitive manufacturing community through improved collaboration and knowledge sharing. MIN's three driving growth principles are to do the following:

- *Build awareness.* Raise awareness of products and services manufactured in the region, on both a local and a global scale.
- *Improve collaboration and knowledge sharing* between companies and industry professionals in an effort to create shared best practices, standard protocols, and new innovations. Members can join peer groups, create professional profiles, and access experts in blogs and online discussion forums.
- *Increase trade.* A centralized e-marketplace for buying, selling, and promoting goods and services online, such as classified ads, a job board, and a comprehensive company directory.

It is the place to go to find out what is happening in the region's dynamic manufacturing sector and to get connected with resources and people from across the region and beyond. MIN is also viewed in Canada as one of the most successful collaborative ecosystems using collaborative technologies.

Basille's passion for collaboration excellence in his external community is just as pervasive in his leadership style with his employees. One of his current corporate mantras internally with his employees is "Collaborate or die." Although Basille was not the first to coin this phrase, he, like many smart CEOs, understand that growth from networks and community ecosystem knowledge flows will drive more value than simply investing in only products for distribution.

In early 2009, RIM made a strategic decision to improve its global collaboration footprint worldwide and engaged in a comprehensive request for proposal (RFP) process that resulted in selecting the IBM footprint for its collaboration solutions. IBM and RIM have partnered heavily to ensure the RIM mobile stack is interoperable with the IBM stack increasing ease of communicating with others' respective platforms. The program was led by Rex Lee, director of eCollaboration at RIM, and supported by a cross functional team. Lee is well known in the industry for his depth of knowledge in collaboration and portal business practices, having had prior success at Bell Canada leading their collaboration IT strategies. He was able to learn firsthand the importance of front line employee engagement and executive alignment.

Over 12 months, the team worked night and day supported by Helix Commerce (strategy and change management consultants) supported by IBM (technology solutions provider) to design a robust program that would result in all employees having access to the IBM Lotus Collaboration Suite, supported by strong communication, training, and a center of excellence (COE) to sustain the ongoing operational requirements.

RIM has made major investments in their global eCollaboration program to evolve their organization's capabilities and to support their requirements for global scale. They have learned firsthand that a collaboration leadership approach to business practices and processes will help them achieve a stronger competitive advantage.

The following lessons can be learned from RIM:

- *Executive leadership and accountability are key.* A senior executive council was established to provide stakeholder governance and included diverse executives from information technology, human resources, engineering, security, legal, research and development, and other departments. They met monthly to review the status of the collaboration program activities, to help remove barriers, and manage internal communication requirements.
- *Lead with leading practices.* RIM was very astute in developing their change management program practices as they realized from the "get go" that having embedded leading practices would make a major difference to the success of the overall program. Seeding this with knowledge and depth from Helix and IBM's global collaboration experiences helped reduce the risk of making mistakes, and transferring knowledge from proven programs to support the design and execution of customized approaches at RIM was invaluable.
- *Drive adoption rapidly.* RIM compressed its deployment programs significantly from an initial pilot phase to deploying a full roll out program. Their view was iterative in design, having a young work force hungry to use the tools would be smart enough to apply the technology effectively. Being perfect is

simply not in the RIM cultural DNA. Getting out with a more agile approach and learning and adapting are more in line with the strong entrepreneurial DNA of the culture.

Further Innovation and Social Enterprise Research

The scope of this book precludes an extensive overview of the many noteworthy companies with leading collaboration and social practices, driving culture change, leadership, and innovation focus. For more information on what companies such as Cisco, Google, IBM, and many others are doing, please see Helix's recent report on innovation and social enterprise.[12] An extract of the report is available as an appendix.

Creating a Social Workplace: Leadership Behaviors Remain Problematic

IBM recently completed a study on the social workplace based on conversations with over 700 chief human resource officers worldwide.[13] The study is focused on the following:

- Cultivating creative leaders who can more nimbly lead in complex, global environments
- Mobilizing for greater speed and flexibility—producing significantly greater capability to adjust underlying costs and faster ways to allocate talent
- Capitalizing on collective intelligence—through much more effective collaboration across increasingly global teams

From in-depth conversations with hundreds of HR leaders, they found that numerous boundaries are restricting the ability of organizations to effectively match resources with opportunities. Comprehensive research outlines that key gaps exist in the ability of their companies to develop future leaders, rapidly develop workforce skills and capabilities, and effectively collaborate and share knowledge-flowing technology capabilities. What is clear is that workers are feeling overwhelmed, attention deficit is on the rise, and that leadership needs to start developing stronger competencies in creating and sustaining smart and adaptive virtual organizations.

Now You Know

- Jeff Howe coined the term crowdsourcing to describe "everyday people using their spare cycles to create content, solve problems, and even do corporate R & D."[14]
- Walking-the-talk lessons learned, based on our Cisco case study, include the following:
  - Collaboration requires robust and networked infrastructure to be effective.
  - Collaboration fuels accelerated team performance.
  - Collaboration requires leadership alignment.
- Social media lesson learned, based on our Molson Coors case study include the following:
  - Early objectives are key and success should be measured.
  - Speak to, not at, an audience.
  - Social media success can be iterative.
- eCollaboration lessons learned, based on our RIM case study, include the following:
  - Executive leadership and accountability are key.
  - Lead with leading practices.
  - Drive adoption rapidly.
- Collaboration and social media lessons learned are the following:
  - In executive leadership, walking the talk is key!
  - Collaboration and social technology toolkits need integration.
  - This journey takes time to get right!

CHAPTER 9

Real in the Virtual World

Small startup companies as well as global 1000 giants are recognizing that virtual environments can help improve the bottom line, by reducing costs and increasing revenues by extending reach to customers. The signs are clear: Virtual Worlds @ Work is becoming standard business practice.

—Eilif Trondsen, PhD, SRI Consulting Business Intelligence, 2008[1]

Strategy 4: Second Life Virtual Worlds

Virtual worlds represent a new form of 3D web-based human interaction experiences. Ignoring these richer forms of media consumer, employee, and partner relationship approaches will impact an organization's ability to successfully attract, develop, and retain not only Gen X and Y talent but the next generation of Gen V (Virtual) talent. Gen Vs will further transform the ubiquity of rich media and gaming-like experiences into real-life experiences. This will continue to unfold as the human condition searches for greater collaboration and social mediated connections. In time, all forms of digital interaction will be 3D with integrated personas.

Our examination of this rich form of social interaction concentrates on SL virtual worlds and includes two parts: inspirations and memories. This chapter focuses on the inspirations—that is, the SL implementations that are active today. We recommend you visit each of these islands to see how businesses are reaping the benefits of this powerful alternative existence. In addition to the active worlds, there are many that have left SL in the last 12 months. Despite their fading, their stories are so compelling in innovation and experimentation that we have chosen to ensure their virtual histories are not lost and are recorded for ongoing insight and learning as early stage pioneers. The lessons from these memories are many and worth your attention. We have chronicled their tales in an appendix and highly recommend you take the time to learn from these early adopters. Together, the active and inactive provide valuable insights, inspirations, and memories to help businesses, profit or nonprofit, appreciate the value that virtual worlds hold in developing new business models to support the continued virtualization of business.

Real Biz in Second Life

Dell Inc. is a multinational technology corporation that develops, manufactures, sells, and supports personal computers and other computer-related products. Dell is based in Round Rock, Texas. Dell is treating SL as an extension to their web presence. Similar to IBM's Sims, users can order real products online as well as participate in interactive activities. The islands feature a welcome area, an orientation island, a theater, promotional pavilion, and a conference center.

The environment is unusual; when it comes to brand presence in SL, unusual is a good thing. The actual appearance of the island is striking, in that it blends a medieval style village with a very futuristic design. At the central hub, instead of having a map that allows the user to transport instantly to their desired location, they have designed a flying white transport pod in which a user's avatar can become enveloped and transported.

The original presence was largely centered on a virtual factory. Here users could begin the buying process of a new computer by picking parts and watching them assemble. Then they were directed to the web to complete the purchasing process. This area was created to coincide with the release of Dell's crystal display monitors and developed to appeal to the SL community. Also included on the island is an SL orientation station. We estimate Dell is receiving over 800 visitors a week.

Last year, Dell began staging an increasing number of events on their island. These included a promotion for the film *Evan Almighty* and a "Plant a Tree for Me" environmental initiative where users could donate and plant a virtual or real tree. These events, along with the already present interactivity, are promising. The island, however, lacks an in-world event schedule; hence, future events are unknown.

For the most part, the island has been designed to engage residents automatically. While residents used to be able to begin purchases in world, Dell found that not enough people were using the service to justify the costs of keeping it up to date and dynamic. Recently, however, Dell has been working with in-world staff. The center of the Sim has posted "tech support" hours. Five days a week for 4 hours a day, Dell has in-world support staff available for discussion and information. An innovative highlight experience on their island is the oversized Dell computer where users can enter and explore inside a computer several stories high.

The community experience on this island is facilitated by three features: regular staff hours, a Dell SL group, and occasional large-scale events. Dell's in-world staff offers the company an opportunity to have consistent dialogue with older tech-savvy consumers and give residents a reason to return to Dell's island even when there are no events or updates. Similarly, the Dell SL group facilitates a way for Dell to keep in touch with residents and inform them of upcoming events and changes. Laura P. Thomas of Dell's global e-commerce has said that in-world community events have been very strategic in their relevance to both the company and SL.[2] As such, these have been large but intentionally very spaced out. An area for improvement in terms of community experience is the frequency of events. In this regard, Dell could learn something from Microsoft's new island where events here are kept relevant by allowing a concentrated user group to organize frequent small events and seminars.

The design of the island is original and engaging. It is also constructed to have a minimal amount of lag. However, it does still lack a greater level of interactivity. The space has potential to be more meaningful. There are several video feeds on the island including an e-seminar on the value of Windows Vista. The Dell factory is quite innovative, and there are definitely some elements of interest on the island (e.g., Michael Dell's college dorm room). Also, by clicking on a certain virtual PC, residents will initiate a psychedelic adventure to the giant PC at the other end of the Sim. In the main village, there is a freebie store where residents can pick up Dell backpacks.

Visit Dell Island at http://slurl.com/secondlife/Dell%20Island%204/2/236/40.

Real City in the Virtual World

At the end of March 2007, Amsterdam, a popular SL location and re-creation of Amsterdam, Holland, was sold on eBay for $50,000 to the Dutch company Nested Group. The Amsterdam Sims, a popular SL destination with canals, houseboats, and an adult explicit red light district was one of the largest sales of a SL business by a private developer.[3]

The Amsterdam Sim was created by SL resident, Kevin Alderman (also known as "Striker Serpentine"), with high resolution photos of the city and included several Amsterdam streets lined with hundreds of shops and detailed squares. Although the initial deal fell through shortly after purchase due to disagreements over property rights, the Sim was purchased by the Dutch media company Boom. This sale is indicative of how much value developers place on popular SL locations. At this point, most major developers are not likely to take on a corporate campaign for less than $10,000, and this would only produce a modest island. The average price for a complex development is in the $50,000 to $100,000 range in American dollars.

To visit the Amsterdam Sims, see http://slurl.com/secondlife/Amsterdam%202/182/188/26.

The Million-Dollar Avatar

Anshe Chung is the avatar and brand name of real-life Ailin Graef. She is the CEO of Anshe Chung Studios and the first person to earn over $1 million in assets in SL. Described as the "Rockefeller of Second Life" by a CNN journalist, she sells and develops virtual real estate. Anshe Chung started her SL career in 2004 with a $10 investment in a premium account. The virtual funds she earned selling her designs were reinvested in buying and developing virtual land. Initially, Anshe wanted to make money in SL to support her church's charitable work. Before long, however, she began making enough to reinvest her funds, and now Anshe Chung "owns" over 500 servers worth of land that she develops and rents out. Most of the land is rented as part of her "Dreamland" series of developments. Her real-life company, Anshe Chung Studios in China, now has over 60 employees. According to several sources, including a title in the October 2009 issue of *Avenue Magazine*, Anshe Chung joined the founders of Skype as a key investor behind the new 3D avatar fashion site Frenzoo.[4]

To visit Chung Central Park in Dreamland, see http://slurl.com/secondlife/Dreamland/135/181/22.

Where the Best-Dressed Avatars Meet

Modavia Productions, the fashion show production division of Modavia Fashion Marketing, announced the lineup of designers participating in the Modavia Fashion Week 2010 event. The fashion shows fall collections covered some of SL's very best labels. Fashion Week Fall 2010 is sponsored by LeLutka and supported by media partners *Deja Vu International* magazine and Wilder Public Relations. The event is also be supported by treet.tv.

This event occurs in parallel with Fashion Week in New York City and includes 35 shows over 8 days with over 400 Virtual Fashion outfits in a new multi-Sim venue, resulting in 4 to 5 fashion events a day. SL Fashion houses participating in Modavia Fashion Week 2010 included A la Folie, Angel Dessous, Anubis Style, Baiastice, B! Fashion, Bliss Couture, Boudoir, Casa del Shai, Chantkare, CheerNo, [dekade.], Dojo, Eshi Otawara, Gabriel, Gasqhe, Gems & Kisses, House of Fox, Indyra Originals, Kunglers, L'Abel, LeeZu!, MEB, Miamai, Modern Gypsy, My Precious, Niven Collection, Orage Creations, Paper Couture, Ricielli, SHIKI, Sonatta Morales, Son!a, and Violator. For more information on Fashion Week, visit the Modavia Fashion Week website.[5]

This is the second Fashion Week produced by Modavia and, as in 2009, will be held in conjunction with the Mercedes-Benz Fashion Week taking place in New York City at the same time. The event last year, set in Bryant Park SL, was well attended and attracted an unprecedented level of media coverage.

Modavia Fashion Marketing CEO Poptart Lilliehook coordinates this highly anticipated event and became aware of the existence of haute couture design in SL from the experience of shopping at LeeZu Baxter Designs (now LeeZu!) SL store in December 2007. What started out as a random shopping trip turned into a full-fledged obsession with Modavia Productions, which started in collaboration with Payton Heron and was inspired by the iconic New York City Fashion event. The first Modavia Fashion Week was born in 2009.

To appreciate the growth of fashion in SL, one only has to look at the number of fashion virtual goods available at the SL Marketplace and check the apparel inventory, and you will quickly see fashion business in virtual worlds is booming: with children's wear at over 11,284 items to choose from; clothing textures, 6591 goods; men's clothing, 64, 712 items; unisex, 37,905 items; and women's clothing the largest goods inventory totally over 346,123 virtual goods.[6]

SL also offers most popular directories for all the different online experiences in SL and monitor the most popular destination sites. For keeping track of fashion trends, check out this link and you can be kept current on SL fashion activities: http://secondlife.com/destinations/fashion.

Finding Real Careers in the Virtual World

Ontario Public Services (OPS) Careers is an organization that works with the provincial government and employs people in public service jobs in Ontario, Canada. OPS designed their SL Sim with the goal of creating an interactive island to drive interest and inquiries for Real World career positions and to direct users to the OPS Central Careers website to view available job opportunities. It is currently in pilot phase and remains experimental for the Ontario government. The island came to be in an effort by OPS to have an early stage presence in the virtual world. Since its launch, it has received over 4,000 visitors with an average visitor dwelling time of 23 minutes. OPS was given a government innovation award for the build.

The OPS Island is one Sim ordered into six areas and buildings: the Medical Center, Firefighting Area, Laboratory, Central Terminal, Traffic Center, and Business Center. Upon transporting into the Sim, one arrives in the Central Terminal. There is a semicircle of organized kiosks, each with the name of a different career discipline available through OPS. When clicked on, these kiosks open a browser and send the user to the corresponding website. In a tighter semicircle around the transport-in point are smaller kiosks that act as teleport vehicles to each area on the island. This main building sits in a virtual airfield with two propeller planes, a helicopter, and a hangar. Residents can enter and sit inside the vehicles in various positions, but the planes cannot fly. Outside of this area, roads connect the other sections of the island located in the four corners of the Sim. The exception is the firefighting area, which is just next to the central building. At each building, there is a Sim map that can assist users in teleporting around, which makes visiting each location easy.

The Medical Center sits in the northwest corner of the Sim. As with the other buildings at OPS Careers, the aesthetic aim seems to be a realistic design. Residents walk into a reception area complete with a "no cell phones" sign, a coffee machine, waiting chairs, and plants. Importantly, halfway up the wall, an LED-style sign scrolls the names of medicine-related jobs available in the public services. Also, there are two kiosks: one taking residents to the OPS Careers website, the other taking them to a survey about the online presence. The building features include a short video feed, a room demonstrating CPR using dynamic drawings and avatar animations, a meeting room, and many hospital rooms.

In the southwest corner, the Traffic Center offers a very interesting environment. The hexagonal room demonstrates what a job in the traffic sector might resemble. On the wall is a large screen that shows changing traffic camera shots. Twenty-four computer screens take up the adjacent wall, each displaying a still traffic scene. Clicking on each respective TV screen opens up a web browser with current traffic screenshots. Throughout the room, there are various bits of computer equipment, along with maps and phones. Residents can pick up a free Ontario license plate that says "GR8 2 WRK." At the other end of the building, there is a conference room and an interviewer's office.

The OPS Business Center contains career information, in the same style of moving LED text as at the other buildings, along with a free in-world booklet. The main feature of this building is the OPS knowledge survey, found on the first and second floors. One room features a large TV screen with a short video feed. The other rooms in the building consist mostly of meeting rooms. The structure seems to be made to resemble a real-life 1970s government building.

The laboratory is a small building in the northeast corner of the Sim filled with recreated virtual science equipment. The activity here involves water testing: Residents pick up a beaker and bring it to a source of water on the Sim. After filling it up, they bring it back to the building, where a machine analyzes the contents.

In the forest fire simulation area, users receive a water hose and must stop a burgeoning fire before it consumes the dozen trees in the area.

Information on real-life OPS job opportunities is organized into clear sections throughout the Sim. While residents have the opportunity to review the type of jobs that are available at OPS, important details such as location, experience needed, and job descriptions are not included, thus limiting the value of the recruiting experience. This information can, however, be retrieved from the web through in-world links.

There are many freebies throughout the island. The careers booklet is an excellent idea and takes advantage of an SL capability that is often overlooked by real-life businesses. Free goods are great in-world incentive strategies and are inexpensive methods of promotion if residents take them around SL. A suggestion for the OPS freebies would be to include interactive or coded items. Apart from the outfits, which are always popular, static objects such as coffee cups usually do not receive as much in-world visibility.

The various activities on the island are relevant to the OPS presence and are a great incentive for residents to visit. The firefighting activity is relatively unique among public real-life Sims and is definitely a strong point.

To visit OPS Island, see Ontario Public Services at http://slurl.com/secondlife/OPS%20Careers/44/216/51.

Virtual Project Incubator

The National Aeronautics and Space Administration (NASA) is an agency of the United States government responsible for the country's public space program. The CoLab site is a proposed NASA-sponsored coworking and project incubation facility for NASA staff and the "entrepreneurial technology community," initially located in SL. The SL site is part of an exploratory study commissioned by NASA Ames Research Center. This is one of two NASA forays into SL: the second is called Explorer Island.

According to NASA, the purpose of this online presence is to "catalyze and incubate projects that will help NASA leverage the entrepreneurial talent of the SL community to reduce the cost of space exploration and return more value from NASA's work directly to the public, and in so doing, raise the public profile of NASA." Their stated lists of goals are

- to increase public knowledge of and involvement in space science and space exploration;

- to encourage and facilitate cross-disciplinary collaborations and projects that leverage NASA's scientific and technical resources;
- to tap into the cultural and technical know-how of SL's creative and technical entrepreneurial community to speed the identification and adoption of technical and business process innovations within NASA;
- to create a more intimate and tangible experience of NASA with the public;
- to complement the offline physical NASA CoLab (once built) with an online space that people outside of San Francisco can use to participate in CoLab.

The island is one Sim surrounded by islands based on similar interests. Upon transporting into CoLab, residents find themselves at the entrance of a wheel-shaped building, the CoLab Headquarters. To the left of the teleport point, there is a sign that prompts users to join the CoLab Group, attend weekly meetings on Tuesdays, and to explore. Just next to the sign is a teleportation pad that takes residents to the meeting location and a welcome sign. If a user touches the sign, he or she receives a note card containing six subnote cards, with the following titles: "Welcome to NASA CoLab"; "NASA CoLab Vision and Mission"; "NASA CoLab SL Groups"; "NASA Landmarks—Facilities and Services"; "Learn about CoLab"; and "NASA CoLab Videos." Upon entering the building, there is a Sim teleportation map. The headquarters has a design reminiscent of Space Colony art of the 1970s and contains eight rooms of varying purpose, each with ceiling exits. These are numbered 1–8:

1. The hub of the building. It contains some information, a recreated satellite, and an exit through the ceiling; though it acts mostly as an intersection point of four spoke-like corridors.
2. An unnamed meeting room with a star chart texture.
3. Educator Resource Center. This is a room dedicated to space exploration information, mostly in coded booklets whose pages turn with each click. There are also links to educational resources.
4. MOC-UP (Massive Online Collaboration with Universe Presence) Room. A sign at the entrance to this room reads, "This is the rigging area for prototyping various layouts and tools for room functions

like meetings, presentations, education displays/exhibits, or offices for NASAS Centers and Directorates." The room contains chairs, telescopes, textures, and various prototypes.

5. CoLab Conference Room.

6. National Space Society (NSS) Room. This room acts like a portal to the NSS Sim and contains several displays and a video display screen.

7. Jet Propulsion Laboratory Mission Preview Room. This room contains a set of exhibits about the ion propulsion engine. There are photos, a diagram, a virtual recreation of the engine, and a virtual model of a satellite with the engine running.

8. Unoccupied room, reserved for Global Warming.

Outside of the headquarters building, there is a wealth of information, along with presentation areas and complex interactive content. The south side is occupied by the NASA Solar Amphitheater and weekly meeting area. Next to it, the southwest corner contains a sandbox test bed for NASA co-op creations. Toward the northeast corner, the "Back to the Moon" exhibit/building sits under construction.

Since NASA aims to increase public knowledge and involvement in space science and to tap into the collective knowledge of SL, events are a must. NASA has executed its balance of small-scale weekly meetings and less frequent (once or twice a month) larger scale events perfectly. Large events such as keynote speakers and presentations have been promoted via the NASA website, and many of the feeds are available on YouTube. Some of these events, such as the NASA Future Forum, have been mixed reality events wherein live presentations are streamed into SL and SL audiences and questions are streaming in real life. The experiences are relevant and well promoted. Throughout the Sim, NASA encourages users to fill out an online survey regarding the presence.

This island is filled with rich and interactive media experiences; there is a myriad of exhibitions, and very few of them are static or without scripting. An excellent example of one of NASA's rich experiences is the Victoria Crater center. At 600 meters above the Sim, this area showcases a virtual re-creation of the Victoria Crater on Mars, created by mapping real data into sculpted prims (sculpties). The result is a 3D recreation of the landscape, one-third of the actual size. This exhibit is impressive because it is very complex and is more or less on the leading edge of what can be done in SL.

CoLab is a development aimed largely at collaboration and project incubation. Helix believes that they have indeed succeeded in creating dynamic collaborative experiences in their SL presence. For instance, in the CoLab headquarters four of the rooms are collaborative efforts with related entities, such as the International Space Museum and the National Space Society. As well, there is a conversation area where CoLab stages weekly meetings for collaboration and e-learning. Throughout the island there are various forms of e-learning, including in-world text books, dynamic re-creations (such as coded satellites with textual labels and moving parts), audio and video feeds, and multilingual kiosks.

NASA's CoLab is an excellent example of a real-life brand that has to successfully develop and engage an SL community. They have maintained such a community by running weekly meetings, staging relevant large scale events, encouraging SL users to contribute ideas and creations, and writing in collaboration. An important point here is that the SL community has played a significant role in the implementation of the CoLab island and its exhibits and builds.

In terms of services, the CoLab Sim contains a wide array of information regarding NASA's current and future endeavors. Concurrently, NASA actively engages the SL community by welcoming ideas and creations. At present, there are neither products for sale in-world nor in-world sales agents. There are no posted hours when staff has office hours, though the times of weekly in-world meetings are widely publicized throughout the Sim. An impressive products and services aspect is the amount of cross promotion from the web to SL and vice versa. As well, there are some freebies scattered around the island.

To visit NASA Island, see http://slurl.com/secondlife/nasa%20e Education/124/154/43.

You Only Live Twice

The Australian Broadcasting Corporation (ABC) is Australia's national public broadcaster. Their island consists of one Sim, which was revamped in October 2007. Upon transporting into the Sim, the user arrives in an entrance area at the base of a floating broadcast tower. In this area, there is an introductory video and a map. An optional flying guided tour reveals the different activities that ABC offers in SL. These include the following:

- Info-Dome: Headlines and real world clips of news stories float around the inside of the dome. If one has his or her avatar sit down on a pillow in the middle of the room, he or she can go into mouselook and explore the ever changing news stories that appear and scroll inside the dome. Clicking on the snippets will bring the user to the full story on the 2D web.
- Sandboxes: This multistory area encourages users to experiment with creating objects in SL and offers design challenges. For example, the 2007 Furnish the Eco House contest challenged residents to make the best furniture for their "Eco House."
- Hidden "unearthed" dance club.
- "Dreamtime Theater": A campfire area that has a screen on which you can watch animated retelling of indigenous and traditional stories.
- Melbourne Laneways: A detailed re-creation of downtown Melbourne.

ABC-TV holds regular large events in SL. At present, events consist of building tutorials and contests. Users who join the ABC group in SL receive regular updates on events and ABC-related news.

The island is certainly a place for users to review ABC-TV's services in a very immersive and interactive way. However, one cannot purchase any real world goods or services here. Melbourne Laneways offers several freebies. This area could become more popular if the ABC were to have metabrands rent spaces and sell their goods rather than have just have pictures of stores.

The site itself acts as a social hub, with areas to converse while watching or listening to ABC feeds (e.g., the hidden dance club and campfire tales). Along with their sandbox, ABC has building tutorial note cards to aid novice users. Most noteworthy, though is the community blog on the 2D web. There are now semiregular updates online as well as forums to discuss what sort of event should be run next.

ABC's island is richly designed and very immersive. SL blogger Tateru Nino touted it as having a "Second Life feel" to it, something that many corporate sites have struggled with. At the transport-in point, there is a video screen that plays the virtual-world documentary *You Only Live Twice*. ABC has included interactive kiosks as well as many of audio and video feeds. Their info-dome is an innovative idea that presents users with snippets of news stories and offers the curious avatar the option of reading the rest online. They also have a guided tour of the island.

To visit the Australian Broadcasting Corporation, see http://slurl .com/secondlife/ABC%20Island/131/137/42.

Real Brands in the Virtual World

Accenture is a global management consulting, technology services, and outsourcing company based in Hamilton, Bermuda. Its revenue in 2008 was upward of $23 billion. Accenture built this island to extend its real-life brand experience to SL for brand engagement with and recruitment of tech enthusiasts.

This island is the most recently developed of nine Accenture-owned Sims in SL. It is located within a cluster of six Sims, but four of these are still undeveloped. According to Susan Raycroft, Accenture's Internet marketing lead, Careers Island exists as an opportunity for the company to meet and form relationships with technology enthusiasts. They are using it primarily for recruiting but also for extending the Accenture brand into the virtual world. The island is made up of one Sim plus some of a second. It is split up into a number of areas: Careers Central; interview building; event auditorium; and the Accenture Challenge area (taking up the majority of the Sim).

The Accenture Careers Island development is fairly new, so it is difficult to measure event density. Accenture is a company located in 49 countries, and the island is meant to be used by branches in any of them. At the time of writing, there has been one in-world event and supposedly many planned for the future ("RealBiz in SL"), but there is no event board listing. It is important to note that in June 2007, the French Accenture Island held a recruitment drive called "Accenture Speed Recruiting" targeted at the Francophone segment of SL. This suggests that virtual recruitment has been successful in the past for Accenture, and similar efforts will take place on Careers Island. Other features of the island that contribute to Accenture's event density rating include a kiosk wherein users can give feedback and complex automated user experiences (e.g., games).

At present, Accenture is not selling any real-life (RL) or SL goods on Careers Island. In terms of services, the island offers a lot of information regarding the company's RL affairs. For instance, users can browse kiosks that review what Accenture does in RL and who runs the company. According to Raycroft, Accenture values employing in-world staff during virtual events. However, there is no in-world staff working specific hours between events. In lieu of staff, Accenture has a number of bots placed throughout the island. Bots are programmed to help users navigate but are very limited in their Accenture-related capabilities. Interacting with the bots is similar to playing text adventures like Hitchhikers Guide to the Galaxy on a Mac Classic. All the information on the island is available in five different languages. There are various freebies around the Sim (mostly T-shirts and the like), the most interesting of which is a giant Accenture Rubik's cube.

Part of the aim of Accenture's Career Sim is to engage with a specific community of technology enthusiasts ("Realbiz in SL"). The island is very well suited for future virtual recruitment campaigns. However, at this point it is difficult to rate the breadth of such community experiences. According to Raycroft, Accenture recently hosted an event aimed at graduate students for which the island was redecorated with relevant interactive kiosks and banners. The main thing that the island lacks is a community events listing, a factor that would greatly improve the community's experience. Currently, there is an area to leave detailed feedback, via a note card.

Interactively, the Careers Island experience is very rich with automatic engagement. The majority of the island is dedicated to nine games that are at least somewhat relevant to Accenture. These are games that "push you physically and mentally and test your ability to work as a team member" and are designed to have users engage with the brand in a fun way ("Realbiz in SL"). As mentioned, there are bots placed throughout the Sim. There is also an automatic tour of the island that informs the user about different areas of the Sim.

To visit Accenture's Island, see http://slurl.com/secondlife/accenture %20Italia/89/45/27.

Other Second Life Sites Recommended

Additional case studies can be found at http://secondlifegrid.net/ casestudies. The following are some of our favorites:[7]

- *The Tech Museum of Innovation in San Jose.* The Tech Virtual launched in 2007 with the mission of bringing faster and more collaborative exhibit development to museums worldwide using an online platform. Last year, the core concept of Tech Virtual was extended beyond prototype exhibits to virtually prototyping an entire museum gallery to share that with stakeholders such as administrators, curators, exhibit designers, and sponsors. In 2010, The Tech Virtual began to prototype and test a new and participatory exhibition, called Expolab, to institutions such as Citilab Cornella, the Science Centre Singapore, and the Lemelson Center for the Study of Invention and Innovation at the National Museum of American History who built Places of Invention. The Tech Virtual has gone beyond the "virtual museum" concept into one in which the virtual exhibits become a precursor of the real construction. These are results that those in both the virtual and real worlds can experience and appreciate—a core requirement for the Linden Prize.

  They also opened a contest to the residents of SL to create a virtual in-world exhibit. The winner of the contest was flown to San Jose to create the exhibit in RL. The virtual building is a close replica of the museum in San Jose, which is home to a virtual world exhibit featuring SL. There is a camera and screen set up in the RL exhibit that monitors visitors movements to make avatars in SL mimic the same movements. For more information, see http://www.thetech.org/techvirtual.

  Also, The Tech Museum of Innovation received the 2010 Linden Award (http://blogs.secondlife.com/community/ community/blog/2010/06/01/announcing-the-winner-of-the -2010-linden-prize).

- *CNN iReport.* CNN iReport provides alert news to virtual world subscribers. You can subscribe to notifications or attend special news reports in SL. iReport has weekly meetings on their island every Tuesday. Avatars actively write about events that happen in SL; it is the same as the real-life iReport except it reports on virtual world stories. They have discussions in the group chat. For more information, see http://slurl.com/ secondlife/CNN%20iReport%20Island/98/96/24.

Putting All the Pieces Together

Second Life recently turned 8 years old. Yet in many ways, the virtual worlds market is still emerging and, some will argue, still in its infancy. The current state of virtual worlds is similar to the World Wide Web from a decade ago. In the early days, many large corporations such as Reebok, Sony BMG, and Nissan set up shop in SL in very bold and costly ways. Like the web prior to the dot-com bust, the majority of these companies made a large monetary investment on full islands and multiple Sim builds that proved to have little relevance to the SL culture.

While such islands made public relations splashes, many quickly turned into ghost towns. Some companies gave up on SL, others learned and revamped, and a select few actually got it right the first time. In the past 5 years, we have learned a great deal about what works and what does not work in SL. Learning insights include the following:

- Virtual worlds are about interaction and engagement.
- Events drive traffic.
- In-world staff are better than bots.
- Second Life offers unprecedented room for innovation.
- Community experience is crucial.

The Sims with the most traffic in SL are never static. A Sim must be engaging automatically and, where possible, through real people (i.e., staff). As seen with automotive industry Sims, automatic engagement has shown to work very well. The Nissan Sims, for example, have consistently received a high volume of visitors because they offer automatic engagement in the form of innovative freebies. Residents continue to visit the island to take away the two brands of virtual cars and drive both within the Sim and elsewhere in SL.

Avatar-to-avatar engagement has worked very well for IBM's Business Center and seems to be an integral part of their business model. IBM's success strategy is to make in-world representatives available to answer questions, much as they would in RL by e-mail or by phone. Similarly, while ABN AMRO has gone through several revisions of their SL presence, the one consistent feature of their island that they have maintained is a live staff member to answer questions and show visitors around. Not only does this type of interaction engage residents in a company's brand, but it also gives the corporation an unprecedented opportunity to connect with its customers. When asked about the value for Cisco in SL, Christian Renaud, Cisco's Chief architect of networked virtual environment, remarked, "The ROI that we get is we have an event every week to two weeks, we will fill up our Sim, talk with our customers and talk to our partners; that kind of investment is like a focus group or a birds-of-a-feather or a breakout at any other tradeshow—and that's invaluable . . . That's the ROI that we get."[8]

Community experience is crucial, and events are a large part of this. Staging events on a regular basis gives residents a reason to visit your island, even if they have already experienced the automatic engagement it offers. It also shows SL users that your company is actively involved in the virtual world and is not "just another RL company in SL." Regular meetings and events is an excellent method to build community around one's brand. It brings together groups of residents that share similar interests and allows them to interact together on the same Sim. With that in mind, it is important to have a company group through which members can be contacted about upcoming events and meetings.

Utilization of social media sites on the web can also be a powerful tool in community building. A strong example of this can be found in the Australian Broadcasting Corporation (ABC) case study. As a revamp of their presence, ABC created a user group to receive feedback and assist in the planning process of the island. Along with the group, there is a community forum and calendar on ABC's SL-related website. Through the user group, ABC was able to improve and plan for their Sim with their SL community playing an active role. Microsoft's newest user group island is based entirely around this sort of community contribution.

In terms of design, many of the earlier RL businesses that entered SL failed to take advantage of the creative possibilities that the SL environment has to offer. For instance, Reebok designed their Sim to resemble an urban environment with a store in which they sold customizable avatar shoes that closely resembled the real world product. However, the majority of Reebok Island was unused space that could have been built upon with more innovation and creativity. Many of the subcultures in SL appreciate imaginative builds with innovative structures and coding.

An example of an imaginative build is the recent Intel addition to their island. While the new area houses activities and has realistic aesthetics on the ground level, it also has multiple secret floors underneath that take residents deep into the Sim. Using these areas, Intel allowed their designers to let loose and create fantastical environments used for meetings, dance clubs, and even product information. Even simply updating a company Sim (such as by removing features that are out of date such as advertisements for events that have long since occurred and updating event calendars) can significantly improve a Sim and demonstrate that it has not been neglected by the parent company.

Recommendations for Getting Started Successfully in Second Life

There are several practical ways of embracing virtual worlds and massively multiplayer online games (MMOGs) that we recommend organizations start with:

- Set a clear vision in your organization to embrace new virtual-world capabilities:
  - Attract, retain, and develop your talent by leveraging innovative recruiting approaches.
  - Increase your employees' collaboration, project management skills, and their sense of fun in the workplace.
  - Promote your products and services to diverse stakeholders.
  - Facilitate using new virtual tools to extend your customer relationships.
  - Improve employee communication, training, and development via employee engagement experiences using virtual worlds.

- It is imperative to develop, early on, clear goals and objectives with effective and relevant performance metrics. Start simple, gain some success, and build momentum.
- Evaluate and experiment with virtual world experiences to learn.
- The best way to optimize learning is to develop a learning lab or a pilot to interact online with external customers or recruits. As the numerous case studies have shown, learning labs and pilots are effective in SL. Having relevant performance metrics and reporting approaches to gain further executive support is also a key success factor.
- Develop a collaboration competency. Collaboration competency is necessary in order to leverage virtual worlds solutions. This is the ability to collaboratively solve problems of mutual interest and work toward win-win outcomes. True collaboration requires the development of leadership behaviors that work in a virtual world. The leadership behaviors include the following:
  - The ability to develop rapid trust with people that you may never have physically interacted with.
  - The ability to hone communication and visioning skills to effectively communicate to a global work force. Company resources are engulfed in constant change and require effective communication interchanges to keep them focused, motivated, and executing effectively.
  - The ability to recognize that the wisdom of the crowd and their competence to execute is stronger than traditional hierarchical cultures. "We are smarter than I" needs to be the cultural orientation underpinning in a virtual-world experience.
- Ensure your SL strategy is integrated into your Web 2.0, social mediated, and knowledge management strategies.
  - Create islands of experiences that are effectively positioned under a unified Web 2.0 collaboration or knowledge management strategy; otherwise, there will be confusion and fragmentation in strategy.

- Integrate existing blogs and podcasting, if they are relevant to the virtual worlds experience design. This will further increase audience reach and help unify Web 2.0 brand experiences.
- Develop collaborative work spaces to gather knowledge, express ideas, and concerns and share collective know-how. There are a variety of solutions that support collaborative knowledge generation activities:
  - Web conferencing solutions (e.g., WebEx, Live Meeting)
  - Document creation collaboration solutions (e.g., Atlassian, Confluence Social Text, IBM Lotus Connections, Igloo, Jive, Microsoft SharePoint)
- It is also important to ensure that your organization has a point of collaboration to enable the interaction between your employees, customers, and suppliers. Companies that are first to solve this challenge are better positioned to subsequently embark on virtual world projects.
- Start small, yet think big!
  - Too many organizations find excuses not to leverage Web 2.0 and social mediated approaches in conducting business.
  - Adding an experiential dynamic of interacting with avatars is seen by many executives as a waste of time. These are some of the hurdles that champions of implementing virtual worlds will need to define and overcome.
  - A small and tightly focused project with clearly defined goals and objectives is usually the best way to get started. Suitable application areas for getting started include the following:
    - Recruiting islands—such islands offer an effective means of attracting users, particularly web-savvy and technically skilled talent (Gen X and Y).
    - Product engineering learning and training labs—these labs attract technical resources that typically have existing computing functionality and the required graphic cards.
    - Training and conference sites—these sites provide a low cost alternative to webinars, as they provide integrated

communication experiences with instant messaging, Skype, interactive voice, and avatar engagement. These environments provide a low cost and high retention learning space.

Food for Thought

Even though the approach to virtual worlds (VWs) is in its infancy, organizations that experiment early on with VWs will learn from their experiences. As VWs become more mainstream, early adopters will be uniquely positioned to successfully take advantage of the new forms of rich media experience platforms. The World Wide Web is rapidly becoming the 3D web, a platform where information that is contained in flat pages today will be presented as a VW, on the screen in front of us.

We continually hear people question whether VWs will become another killer application in the business world. To that we simply say, take a look at the next generation of Generation Virtual. Gen Vs have been growing up on Webkinz, Club Penguin, and World of Warcraft—an evolution in human conditioning using avatars for web interactions.

The real question executives need to be asking is, "How rapidly will these new technologies evolve before they become mainstream?" Companies such as Cisco, Dell, the U.S. government (Department of Defense, military), IBM, and others are not waiting for VWs to become widely adopted. They want to be ahead of the pack by helping create the standards and platforms for enabling this next generation of 3D web virtual interaction experiences.

Virtual worlds are also ideal for RL simulation experiences. For example, hospitals can design an experience that looks like a RL experience and demonstrate effective learning practices with experts around the world using a combination of RL and SL learning methods. This innovation is already under way, and we expect more to come onstream rapidly.

Virtual worlds are also going to help drive the next wave of web-based delivery services. This will be a multibillion-dollar market, so it is not surprising that companies such as IBM, Cisco, or Sun are active in this space. Dr. Cindy Gordon, lead researcher of the Helix Virtual World's research project, predicts that

In less than ten years, Virtual Worlds will be pervasive and highly ubiquitous with integrated RL and VW and ultra-mobile, geo-local experiences. As the standards and infrastructure evolve to a more open and decentralized architecture, these VWs will become more mainstream.[9]

Virtual worlds offer many forms of revenue generating opportunities to companies, well beyond just for infrastructure. Content creation is a big VW business. According to Linden Lab, SL residents transact more than $3 million a day. In some SL stores, residents are making more than $1,000 per month by simply selling virtual clothing.

According to the British Computer Society (BCS), the secondary market value for virtual goods has been estimated at now a multibillion U.S. market. Designing and purchasing digital objects that mirror RL objects will continue to be a source of innovation as VWs continue to evolve. We have already seen virtual trading markets spring up through sites such as eBay and IGE.com, and assets are regularly bought and sold for real cash.[10]

As these worlds function primarily as social spaces rather than games, there are fewer incentives for users to maintain a strict boundary between the virtual and the real. In contrast to the warriors found in gaming worlds such as World of Warcraft, VW avatars are more likely to take on human forms. Avatars appear in real-day dress, based on recognizable real-world fashion trends, and interact in VW experiences similar to RL experiences. As well, many avatars are being customized as mini replicas of their RL personas. Since a user's RL personal reputation may be affected by their virtual representation in a social VW, they are even more likely to spend time and money on avatars.

For better or for worse, VWs will increasingly function as centers of commerce, trade, and business. RL brands in every vertical market are experimenting using VWs to prototype, advertise, and sell goods. Major consumer brands that have already appeared in VWs include Coca-Cola, Levi's, McDonald's, Pontiac, Nike, and DaimlerChrysler. Canadian market leaders are lagging in this area with only a few entrants from organizations such as Canada Post, Ontario Government, and The Weather Channel.

Now You Know

- *Start with a simple application.* You will be surprised at what is possible. Engage your youth on this project, perhaps a local university, community college, or even high school, to support your "imagineering" efforts. If your business is dependent on web channel interactions, you cannot ignore that your business plan will need to start planning for VWs. They will augment your brand and user reach, both for customers and for employee engagement practices.
- *Integrate VWs with your overall Web 2.0 and knowledge management strategy.* These different collaboration experiences should not be treated in isolation from one another in terms of branding, communication engagement practices, and architecture planning strategies.
- *Develop a learning and experimentation innovation attitude.* The majority of organizations are failing in their entry into VWs simply because they have poor innovation and experimentation practices, supported with effective operating practices (i.e., governance, nonsustainable budgets, or ill-defined performance metrics). When an organization enters a virtual online world, it is extremely visible. Avatar communities are well educated, and word spreads quickly when another poor entrant is found. Active bloggers are pervasive in VWs, and they spread the word (good or bad) quickly.

With good planning, strong communication practices, and changing community interaction experiences, organizations can increase their success. They can also ask their visitors to help evolve the experience; seeking avatars' feedback can increase their sense of belonging to the community. As well, communities require a purpose that resonates with its visitors or the avatar will simply go elsewhere. Without a reason for a return visit, avatars seldom return.

PART III
The Way Ahead

CHAPTER 10

What Every Leader Needs to Know

The future cannot be predicted, but futures can be invented.

—Dennis Gabor, *Inventing the Future*, 1963

Learning From Challenges Along the Way

Words are easy to read. Putting into action and realizing results is the challenge to lead the way forward. Creating a compelling and visionary pathway forward is what role model leadership is all about. Yet when one steps back time and time again with new business models or technology capabilities that enter the market, leaders more often stumble than succeed. Unfortunately, they continue to stumble on the same bumps in the road. Over the past 20 years, in leading global changes in major organizations, both publicly and privately held, the top four challenges we can distill from the insights of our collective learnings to share with you are summarized in this next section.

We have called these challenges "The High Five." We hope by sharing these top of mind challenges you will be more successful in going virtual.

Challenge #1—Cracking the Big Nut: Unlocking the Power of Your Talent

The biggest nut in intensifying your strategy to go virtual is aligning your talent. Mobilizing change to do work differently using new approaches and toolkits to evolve work practices, processes, and procedures to leverage virtual, social, and collaboration approaches is a tough nut to crack.

Create a compelling vision that frames what's in it for me. Everyone is overloaded today in business with communication stimuli. Just think of how many e-mails you have every day, compounded by adding in the diverse social networks you likely already belong to like LinkedIn, Facebook, Twitter, Plaxo, and Ning, to name just a few, let alone adding on Orkut, MySpace, and the new XYZ. Then your leadership team communicates that you are going to be investing in a new collaboration virtual environment. The aim, they say, is to give you access to a new set of tools to increase your office productivity, whether you have chosen IBM Lotus Connections; Microsoft's SharePoint Platform; Cisco's new Telepresence solutions; new web-centric models like Jive, Igloo, or Social Text; or some other collaboration and social technology platform. The reality is that your employees are overloaded, so how do you create a compelling vision that motivates them to execute and to stop using older and often "proven" work practices? After all, many will have the view of "if it is not broken, don't fix it."

We recommend the agile approach of giving a target team of employees collaboration capabilities and, by partnering with them, exploring diverse-use case scenarios that they are passionate about and "focusing" on the passion opportunity area. Having no sense of desire to change and an approach that intuitively feels like more work are simply a case of rolling a rock uphill. It is not worth it for the leader or the employees.

Organizations that are leading the way in going virtual have an uncanny ability to listen to their talent and engage them iteratively. They are highly adaptive or resilient to change. They also respect and trust their voices, and trust is at the core of enablement for change realization, our challenge #2.

Challenge #2—Learning to Let Go and to Trust

Trust in organizations across the world is at an all-time low in the majority of employee satisfaction scores conducted in the Fortune 500. How often have we continued to hear the emperor has no clothes on?

In a 2009 IBM global innovation survey[1] asked senior executives if they were confident in their organizations' ability to innovate successfully, and the majority of executives said they were not confident. In many Fortune 500 companies employees do not trust their employers and the senior leaders also do not believe their talent have what it takes to successfully innovate. We know from many research studies on effective change that over 30% of an organization's employee base will not be successful in making the trip to the new promised land. However, with executives not expressing confidence, they can make the turn with the majority of the employees they have to still row the organization forward, which is worrisome. The shadows often are our organizational reality. Perhaps it should be no surprise then that the most successful companies in the world are those that have the healthiest human capital and employee engagement practices in terms of investment, confidence, and trust in their talent.

So how do you ensure as you are creating your virtual business that you get your trust health equation right? First, it is critical to ensure that the fundamentals that affect trust are healthy, including your core values; behaviors; and organizational structures, such as your business hierarchies and business processes. The values and the culture are the foundational glue so critical to understanding the importance of embracing new ways of working. However, often prior attempts have left carnage in an organization's memory from failed attempts or promises not delivered, continual downsizing, or rightsizing, so depending on the organization's history the complexity of the pathways forward will vary and need to be customized to the degree of the challenge that is ahead.

Values are fundamental, as these form the foundation for attracting, developing, and retaining talent in an organization. Values determine how talent interacts, the shoulds, the should-nots, the musts, must-nots, rights, wrongs, and so on. There are often formal values written down and often unwritten rules that are locked in stories, rituals, and organizational artifacts. They are more often than not aligned, so unlocking the unwritten rules to align with the vision for creating a stronger virtual and more competitive organization is the most important area for leaders to focus their attention.

Values that support trust are those that reinforce the importance of collaboration. The interdependency of working together and supporting one another to ensure the right work is done in the right way are important signals to send. If employees are rewarded for cutting corners and leaders disrespect their employees and have weak listening skills, the confidence in the employee base is eroded and new programs that intensify collaboration and virtualize the business will be implemented. Trust, we believe, must be explicitly mentioned in corporate values and in leadership behaviors and be fundamental for promotion in selecting future leaders. When people are rewarded more for the achievement of individual excellence over compromising group goals, this divisive paradox will lead to noncollaborative and untrustworthy behavior.

Trust is highly integrated with interdependence when employees require support from one another. This dynamic where I help you and you help me is rooted in reciprocity and is strengthened or weakened depending on the limitations of skill, time, or control that individuals have. Irrespective, if employees understand that each exchange needs to be a mutually satisfying exchange where respect and open transparent communication is shared, trust will strengthen between organizational ties and networks across the organization. When power behaviors are rewarded in an organizational culture, the implications to creating healthy trusting and collaborative cultures are impacted.

Challenge #3—Ensuring Goal Clarity and Vision Visibility Alignment

Once you have your vision on growing your business more virtually, you can start your execution pathway. Keeping visible your vision and aligning the organizational goals to achieve congruence will be a compelling requirement and challenge.

Goal clarity means stating the desired end-point vision clearly at the same time and ensuring the operating goals align with the overall direction while roles and processes are methods of achieving the goal.

Goal clarity and vision alignment help to ensure trust is also being practiced, as does increased clarity of the change journey roadmap to go visible. This in turn helps your talent to understand the vision and the expectations of them in the vision path and to participate in helping to shape the direction and give feedback.

When trust is given and it is clearly a core value—and when organizations communicate the vision and goal clearly, ask for feedback genuinely and openly, and listen and implement the changes—belief systems and alignment increases.

The opposite is also true and is to be avoided at all costs. When the actions and results of decisions and behaviors are hidden, and when there are other structural factors that encourage untrustworthy behavior, then the temptation to manipulate others is higher.

Challenge #4—Having the Courage
to Shape Consequences

At the end of the day, striving to have your business go virtual and evolve its practices to be more collaborative requires a realistic perspective on shaping consequences when alignment is not being realized.

Many organizations take the time to create a compelling vision, architect a clear change journey road, work hard on goal congruence and cultural alignment, and set new reward and recognition systems up, but then they fail at consequences being clearly defined and practiced.

In other words, if I trust you and you fail to meet our agreed actions, then what happens? If there is nothing else I can do, if there are no consequences for you as a result of this failure, then why should you worry? A system that has no punishment for trust failure will collapse and be "lip service."

Consequence management can take two forms. If I report to your supervisor and complain on how you are acting, what are the consequences?

Is this simply a mild reprimand and coaching moment or a more serious warning or an expulsion from the business? There are also social consequences of reputation as employees usually share their experiences with others, and there are often implications in social peer networks for building deeper trust.

What is important, however, is to ensure that you are building a learning culture in leadership behavior and helping to clearly understand the facts from both employee perspectives and not making generalized assumptions or leaping to action without an effective communication with all parties involved. Also, a key leadership behavior is to ensure the employee who has tabled his or her concern has also respectfully communicated before raising the complaint to more senior levels. Of course, the nature of the transgression will also determine the employee's comfort in having this authentic and open conversation.

Developing a culture that views feedback as a gift for improvement is a healthy environment to work in. At the same time, lacking the will to change and to genuinely make an effort to use new virtual and collaborative ways of working after multiple learning interventions and coaching moments, there needs to be demonstrated consequences to the culture that this is no longer acceptable behavior, and leadership needs to step up to the requirements for refreshing talent.

Challenge #5—Harnessing Social Power

Most undergraduate organizational behavior classes include a segment on power as it relates to organizations. The basis of this section of the class will almost certainly include a review of John French and Bertam Raven's 1959 seminal work on the subject in which they described their five bases of power.[2] Here is our terse and oversimplified overview of the five bases of power:

- *Coercive.* Power that relies on threats to force someone to complete a task that they do not want to do.
- *Reward.* Power resulting from people's desire to receive some benefit (reward) for completing a task and recognizing that the reward holders have some degree of power.
- *Legitimate.* Power based on role in an organization. Think of an organization chart: the higher one is in the hierarchy, the more power they have to make decisions and take action.
- *Referent.* Power derived from respect.
- *Expert.* Power based on knowledge or expertise.

Most seasoned leaders are aware that most of the bases of power are common in their organizations. However, leaders are quickly becoming aware of another type of power that is emerging both inside and outside their organization. Sometimes called the power of the people, the basis of this power is the ability of people to organize and have their opinion heard. Of course, the idea of groups of people massing to spark change is nothing new. In fact, this is really the basis of organized labor, but this new massing is happening at lightning speed and with viral distribution through social media.

One of the first major examples of the social power was chronicled in a *USA Today* article titled "Offended Moms Get Tweet Revenge Over Motrin Ads." The story described how a group of mothers used social media, primarily Twitter and YouTube, to show their displeasure about an advertisement for the drug Motrin. The article included this passage:

The ads, launched in magazines and online on Sept. 30, centered on new moms who carry their babies in slings (and might need Motrin). They likened the sling to a fashion accessory and said that while toting the baby can be tough, it "totally makes me look like an official mom."

Some moms saw the ads as snarky pokes at motherhood. Backlash hit a boiling point by Sunday, particularly with Twitter bloggers, even though some warned about overreacting.

By Sunday night, McNeil had sent an apology to bloggers and on Monday posted a separate apology on Motrin.com. "We have heard your concerns about the ad," says a statement by Kathy Widmer, marketing vice president. "We are parents ourselves and take feedback from moms very seriously. We are in the process of removing this ad from all media."[3]

Suddenly, corporate officers around the world realized the power of social media. They were used to dealing with upset or concerned consumers in traditional means such as letter writing campaigns, telephone calls, face-to-face protests, and the like; however, most were not prepared for speed or voracity of a social media campaign organized by everyday people. This is why social power and organizational leaders must pay attention or pay the consequences.

Big Benefits and Payoffs: Recognizing the Patterns Is Half the Battle

Throughout this book, we have been providing rich examples of leaders recognizing and understanding that people are social animals. Throughout our lives, we thrive on building communities through diverse social interactions with family members, classmates, coworkers, and through our personal interests. We constantly seek to create networks of people whom we can identify with; have personal contact with; and rely on to look for a job, to seek advice or source information, and to seek insight. This reality is no different in the world of work. When we make contact with someone at work and it is pleasant and respectful, we feel the wind at our back, we are more confident to engage and participate, and we bring our best ideas forward. It makes no sense for businesses not to encourage employees to get to know one another, even though they might not encounter these individuals during the course of the typical workday. Providing a forum such as a company-only Facebook- or YouTube-style social networking tool will encourage employees to reach out to one other. Too often we do not bring our full focus to work; now with social networking and collaboration approaches, we have an opportunity to increase the hidden potential of people.

Senior executives like to see reports from leading organizations like McKinsey in helping to demonstrate payoffs, so we wanted to ensure we added to the already get on with it messaging some perspectives from McKinsey.[4] McKinsey cites the following benefits of increased collaboration and communications to the enterprise:

- Generating revenue by uncovering the "hidden" people who have contributed to cross-selling or closing deals
- Improving cross-selling by identifying others' expertise and drawing upon it during the selling process
- Enhancing career paths by more accurately identifying top performers
- Boosting productivity by sharing best practices and facilitating the transfer of advice and information from colleagues
- Improving the allocation of resources through analysis of various networking and collaboration tools
- Eliminating inefficiencies by reducing redundant efforts and sharing information

In addition to these generalized benefits, social computing and collaboration also support strategic business goals and scenarios. The benefits according to Microsoft global research from use of these tools are as follows:

- Providing natural ways to capture and share tacit knowledge— critical to the continuity and competitiveness of businesses faced with the retirement of baby boomers during the next 10–15 years and the virtualization of organizations through outsourcing and telework

- Enabling people to find and engage experts inside and outside the organization to generate ideas and facilitate the conversations that lead to rapid innovation
- Helping organizations attract and retain young talent by providing people with a familiar infrastructure of collaborative and social media to effectively blend work and life priorities and be productive
- Increasing organizational productivity, providing managers with clear vision into team dynamics and giving knowledge workers easy, natural ways to share insights and collaborate[5]

Creating an Intelligent and Smarter Planet

With over half of our world's population now living in cities, our governments, universities, and businesses need not only to collaborate but to invent and innovate in new ways that make our cities more vibrant, prosperous, sustainable, secure, and more intelligent.

According to Wikipedia, intelligent city (IC) is a term that has various meanings. It is defined broadly as an equivalent of "digital city," "information city," "wired city," "telecity," "knowledge-based city," "electronic communities," "electronic community spaces," "flexicity," "teletopia," and "cyberville," covering a wide range of electronic and digital applications related to digital spaces of communities and cities.[6]

Looking ahead—imagine a world where business goes virtual at every level. Connectedness, collaboration, and continual continuity will be a reality. Over time, we will eventually become a much smarter and more intelligent planet. One of the most impressive virtual leadership forums driving a strong global vision for creating more intelligent cities is the Intelligent Community Forum (ICF).[7] It is a global think tank that studies the economic and social development of the 21st-century community. Whether in industrialized or developing nations, communities are challenged to create prosperity, stability, and cultural meaning in a world where jobs, investment, and knowledge increasingly depend on advances in communications. ICF shares best practices of the world's intelligent communities in order to help communities everywhere find sustainable renewal and growth.

The Intelligent Community Forum (2006) has developed a list of indicators that provide a framework for understanding how communities and regions can gain a competitive edge in today's broadband economy. Being an IC takes a combination of (a) significant deployment of broadband communications to businesses, government facilities, and residences; (b) effective education, training, and a workforce able to perform knowledge work; (c) policies and programs that promote digital democracy by bridging the digital divide to ensure that all sectors of the society and citizens benefit from the broadband revolution; (d) innovation in the public and private sectors and efforts to create economic clusters and risk capital to fund the development of new businesses; and (e) effective economic development marketing that leverages the community's broadband to attract talented employment and investments.

As business goes increasingly virtual, there will be opportunities for countries to create more intelligent nations. Countries like Taiwan have recently declared they are striving to be an intelligent nation.[8] With an investment of over 3.99 trillion Taiwanese dollars over 8 years, the vision is all encompassing, from a new rail transportation network, increasing free trade, developing an ecopark and marine technology center, strengthening education, developing a complete wireless broadband country, increasing green forestry, and ensuring increased skills in IT and digital media literacy as the intensification of the world going virtual will required increased technology capabilities.

Canada has also recently declared it will also become an intelligent nation, iCANADA.[9] The organization is chaired by Bill Hutchison, the vice chair is Dr. Cindy Gordon, and other Canadian global leaders are rapidly coming on board like Terry Matthews, founder of Mitel. Currently the goal is to create an advocacy movement to create a more intelligent Canada and increase broadband access to all homes in order to run the advanced applications of virtual environments. Community citizenship leadership activities like this will be key to creating urban centers that are smarter, cleaner, safer, and connected.

One cannot ignore the trend in integrated intelligent digital signage into office real estate and also setting up immersive digital signage experiences for consumers—it won't be long before we are all driving down the road and our cars change the ads in real time based on personal profiles or our cells pick up a digital signage signal and send us a Twitter alert with a location address to take us to the nearest store to buy a business suit on sale. Even if we are busy, our virtual assistants can help our virtual avatars with the dimensions, as the Twitter alert also has a virtual clothing code identifier. Life will never be the same as business increasingly goes virtual. What we can count on is as leaders we will need to learn, listen, and lead every day.

Learn, Listen, and Lead

We recommend all organizational leaders simply get started by adopting a learn, listen, and lead social and innovation plan. This should start by the leader learning how social media works. We believe leaders should learn how Facebook, Twitter, Google, and other tools work. Frequently we hear executives say they do not have time to learn and delegate these tasks to subordinates. We would suggest it is a good investment of your time! Yes, we need to focus on a bigger picture that we can aspire to with intelligent cities, but to get there we need to also learn how to use social innovation toolkits that will further our imaginations to discover new ways of working and playing.

Next, leaders should personally discover what is being said about the organization. There are many tools to help with this task, many of which are free and easy to use. For example, Google Alerts (http://www.google.com/alerts) allows leaders to submit key words and receive e-mail updates based on Google results of news stories, blog posts, web pages, and the like. In the listening phase, focus on the tone: Is it positive, negative, or indifferent? Remember, this is the listening, not acting phase.

Finally, once you have learned the tools and have listened to the conversation, you will be in a position to lead or at least influence the discussion. We recommend the use of blogs, microblogs, and social networking tools. Fortunately, there are many tools to make this very efficient. For example, a message can be entered in one tool and automatically disseminated to many social media outlets. In our opinion, two mistakes are commonplace. First, many senior leaders ignore social media and use the ostrich theory: If I put my head in the sand, then nothing will happen. That is usually when a network army will launch a major campaign. The second error is to try to influence the conversation before you have learned and listened—invest the time now. The power of the social

media must not be underestimated. The wise leader will learn to influence the conversation through the sharing of valuable content.

Enjoy the virtual world!

What You Know

The final Now You Know section is different in that we wanted to summarize what we have learned along the journey. Here is a recap of the
major takeaways:

Virtual Business: Real or Imaginary?

- Virtual business is driven by a melding of three critical
  enablers: social technology, visionary leadership, and a culture
  of collaboration.
- The "any place, any time" strategy focuses on providing
  high quality service 24/7 by ignoring traditional geographic
  challenges.
- The "people know best" strategy harnesses power of the everyday people to create value. The "everyone has a stake" strategy,
  which considers the stakeholder view of the organization,
  guides leaders in tapping this vast store of wisdom.
- The "real in the virtual world" strategy offers incredible opportunity for real businesses to sell their wares in the virtual world.
- A convergence of ubiquitous communication networks, low-
  cost appliances, exponential web-based content growth, and a
  cultural shift toward sharing has created an always-on, always-
  connected, always-sharing environment.

The New Face(book) of Organizations

- The single largest cultural-technological innovation of the 21st
  century may be the social networking website.
- Facebook popularity and impact continues to grow. By the
  end of 2010, Facebook had more than 500 million active users;
  about 50% of their users access the site every day.

- LinkedIn, the social networking site for professionals, now boasts more than 85 million users.
- Eight percent of American adults who use the Internet are Twitter users. Many companies now have more than one million Twitter followers.
- There are more than 100 million blogs in the world.
- Wikipedia commands an impressive online following with about 13% of global Internet users visiting the site every day.[10] At present, the English-language version includes more than 3.5 million articles totaling almost 23 million pages. The wiki has been edited more than 433 million times; there have been more than 850,000 files uploaded.
- The *Groundswell* movements reminds us that we should cater to different categories of social computing users, including the following:
  - *Creators* make social content go.
  - *Critics* respond to content from others.
  - *Collectors* organize content for themselves or others using RSS feeds, tags, and voting sites like Digg.com.
  - *Joiners* connect in social networks like MySpace and Facebook.
  - *Spectators* consume social content including blogs, user-generated video, podcasts, forums, or reviews.
  - *Inactives* neither create nor consume social content of any kind.
- Leaders must not allow technical obstacles to thwart great business ideas.

Real Leadership in the Virtual World

- One of the best aspects of social media marketing through sites like Tripadvisor.com is that it is free of charge. However, leaders must be aware that it is a two-edged sword that can be wielded by a fickle foe. It is not possible to please everybody all the time, but as far as is possible, leaders must attempt to satisfy even the most fastidious of critics. When not possible, then a gracious apology and the promise of a "try harder" attitude goes a long way.

- Everyone has the chance to make money while they sleep. You just have to simply plan and execute. Stop procrastinating and get going with it. Start it up. Promote it. Sell it. And make money from it.

- The top tip from one of our pioneers: Crowdsourcing is a key way to handle elastic projects and manage knowledge effectively.

- Always know what you are getting upfront. You write the contracts, you set the timeline. When other people are in control, it is bad for your business.

- Never outsource your core competencies

- Always remember, the most intelligent people always realize how little they actually know.

- Even with detailed planning and creative marketing, some innovative virtual business ideas will not succeed, likely because they were before their time.

- Finally, one of our pioneers suggested her secrets to success included virtualization, passion, values, a can-do attitude, determination, education, willingness to share and mentor, concentrating on following your dreams and not chasing others, believing in yourself, giving back to others, joining groups and organizations that pertain to your field, and always being the best that you can be.

The Power of Sharing

- A convergence of ubiquitous communication networks, low-cost appliances, exponential web-based content growth, and a cultural shift toward sharing has created an always-on, always-connected, always-sharing environment.

- When you implement more efficient processes, achieve faster time to market, and reduce cycle times, you extract more value from your collaboration investment. We referred in chapter 4 to the study called *Meetings Around the World 2: Charting the Course of Advanced Collaboration* as it provided strong evidence of the value of business going virtual. There is sufficient validity to act; these are positive and strong reasons for leaders to chart the future of work more rapidly.

- *Collaboration technologies can help reduce stress.* More than half of the 3,500 respondents in this survey say collaboration tools allow for greater balance between work and personal life and help them gain more control over their busy lives.
- *Confidence in virtual meetings is growing.* More than half of respondents think conferencing tools are a good alternative to visiting business contacts face to face.
- *Telecommuting is becoming more popular.* Almost half (47%) of respondents report having a formal telecommuting policy in place. However, less than a third (27%) telecommute at least once a week, and 22% telecommute on a daily basis. This tallies with the numbers in a Forrester study, which reported that one-third of workers telecommute at least some of the time.
- *The environment is a priority.* More than half (53%) say reducing an organization's carbon footprint and other environmental concerns are important factors in determining collaborative technology requirements.

Making Sense of Virtual Worlds

- These approaches are relatively low cost and can interrelate easily between real-life and Second Life experiences.
- The technology is rapidly evolving; it won't be long before all customer experiences will have an optional engagement experience to use 3D for their online experiences.
- With the tweens growing up rapidly and arriving in the workforce in fewer than 5 years, their quest to experience 3D will continue to alter everything we know about immersion.
- From a business perspective, it is also important to understand that virtual worlds are changing from levying monthly subscriptions to charging small amounts for virtual goods, a practice made popular by FarmVille. Brands are now creating their own virtual worlds to sell their products.

- Virtual goods that carry real-life brands have 10 times the buying power of virtual brands. Brands like Second Life may not continue to dominate the business experience landscape, as new virtual worlds like Blue Mars and Project X evolve their footprint.
- We can also be assured that Google is following this market space very closely as the interplay between GoogleMaps, virtual worlds, and social and geolocal/spatial mobile devices is a powerful overlay that will change even further the world we interact in.
- One thing we can count on is that it will be incredibly rich and immersive and the long awaited entertainment economy will be embedded in the virtualization of business.

Any Place, Any Time

- In our first-place case, we witnessed how Midwest virtual order centers help fast food restaurants on the West Coast. By geographically relocating a mission critical step in the drive-thru process, the restaurateurs created real value for the store and home-based agents alike.
- Our second example featured U.S. board-certified radiologist completing off-hour emergent radiology interpretation. In other words, highly qualified doctors living in Australia read X-rays for American medical facilities. The physicians, who work during Australian daylight (American nighttime), are well rested, alert, and delighted with their work environment.
- Next we reviewed an innovative way to outsource selective steps in the tax return process. Accounting firms are to protect clients' privacy by ensuring no sensitive financial data leaves the United States. This creative use of virtual private networks allows the firm to combat the increasing shortage of U.S.-based CPAs.
- The fourth case described how businesses may expand their call center operations without the cost of huge capital projects normally associated with new places. By employing home agents, the companies are able to forego the need for new buildings.

- Finally, we learned how Web 2.0 tools and techniques can be used to create virtual gathering places.

The People Know Best

- Crowdsourcing is "the act of taking a job traditionally performed by a designated agent (usually an employee) and outsourcing it to an undefined, generally large group of people in the form of an open call."[11]
- Crowdsourcing may be an excellent alternative for organizations lacking the know-how or resources to solve a difficult problem.
- Viral videos can be positive or negative as they tend to move at lightning speed. Is your organizations ready to exploit the momentum of a positive video? Are you ready to quickly deal with an unwanted viral video? Remember to think about squirrels and guitars!
- By the end of 2010, there were more than 700,000 CNN iReporters and at least one story from all 194 countries on the planet.[12]
- TripAdvisor (a good example of *Groundswell*'s critics category) truly has an army of volunteers who rate their travel experiences around the world. Since they launched in 2000, TripAdvisor has witnessed tremendous growth and now boasts a global army of critics including more than 50 million unique monthly users.

Everyone Has a Stake

- Jeff Howe coined the term crowdsourcing to describe "everyday people using their spare cycles to create content, solve problems, even do corporate R & D."[13]
- Walking the talk lessons learned, based on our Cisco case study, include the following: the importance of robust collaboration and networked infrastructure; collaboration fuels accelerated team performance; and collaboration requires leadership alignment..

- Social media lesson learned, based on our Molson Coors case study, include the following: early objectives are key and success should be measured; speak to, not at, an audience; and social media success can be iterative.
- eCollaboration lessons learned, based on our RIM case study, include the following: executive leadership and accountability are key; lead with leading practices; and drive adoption rapidly.

Real in the Virtual World

- *Start with a simple application.* You will be surprised at what is possible. Engage your youth on this project, perhaps a local university, community college, or even high school, to support your "imagineering" efforts. If your business is dependent on web channel interactions, you cannot ignore that your business plan will need to start planning for virtual worlds. They will augment your brand and user reach, both for customer and for employee engagement practices.
- *Integrate VWs with your overall Web 2.0 and knowledge management strategy.* These different collaboration experiences should not be treated in isolation from one another in terms of branding, communication engagement practices, and architecture planning strategies.
- *Develop a learning and experimentation innovation attitude.* The majority of organizations are failing in their entry into virtual worlds simply because they have poor innovation and experimentation practices, supported with effective operating practices (i.e., governance, nonsustainable budgets, or ill-defined performance metrics). When an organization enters a virtual online world, it is extremely visible. Avatar communities are well educated, and word spreads quickly when another poor entrant is found. Active bloggers are pervasive in virtual worlds, and they spread the word (good or bad) quickly.
- *With good planning, strong communication practices, and changing community interaction experiences, organizations can increase their success.* They can also ask their visitors to help evolve the

experience; seeking avatars' feedback can increase their sense of belonging to the community. As well, communities require a purpose that resonates with its visitors or the avatar will simply go elsewhere. Without a reason for a return visit, avatars seldom return.

PART IV

Appendixes

APPENDIX 1

The Big Money Top 50

In November 2009, *The Big Money* (http://www.thebigmoney.com) released *The Big Money* Facebook 50, a ranking of the brands that are currently making the best use of Facebook. *The Big Money* used various metrics—including fan numbers, page growth, frequency of updates, creativity as determined by a panel of judges, and fan engagement—to establish each page's score and ultimate rank on the list.

The table includes the number of Facebook fans for each of the pages as reported by *The Big Money* in November 2009. We have also included the number of Facebook users who "like" the page as of late February 2011. The latter was derived by us visiting each of the pages and recording the number of people who like the page. We should note that in 2010 Facebook moved from a system of "fans" to a system of "likes." Although there is a difference between the two systems, for our purposes, the system in place is not as important as the number of Facebook users who made a conscious effort to connect with the page.

Table A1.1. The Big Money *Facebook* 50

Rank	Company	The Big Money Rationale
1.	Coca-Cola	A Coca-Cola fan created this page last year without much of a strategy. "I sat back and watched it grow and grow and grow," he says. Thanks to the power of the brand, the page eventually became a top page on Facebook. Coca-Cola (KO) has since made the page "official," created some sophisticated apps, and smartly kept the creator and his buddy onboard. The result: An organic fan-centric page without a corporate feel. Fans as of November 15, 2009: 3,996,163 Likes as of February 2, 2011: 22,226,541
2.	Starbucks	Starbucks (SBUX) took over the top spot this summer as the brand with the most fans on Facebook. The coffee company won almost 200,000 new fans in a single week in late July, thanks in part to a free pastry promotion. Fans as of November 15, 2009: 5,034,578 Likes as of February 2, 2011: 19,473,226
3.	Disney	Disney (DIS) fans have uploaded more than 3,400 of their own photos onto the media and entertainment company's page. Fans as of November 15, 2009: 2,119,773 Likes as of February 2, 2011: 16,677,141
4.	Victoria's Secret	Two Victoria's Secret fan pages—the standard page and a separate page devoted to its Pink! line of underwear—are the top-ranked "Fashion" pages in terms of fans. The Limited-Brands-owned (LTD) retailer posts lots of photos and videos starring its models. Fans as of November 15, 2009: 2,151,895 Likes as of February 2, 2011: 11,365,267
5.	iTunes	Within a week of launching this page in May, Apple's (AAPL) digital downloading service iTunes already had more than 1 million fans. Fans as of November 15, 2009: 2,236,306 Likes as of February 2, 2011: 11,365,267
6.	Vitamin-water	The "flavorcreator" doubles as a fun app and a market research tool. Users voted on Coca-Cola (KO)-owned Vitaminwater's next drink flavor and submitted designs for the label. Fans have more than doubled since the promotion launched in September. Fans as of November 15, 2009: 1,087,153 Likes as of February 2, 2011: 2,152,039
7.	YouTube	In July, Google's (GOOG) YouTube publicly set out to get more Facebook fans than celebrities Adam Sandler, Lady Gaga, Will Smith, Megan Fox, and Vin Diesel by the end of September. While the video sharing Web site didn't end up meeting the challenge, it still gained 600,000 new fans in what it called a "friendly celebrity tussle." Fans as of November 15, 2009: 3,733,242 Likes as of February 2, 2011: 26,658,021

Table A1.1. The Big Money *Facebook 50 (continued)*

Rank	Company	The Big Money Rationale
8.	Chick-fil-A	Chick-fil-A was the first restaurant page with 1 million fans on Facebook, reaching this milestone in August. Fans as of November 15, 2009: 1,221,064 Likes as of February 2, 2011: 3,740,011
9.	Red Bull	An appropriately energetic page. Red Bull's latest app, called Red Bull Stash, maps out a real-life scavenger hunt for fans of the drink company. Fans as of November 15, 2009: 1,623,102 Likes as of February 2, 2011: 15,055,143
10.	T.G.I. Friday's	T.G.I. Friday's ran a television ad this fall with an enticing premise: Become a fan of this guy and you get a free burger, but only if the page reaches half a million fans before October. The restaurant chain reached its goal by Sept. 13. Fans as of November 15, 2009: 974,192 Likes as of February 2, 2011: 515,392
11.	Skittles	For a while, the Skittles.com homepage redirected to its Facebook fan page. While the Mars Inc. candy brand doesn't update the page often, it still maintains an enthusiastic following. Fans as of November 15, 2009: 3,523,796 Likes as of February 2, 2011: 14,948,837
12.	Dunkin' Donuts	While most fan pages use corporate logos as their profile pictures, the doughnut and coffee retailer uses the space to honor the winner of its "Fan of the Week" contest. Fans as of November 15, 2009: 953,544 Likes as of February 2, 2011: 3,021,719
13.	Best Buy	With the page's Shop + Share tab, fans of the electronics retailer can browse and discuss Best Buy (BBY) products without leaving Facebook. Fans as of November 15, 2009: 844,927 Likes as of February 2, 2011: 2,429,409
14.	NBA	Basketball leagues rule on Facebook. The NBA and the WNBA pages both beat the NFL and MLB pages in terms of fans. Fans as of November 15, 2009: 1,692,030 Likes as of February 2, 2011: 7,355,844
15.	Adidas Originals	Recognizing its international fan base, sports retailer Adidas occasionally posts updates in languages other than English. Fans as of November 15, 2009: 2,153,845 Likes as of February 2, 2011: 7,005,396

Table A1.1. The Big Money *Facebook 50 (continued)*

Rank	Company	The Big Money Rationale
16.	Kellogg's Pop Tarts	Kellogg's (K) breakfast pastry brand Pop Tarts recently gained more than 15,000 fans in one day during the launch of its Flavor Tournament app. Fans as of November 15, 2009: 987,667 Likes as of February 2, 2011: 2,672,667
17.	Krispy Kreme	The Krispy Kreme Doughnuts (KKD) page demonstrates that asking questions is an easy way to engage fans. Fans as of November 15, 2009: 1,158,693 Likes as of February 2, 2011: 2,884,122
18.	Mountain Dew	PepsiCo.'s (PEP) Mountain Dew keeps fans engaged. The soda company personally congratulated its 500,000th fan in early September. Fans as of November 15, 2009: 610,858 Likes as of February 2, 2011: 4,141,030
19.	JCPenney	When retailer JCPenney (JCP) purchased Facebook ads for the back-to-school shopping season, its fan numbers skyrocketed from 22,000 to almost 500,000. Fans as of November 15, 2009: 570,946 Likes as of February 2, 2011: 1,464,104
20.	Papa John's	A year ago, Papa John's (PZZA) gained 200,000 Facebook fans by offering a free medium pizza deal to anyone who signed up to the pizza chain's page. The promotion was so successful that Papa John's is repeating it this month. Fans as of November 15, 2009: 730,951 Likes as of February 2, 2011: 1,516,578
21.	Disney/Pixar	Soon after Disney's (DIS) animation production company Pixar released a *Toy Story* remix video on YouTube—along with a link back to its Facebook page—it gained more than 9,000 new fans. Fans as of November 15, 2009: 657,917 Likes as of February 2, 2011: 7,279,750
22.	*National Geographic*	National Geographic gets impressive fan feedback—thousands of "likes"—nearly every time the magazine posts its content. Fans as of November 15, 2009: 578,817 Likes as of February 2, 2011: 4,569,161
23.	McDonald's	This summer, McDonald's (MCD) fan numbers spiked. That's probably because the fast food chain folded unofficial McDonald's fan pages into the official page—something Facebook will help companies to do—says InsideFacebook's Justin Smith. Fans as of November 15, 2009: 1,447,163 Likes as of February 2, 2011: 7,070,573

Table A1.1. The Big Money *Facebook 50 (continued)*

Rank	Company	The Big Money Rationale
24.	H&M	High fan interaction. The fashion retailer has had success in generating tens of thousands of responses with polls. Fans as of November 15, 2009: 1,341,742 Likes as of February 2, 2011: 6,137,543
25.	Gap	Gap (GPS) has gained more than 100,000 new fans since it launched its "born to fit" fall ad campaign, which the clothing retailer based on customer feedback and interaction. Fans as of November 15, 2009: 479,101 Likes as of February 2, 2011: 1,323,392
26.	Reese's	There was noticeably more activity on the fan page for Hershey's (HSY) Reese's peanut butter cups around Halloween time. Fans as of November 15, 2009: 1,430,286 Likes as of February 2, 2011: 6,459,776
27.	Dippin' Dots	The ice cream company posts contests and promotions encourage high fan involvement. Fans as of November 15, 2009: 898,760 Likes as of February 2, 2011: 3,575,148
28.	Kohl's	After Kohl's (KSS) purchased a Facebook homepage ad in August, it was named the fastest growing page that week by Inside Facebook. The department store's page had fewer than 10,000 fans before the ad went up, and it gained more than 350,000. Fans as of November 15, 2009: 726,880 Likes as of February 2, 2011: 3,392,726
29.	Forever 21	High frequency updates and a weekly giveaway keep fans of the fashion retailer engaged. Fans as of November 15, 2009: 451,834 Likes as of February 2, 2011: 3,986,740
30.	Ben & Jerry's	An ice cream company would know that you can have too much of a good thing. Ben & Jerry's doesn't overwhelm its Facebook fans with too many posts. "We don't have a magic rule or formula for how often is the 'right' amount," a company spokesperson told *The Big Money* over e-mail. "I can tell you, we over-posted once, and fans didn't like it." Fans as of November 15, 2009: 987,761 Likes as of February 2, 2011: 2,427,786
31.	Puma	Coordination with retail stores keeps employees and customers of the sportswear company involved with the page. Fans as of November 15, 2009: 1,271,064 Likes as of February 2, 2011: 3,725,453

Table A1.1. The Big Money *Facebook 50 (continued)*

Rank	Company	The Big Money Rationale
32.	The Art of Travel by Louis Vuitton	When fashion house Louis Vuitton streamed a live fashion show on its page in early October, it gained more than 60,000 new fans. Fans as of November 15, 2009: 761,342 Likes as of February 2, 2011: 1,843,365
33.	CNN	CNN.com joined forces with Facebook Connect for its coverage of Barack Obama's inauguration. More than 2 million Facebook status updates were published through the news network's live feed during the ceremony. CNN is a division of Time Warner (TWX). Fans as of November 15, 2009: 654,750 Likes as of February 2, 2011: 1,731,770
34.	Pringles	Pringles, the chip company owned by Procter & Gamble (PG), has an impressive fan base even though it rarely updates its page. Fans as of November 15, 2009: 2,788,810 Likes as of February 2, 2011: 8,923,107
35.	Pizza Hut	Pizza Hut, a subsidiary of Yum Brands' (YUM), created a Facebook app that facilitates pizza ordering. Fans as of November 15, 2009: 1,044,408 Likes as of February 2, 2011: 2,697,580
36.	*Vogue*	Condé Nast's fashion magazine gets positive feedback when it promotes its editorial content and magazine-quality images onto the page. Fans of November 15, 2009: 330,220 Likes as of February 2, 2011: 1,208,488
37.	Apple Students	Apple (AAPL) started "Apple Students" as a sponsored group when the Facebook community was almost exclusively college kids. Even though Facebook has since grown, the electronics retailer's page is a good place to deliver targeted messages to this audience. Fans as of November 15, 2009: 1,405,695 Group not active, 10,298 likes
38.	Dr. Pepper	The soda company, owned by the Dr. Pepper Snapple Group (DPS), regularly posts fan-submitted photos to its wall. Fans as of November 15, 2009: 906,910 Likes as of February 2, 2011: 7,744,145
39.	Vans	The footwear retailer does a good job incorporating YouTube videos onto its page. Fans as of November 15, 2009: 337,550 Likes as of February 2, 2011: 1,917,802

Table A1.1. The Big Money *Facebook 50 (continued)*

Rank	Company	The Big Money Rationale
40.	Six Flags	This summer, Six Flags hosted the "Tournament of Thrills" competition on its Facebook page where fans could vote for their favorite roller coasters. More than 85,000 votes were cast, and the amusement park's fan base more than doubled during the promotion. Fans as of November 15, 2009: 379,056 Likes as of February 2, 2011: 1,129,346
41.	MTV	Viacom's (VIAB) MTV page has a good ratio of fan "likes" to comments. The music channel maintains a fast-moving page with consistent fan engagement. Fans as of November 15, 2009: 1,146,737 Likes as of February 2, 2011: 15,192,576
42.	Harley-Davidson	A fan photo gallery includes more than 9,000 photos of fans and their Harley-Davidson (HOG) bikes. Fans as of November 15, 2009: 339,135 Likes as of February 2, 2011: 2,028,011
43.	Target	Target's (TGT) page gained 97,091 new fans through its two-week "Bullseye Gives" campaign, during which fans could vote for which charity they thought most deserved Target's donations. (St. Jude Children's Research Hospital won the most votes.) The retailer reported that daily views of the page jumped by 4,800 percent. Fans as of November 15, 2009: 588,300 Likes as of February 2, 2011: 3,843,477
44.	Audi	Automaker Audi seeks out fan feedback. It hosted a campaign encouraging fans to discuss what its next car should look like, and the company recently posted a survey asking fans what they wanted from the page. Fans as of November 15, 2009: 381,038 Likes as of February 2, 2011: 2,870,415
45.	Gatorade	PepsiCo.'s (PEP) Gatorade set up an app that encouraged users to vote for their favorite moment from Michael Jordan's career. More than 8,000 votes were cast on the sports drink's page. Fans as of November 15, 2009: 360,860 Likes as of February 2, 2011: 2,867,188
46.	Zara	Fans from all over the world express their love for this clothing retailer on its Facebook wall. Fans as of November 15, 2009: 1,580,858 Likes as of February 2, 2011: 7,957,190

Table A1.1. The Big Money *Facebook 50 (continued)*

Rank	Company	The Big Money Rationale
47.	Taco Bell	Yum Brands' (YUM) fast food chain Taco Bell is responsive to fan comments and generates strong positive feedback when it posts promotions. Fans as of November 15, 2009: 664,592 Likes as of February 2, 2011: 5,423,030
48.	Buffalo Wild Wings	This restaurant chain has a fast-growing and devoted fan base. Fans as of November 15, 2009: 913,754 Likes as of February 2, 2011: 3,909,015
49.	Calvin Klein	Phillips-Van Heusen's (PVH) clothing retailer Calvin Klein regularly announces sales and posts coupons. Fans as of November 15, 2009: 332,521 Likes as of February 2, 2011: 1,180,915
50.	*The Onion*	The satirical newspaper doesn't do much besides post its content on its page, but it still maintains a steady, engaged fan following. Fans as of November 15, 2009: 535,411 Likes as of February 2, 2011: 1,491,415

Source: *The Big Money* Facebook 50 (2009).

APPENDIX 2

Guiding Organizations Into the Future

Well that didn't actually happen, but . . . it could have!

—Geena Davis, actor and raconteur

Note: In chapter 3, "Real Leadership in the Virtual World," we featured a series of stories penned by virtual business pioneers. We briefly discussed the power of the written story and promised to include a chapter from John and JoAnn's book *A Leader's Guide to Knowledge Management: Building on the Past to Enhance Future Performance*. The work that follows is from that book and is an adaptation of a paper written by John and Sandy Lambert. Sandy is a former graduate student of John's and is now pursuing a doctorate degree.

In the past 5 years or so, there has been tremendous interest in the value of oral narrative or storytelling as a catalyst for organizational change. Many of these accounts chronicle seasoned executives telling stories that spark massive transformation in their organizations. It seems, so the story goes, that these organizations were apparently reluctant or incapable of considering even the most modest change initiative—that is, until the story was told. With that in mind, we thought a chapter on crafting future-based stories would be a fitting way to commence a glimpse of the future. Consider our interpretation of the classic Cathedral Builder story:

On a foggy autumn day, nearly 800 years ago, a traveler happened upon a large group of workers adjacent to the River Avon. Despite being tardy for an important rendezvous, curiosity convinced the traveler that he should inquire about their work. With a slight detour he moved toward the first of the three tradesmen and said,

"My dear fellow, what is it that you are doing?" The man continued his work and grumbled, "I am cutting stones." Realizing that
the mason did not wish to engage in a conversation, the traveler
moved toward the second of the three and repeated the question.
To the traveler's delight, this time the man stopped his work, ever
so briefly, and stated that he was a stonecutter. He then added, "I
came to Salisbury from the north to work, but as soon as I earn 10
quid, I will return home." The traveler thanked the second mason,
wished him a safe journey home, and began to head to the third
of the trio.

When he reached the third worker, he once again asked the
original question. This time the worker paused, glanced at the
traveler until they made eye contact, and then looked skyward
drawing the traveler's eyes upward. The third mason replied, "I
am a mason and I am building a cathedral." He continued, "I have
journeyed many miles to be part of the team that is constructing
this magnificent cathedral. I have spent many months away from
my family and I miss them dearly. However, I know how important Salisbury Cathedral will be one day and I know how many
people will find sanctuary and solace here. I know this because the
bishop once told me his vision for this great place. He described
how people would come from all parts to worship here. He also
told me that the Cathedral will not be completed in our days but
that the future depends on our hard work." He paused and then
said, "So I am prepared to be away from my family because I know
it is the right thing to do. I hope that one day my son will continue in my footsteps and perhaps even his son if need be."

This story is an adaptation of a legendary example of how a well-told
story can motivate men and women to make great sacrifices if they believe
their work is important. One can imagine that most leaders would wish
to have a team of cathedral builders rather than stonecutters. The question is, can a story really transform stonecutters into cathedral builders?

To date, most of the work in the domain has focused on the value of
telling stories—in other words, oral narrative. Take, for example, Steve
Denning's book *The Springboard*, the subtitle of which is *How Storytelling Ignites Action in Knowledge-Era Organizations*.[1] In this seminal work,

Denning describes his successes in telling face-to-face stories. Denning's work has spawned a host of other papers and books, most of which focus on telling oral stories.

Surely these printed exposés are themselves motivators for change, so why the continued emphasis on the face-to-face storytelling? Perhaps there is value in examining writing stories rather than telling stories that spark change. This chapter is a story of exactly that, writing stories that help guide organizations. We thought this would be a fitting topic to conclude our discussion of what leaders can do to guard the knowledge of their organizations. We believe that well-written stories are an excellent way to guide organizations into the future.

Getting the Message Right

Stories are a primary mode of human communication and thinking—and one that has been used since the dawn of time. Why? Stories have depth and multiple dimensions; they help us create human connections in a world that seems complex, sometimes (or often) threatening, and increasingly dehumanizing. Stories give us context.[2]

Before describing the stories, it is worth reviewing the literature with a view to determining the theoretical foundations of these stories. Much like the cathedral builder's bishop, many leaders use stories to electrify their subordinates and lead them into the future. The ability to relate to an audience using a story is a concept that has passed the test of time. Through a variety of approaches, present-day executives use stories to excite and invigorate their teams much as their predecessors did. Kaye and Jocobson remind us that "stories tap into our emotions and intellect in ways that get us to remember and use the information and wisdom of the past to help us make informed decisions in the future."[3]

There is an enormous difference between relating a message to an audience and sharing a vision to alter the future of an organization. The use of narration or storytelling envisaged within a corporation can grant insight into an alternate course of action. Chartier, LaPointe, and Bonner state, in *Get Real—The Art and Power of Storytelling in Workplace Communities*, "Stories are a way to honour our past, describe our present and shape our future."[4] The impact of conveying an envisioned story, which can change the future of an organization, can be magnificent, in the sense that it can also change lives. Yet how does one know that the envisaged narrative will be received and have the ability to alter the future of an organization? How does the manager know if the message of their narrative has been received and that their team members can relate? In oral stories, the receivers demonstrate an attentive and responsive reaction, sometimes signs of enthusiasm. However, with the written word, the immediate reaction is often lacking.

Throughout time, leaders have used stories to share knowledge, spark change, and generally enlighten an audience. In a *Harvard Business Review* article titled "Telling Tales," Denning provides a catalog of seven types of stories used by leaders, including sparking action, communicating who you are, transmitting values, fostering collaboration, taming the grapevine, sharing knowledge, and leading people into the future.[5]

Some leaders use formal presentations to achieve these tasks. Although there are similarities in the techniques, there are also significant differences. More and more, the evidence is suggesting the PowerPoint style of knowledge transfer is less effective than many believe. Janis Forman argues that "clear communications between executives and their audiences has been declining ever since the advent of souped-up computer graphics and Internet access to vast quantities of data."[6] Neilson and Stouffer claim that PowerPoint presentations lack contextual meaning.[7] According to McKee and Fryer, we should "forget about PowerPoint and statistics. To involve people at the deepest level, you need stories."[8]

Steve Denning, the celebrated guru of storytelling, claims to have moved from PowerPoint–style presentations to storytelling after observing that his audience "merely looked dazed."[9] Larry Prusak, respected knowledge management expert, goes one step further by suggesting, "I've taken PowerPoint off all my computers; it's the enemy of thought."[10] Though Prusak's action may seem extreme, his point is very valid; knowledge sharing is sometimes impeded by an endless stream of charts and graphs.

In their article "Narrating the Vision," Neilson and Stouffer illustrate the effectiveness of using futuristic scenarios as a storytelling technique. They suggest that "futuristic scenarios—stories that paint a vivid picture of a future state—can help provide a vision and leadership in a narrative format as well as communicate the organization vision."[11] The ability to convey a message, as in the article "Narrating the Vision," is a great example of a futuristic scenario. Nevertheless, it is important to examine the effectiveness of the approach of futuristic scenarios within an organization. Steve Denning (2005) stated recently that future scenarios aid in the exploration of other points of view yet concluded that a descriptive narrative to support the scenario is necessary.

Conveying Futuristic Views

As humans, we are wired to respond to stories in deep, sometimes unconscious ways. We actually answer with our attention and focus, when all other efforts may fail. Watch sometime how body language changes when someone starts a joke or story. Notice the slight rise in alertness and increased presence of the listeners. People will almost always put down what they are doing and give full attention. If the teller is particularly good at storytelling, then the response is almost always deep focus.[12]

Visualizing a future organizational course of action entails strategies and tactics to build loyalty, focus effort, and spark creativity.[13] The leader as communicator exemplifies the restructuring of several organizations, each of which uses stories to communicate a holistic viewpoint with one or more different angles. The basis of the story is a problematic statement posing a challenge for the organizations. The story is used to convey a guided future course of action for the organization; a methodical approach occurs prior to this phase. Before the plot line can be portrayed, a data-gathering process is needed. The data-gathering phase will answer questions on the past, current, and future courses of action of the organization. One should also consider the buy-in factor of stakeholders.

According to Forman, one method that can be used to evaluate or test their envisaged narrative is an analysis tree.[14] Determining coherence through a visual analysis illustrates phases within a story. The corporation's past history, current course of action to take, and the envisaged future will be shown along with the structural ideas that show a link to strategic reality. The analysis tree is similar to a storyboard, which allows visualization of how the process relates to another phase. This particular method was used by executives in the health care industry. The advantage of the analysis tree is flexibility to adapt to the storyteller's needs. The storyteller can adapt the analysis tree to the audience or stakeholders. Evaluating narratives through the analysis tree is valuable to an organization based on the effectiveness of the story.

Contrary to Forman's analysis tree, Allen suggests that storytelling will not substitute for analytical thinking but only enhances organizational knowledge.[15] However, sharing of knowledge ignites change, which increases the possibility of success within an organization. Altering duty into passion is a requirement to increase the level of accomplishments. Linking responsibilities with passions prevents burnout and remoteness among employees and therefore benefits the organization. Storytelling provides the means to convey messages to an audience or a method for sharing knowledge. "Storytelling can be the catalyst for change . . . Telling your story complements analytical thinking and allows customers to engage feelings, leading to loyalty."[16]

Storytelling can be advantageous to an organization in a variety of ways. "Stories can be told in a variety of modes that include: visual accounts, ballads, metaphors, text, and voice. Telling good stories serves the organization with an effective means of collecting wisdom through experience."[17] The use of storytelling, along with five other components, becomes useful for an organization to plan a future course of action. This form of planning is called action mapping and consists of assemblage, accumulation, and production of wisdom; actions as hypothesis; conservation of energy; reflection on action; and storytelling. The planning phase will consist of essential components from the data-gathering phase. Creating the story requires past, present, and future knowledge of the organization, which will in turn be used to develop the future course of action. Involving the stakeholders in the process creates an increased success factor of the envisaged narrative. Matsui suggests, "The knowledge and experiences gained from a journey clarify future actions by identifying emerging patterns."[18]

Steve Denning (2001) uses the catalyst approach and takes storytelling a step further, through springboard stories, which provide the audience or stakeholders with a deeper level of understanding. Visualizing through the use of realistic events sustains the attention and consciousness of the audience. The significant aspect of a springboard story is the use of a simplistic approach, using fewer details to allow the audience to imagine the future possibilities that can occur within the organization. This catalyst approach leads the audience without controlling their views based on an individual's field or past experiences. Audience participation in the creation of the organization's future is met with less resistance and more enthusiasm, therefore obtaining buy-in from the participants.

Writing the Future

Snowden's second heuristic of the new knowledge management generation is that "we can always know more than we can tell, and we will
always tell more than we can write down."[19] These wise words seem to
suggest that telling an oral story may be more effective than a written
story. However, before dismissing the written word, it is worth considering the context of his message. Snowden suggests,

> I can speak in five minutes what it will otherwise take me two
> weeks to get round to spending a couple of hours writing it down.
> The process of writing something down is reflective knowledge; it
> involves both adding and taking away from the actual experience
> or original thought. Reflective knowledge has high value, but is
> time consuming and involves loss of control over its subsequent
> use.[20]

This deeper examination of Snowden's second heuristic seems to imply
that once one takes the time to create a written story, the value may be
higher than a less reflective oral story. Snowden's premise is corroborated
by Denning, who wrote, "A story can help take listeners, from where they
are to where they need to be, by making them comfortable with an image
of the future. The problem, of course, lies in crafting a credible narrative
about the future when the future is unknowable."[21] Together, Denning
and Snowden highlight the challenge of writing future stories—one must
take the time to learn about the future and then articulate the ideas using
the reflective knowledge Snowden described.

The overview concludes that, in theory, narratives help guide people
into the future and share knowledge. The question remains: Can one use
this technique in practice? Perhaps more specifically, the question is, can
one use written narratives to share knowledge and guide people into the
future? One way to answer this question is by chronicling the success of
three recently written stories. Each was written with the express aim of
guiding people into the future.

Before describing the stories, it is important to understand that this
chapter is based on our experiences and not based on empirical research,
nor does it report the results of a true experiment, but rather it describes

the use of narratives in real organizations with real people dealing with real challenges. Most of the results are anecdotal in nature; nevertheless, it is believed that stories are a useful tool in some organizations.

There is no disputing the fact that oral narrative is a powerful form of communicating; however, it is not always feasible. In fact, there are times when the written word packs a more powerful punch. Often it is simply not possible to catch the ear of a wide audience simultaneously, or even at all. Many people simply will not take time from their busy schedules to listen to stories, others may be geographically separated, and still others may simply be out to lunch or otherwise predisposed. In these cases, the power of the pen offers a persuasive substitute.

This is a tale about a trio of such stories, which seemed to sow the seed of change, help guide people into the future, and share organizational knowledge. Of course, time will be the real test; however, anecdotal evidence seems to support the proposition that well-written futuristic stories provide an excellent alternative to face-to-face oral narrative. At least in these examples, the written story proved to be a motivator for organizational change and an effective way to share knowledge.

Story 1: Guiding Government Leaders Into the Future

The first story was developed to excite change in a very large bureaucratic organization—Canada's Department of National Defence. At the time, John was leading the Strategic Knowledge Management cell and he was keen to explain how and why knowledge management could help defense leaders. Clearly it would not be possible to meet face to face with all the target audience, so what to do? Against the advice of many colleagues, pen was put to paper to create a story titled "Twelve Hours of Knowledge" (see the full story on page 207). The story was an overwhelming success, and it was eventually included in the *Canadian Military Journal*—the journal read by the target audience (Girard, 2004a).

The story, which was set 5 years in the future, intentionally blurred the real with the imaginary. Many facets of the story were commonplace in defense, such as the type of equipment, ranks, organizations, and jargon. Care was taken not to use any real people's names; instead, position titles were used. The tale was about a Canadian Forces operation on a small Caribbean island nation that was dealing with the aftermath of a natural disaster.

So what made the story a success? Clearly, there were a number of critical success factors; however, one of the most important was the look of the story. The story was designed to resemble the weekly newspaper of the Canadian Forces titled *The Maple Leaf*. With the editor's permission, a story was crafted that appeared to be *The Maple Leaf*'s cover story. This allowed the story to be distributed as a reprint from the paper. The look was especially useful in capturing people's attention, countering to some degree the old cliché, "Don't judge a book by its cover." At least in this case it seems the cover was important to many people. Attracting the target audience is just the first step; clearly, the content is the vital ingredient.

Although the story was set in the future, it did not rely on futuristic technology, but rather, it described technology that is commonplace today. This was a surprise to many readers as they expected some farfetched, ridiculously expensive *Star Trek*–type technology. Instead, the narrative described leadership and culture as the keys to success—another surprise to many readers.

A crucial component of the story's success was executive support. An early draft of the story caught the attention of one very senior executive who was delighted with the format and the message. His endorsement provided the necessary influence to sway a few less enthusiastic managers, who may have otherwise been able to thwart the distribution of the piece. As is the case with other change initiatives, the support of senior executives is critical to the success of motivational stories.

A story must be believable, realistic, and most importantly perceived as achievable. We are often asked if a story must be true. Before answering this very valid question, consider the following:

> In 2006, Geena Davis won the Golden Globe Award for the Best Performance by an Actress in a Television Series—Drama. She won the award for her portrayal of the first woman to be president of the United States of America in the television show Commander in Chief. After being presented the award, she thanked the Hollywood Foreign Press and then stated, "As I was coming in, I felt a little tug on my skirt. I looked and there was a little girl,

maybe 8 or 10, in her first party dress. She said, because of you, I want to be president some day." She paused while the audience, in unison, all said "awww" and then erupted into applause. The camera panned the audience, and many actors were teary-eyed with emotion over the story. She continued, "Well that didn't actually happen, but," she paused again. This time there was laughter and applause. She looked sheepish and then said, "Awww, but, it could have!" The audience laughed even harder, as she continued, "It very well could have, and if I was in the farmlands of Nebraska, or somewhere, there could have been a little girl, tugging at my dress. And were that to be the case, then all of this would be worth it."

Clearly, we do not suggest you make a habit of distorting the truth in your stories; however, as was the case with Geena Davis's acceptance speech, there are times when modest fabrications or white lies add incredible value without creating harm. Much as Geena Davis did, we highly recommend that you remind your audience of your stretching of the truth once the point has been made. Returning to the original question, yes, stories should be true or based on the truth, at least in most cases. Of course, there will be times, especially in future-based stories, where this is not always feasible or even desirable. For example, it is entirely acceptable to create future conditions to emphasize the point you are trying to make. We recommend that you follow the BRAT principle: Stories should be *believable, realistic, achievable,* and based on the truth. It is most important that you consider each of the elements.

Story 2: Guiding Faculty Into the Future

The second story was developed to excite change in an innovative Great Plains university (see the full story on page 211). At the time, John was a new faculty member charged with the responsibility of integrating knowledge management (KM) into the core curriculum of the College of Business. This was no easy task, especially given the number of naysayers who were perfectly content with the status quo. One group believed KM was just a passing fad and they had been involved with enough fads, thank you very much. A second group thought this KM stuff was a good idea, just as long as it did not affect them or their courses. The final group, which was the majority, had bought into the idea but did not really know what to do next.

The story was a mock interview with the dean 5 years hence. The story was published in a trade journal, titled *KM Today*, shortly after the college was the recipient of the Most Innovative Knowledge Educator (MIKE) award. In the interview, the dean described the implementation of the program and how it had improved the quality of education for the students. The final question asked by the interviewer was, "What would you do differently?" to which the dean replies, "I wish we would have started sooner." Grinning, he continued, "The success of the program makes me wish more folks could have benefited, had we started in 2003, we would have helped another cohort. That said I am absolutely delighted with our results."

Both the trade journal and the award in this story were fictitious, as were the other organizations mentioned in the accompanying stories. As a result, they resembled their real alter egos. For example, the genuine trade magazine is titled *KM World* (see http://www.kmworld.com), while the authentic award is the Most Admired Knowledge Enterprise (MAKE; see http://www.knowledgebusiness.com). This allowed the story to be distributed as a reprint from the fictitious, though recognizable, trade journal.

Unlike the first story, this time the story focused on an individual, the dean, who was very well known in the organization. For this reason, the dean's real name was used, and with his permission his style was carefully modeled in the mock interview. This blending of the real and simulated worlds went some way in helping to convince the readers that the story was believable and achievable. Once again, a vital component of the story's success was executive support. The dean reviewed an early draft of the story, and he was delighted with the format and the message.

Story 3: Guiding Students Into the Future

Based on the success of the previous stories, John penned another future-based story (see the full story on page 213). This time the target audience was a group of executive graduate students completing an accelerated master of science in management program of which John was director. A key element to this program is a major research paper that must be completed before graduation. Historically, all students have completed the course work based on the published schedule; however, there tended to be a handful of students who procrastinated on the projects. This procrastination caught the attention of the university administrators who seemed worried that this tardiness may jeopardize the program. In the past, a variety of techniques were used to instill a sense of urgency in the students, but needless to say, the desired results were still not being achieved.

Once again, the use of narrative was selected as the way ahead. This time the story was set just months in the future, unlike the previous stories that were several years in the future. Specifically, the date of the story was the graduation date of the group with the following headline: "Class of 2005—The First Cohort to Graduate as a Group." The story was published in a newspaper with a striking resemblance to the university's student newspaper.

The target audience for this tale was a group of geographically separated students who needed a morale boost. The story was printed and mailed to the students' homes. At the end of the day, the story achieved its aim by helping focus the students on the few remaining months of the program. Several students commented that the story allowed them to see the light at the end of the tunnel. Ultimately, the class of 2005 was the first cohort to graduate as a group—we believe the story helped to achieve this milestone.

Moral of the Story

All good stories should end with a moral, and this story is no different. This saga began by reviewing the timeless story of a stonecutter and a cathedral builder. Given we believe that most executives would wish for an army of cathedral builders rather than stonecutters, we reviewed the literature to see what the gurus were suggesting. The literature is rich with examples of raconteurs guiding the way ahead with oral stories; however, the domain of written stories was far less mature.

After reviewing a trio of future-based written stories, we hope you agree the power of the pen may be as effective as a well-told oral story. In each case, the written word proved to be a powerful motivator by capturing the imagination and attention of the target audience. Perhaps these types of stories are not well suited to all audiences; however, for some groups the written word is more powerful than even the best oral story. To quote a faculty member who was initially against the change and now a supporter of the idea, "Now I get it." Just four words, but four words that mean one more team member is a supporter—those are four important words! The target audience seems to be a key to the success of these stories.

For some groups it is simply not possible to capture the attention of all group members with an oral rendition. This is certainly the case with the three groups described in this chapter. Two of the groups, the military and student groups, were separated geographically and it would have been extremely difficult to have them meet to hear the story. The majority of the third group, the faculty, were geographically collocated but as a group were not very receptive to a gathering to discuss the subject. Anecdotal evidence seems to support the premise that the target audiences for these stories prefer the written word to the spoken word.

The moral of this story is that both written and oral stories are effective tools in sharing organizational knowledge, sparking change, and guiding people into the future. The wise executive should consider both forms of stories to help guide their organizations.

Remember the Cathedral Builder

The classic cathedral builder story is an example of how a well-told story can motivate men and women to make great sacrifices if they believe their work is important. One can imagine that most leaders would wish to have a team of cathedral builders rather than stonecutters. Will such stories resonate in your organization?

Now You Know

- Stories are a primary mode of human communication and thinking.
- There are seven types of stories used by leaders, including sparking action, communicating who you are, transmitting values, fostering collaboration, taming the grapevine, shar-

ing knowledge, and leading people into the future (Denning, 2004).

- A crucial component of future-based stories' success is executive support.
- People do judge the book by the cover—make sure your future-based story is aesthetically pleasing.
- Stories should follow the BRAT principle—they should be *believable, realistic, achievable,* and based on the *truth.*
- A blending of the real and simulated worlds may help to convince the readers that the story was believable and achievable.

The MAPLE LEAF 🍁 La FEUILLE D'ÉRABLE

31 October 2007, Vol. 12, No. 17 | Le 31 octobre 2007, vol. 12, n°. 17

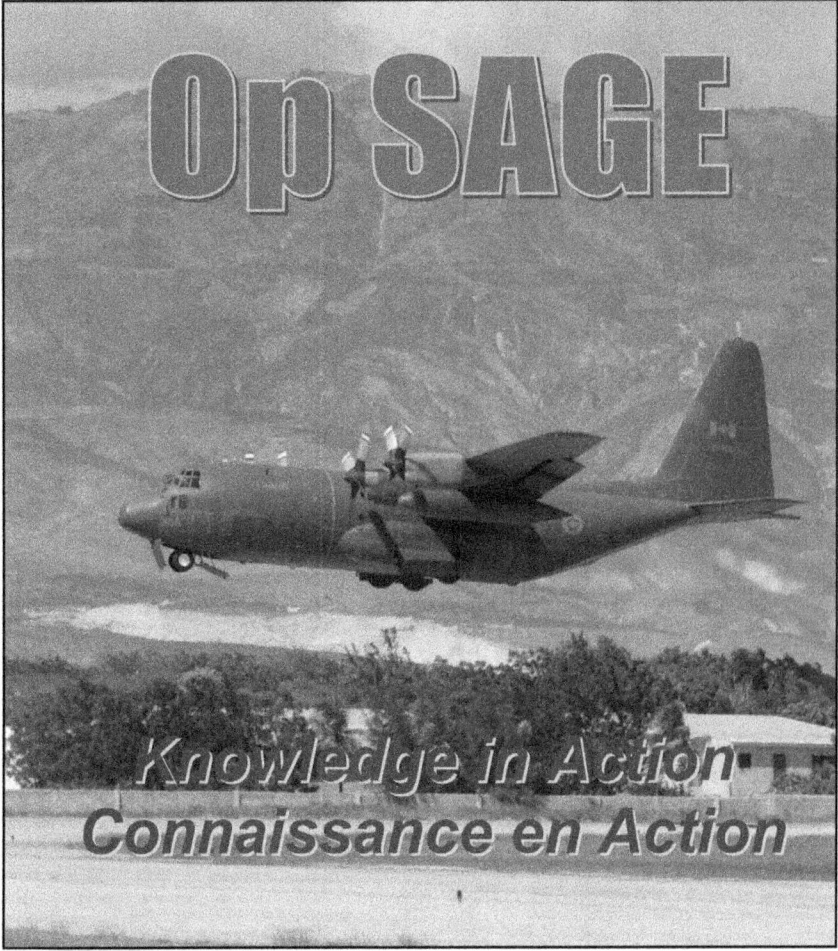

Op SAGE

Knowledge in Action
Connaissance en Action

In this issue / Dans ce numéro

Knowledge in action / Connaissance en action 2-3   Knowledge News / Nouvelles de la connaissance ... 4

This **fictitious** story describes the power of knowledge management in action.
It was created with the kind permission of the **Maple Leaf**.

Twelve hours of Knowledge:
How knowledge sharing helped Op SAGE

(Ottawa) On Monday 29 October 2007, the Canadian Forces' Humanitarian Emergency Relief Team (HERT) arrived in Haiti to help the island nation deal with the aftermath of a natural disaster. HERT was the first international force to answer Haiti's call for assistance. This speedy response, called Operation SAGE, was made possible by connecting people with people to share knowledge. Their story is below.

On Sunday, the Commanding Officer (CO) awoke to the ringing of his personal data assistant. It was 0615 and his Operations Officer had just sent him a priority email. The note contained a news feed describing a hurricane, which suddenly changed course and was heading toward the small Caribbean island nation of Haiti. The CO was surprised by the news as he and his team had been watching the storm for a number of days and most experts believed the storm would not reach land.

After reading the note, CO HERT opened his tablet PC, inserted his Public Key Infrastructure (PKI) card and turned on his computer. Within minutes, through a wireless connection, the CO's personal knowledgespace appeared, which included a dashboard showing the status of his unit. The dashboard was a collection of critical data and information maintained by his staff. The presentation of knowledge in an intuitive manner allowed the CO to quickly decide if he needed to take action or make any decisions. He was delighted to determine that his command group was available, less one officer who was leading a reconnaissance team on another Caribbean island.

Next, he read news from several sites reporting on the conditions in Haiti and the weather forecast for the next 72 hours. Sensing that this may be a mission for the HERT, he created a collaborative workspace for the contingency operation. The content of the workspace was based on the lessons learned from previous missions. After each mission, an After-action Review (AAR) identified the deficiencies and helped redefine the requirements of the workspace.

Returning to his knowledgespace, the CO typed the words *CF operations Haiti* and quickly rediscovered that the CF deployed to Haiti in 1997 and 2004. A synopsis of each operation was available as well as a series of links. To ensure this information was readily available to the other members of his team, he dragged the links into the contingency collaborative workspace. He also saw a list of *experts* on Haiti, including a policy officer from Western Hemisphere Policy, a member of the intelligence staff, a lawyer from Director of International Law and others. He added the list of names to the collaborative workspace.

Eye of the hurricane over Haiti

Next, he opened the staff list for the 1997 operation, but he did not recognize any of the names; in any case, he dragged the link to the staff list into the collaborative workspace. He decided to connect to the CF People Finder application to see where the 1997 battlegroup commander was now. Before being given access to the application, his profile was reviewed to see if he should be given access to the sensitive data. This is a relatively new improvement to the People Finder. In the past he would have had to contact ADM(HR-Mil) to gain access to the information. However, in 2005 decided that a more trusted environment was necessary to support operations. To guard against potential abuses, a sophisticated algorithm monitors all accesses to the People Finder and will lock out and report abusers.

The CO determined that the battlegroup commander retired in 2006 as brigadier-general; however, he remained a member of the Supplementary Reserve and had agreed to be contacted for operational reasons. CO HERT added these details to the collaborative workspace. When he clicked on the 2004 staff list, he was surprised to find that a Staff College friend of his was the deputy commanding officer of the operation. Using People Finder, he determined that his friend is in Ottawa – this fact was added to the workspace.

The CO saw a small flashing icon beside his friend's name, indicating that he was online. Clicking on this icon an Instant Messaging (IM) box appeared and he typed a quick note to his friend. He asked if his friend had heard about the storm and received a quick response saying "AFK – WIMU 10" – which of course is shorthand for "I am away from my keyboard, I will instant message you in 10 minutes" – such shorthand is used when one is using a cellular telephone or other handheld device.

While waiting for his friend to return the IM, he clicked on a link to the lessons learned library. The genesis of the library was an idea from a Community of Practice in 2005. With members from a variety of organizations that collect and analyse lessons, for example the Army Lesson Learned Centre, Director General Safety, Flight Safety, the community thought it would be a great idea to share information amongst each other. The

Director Knowledge Management built on this great idea by sponsoring a project to consolidate the various sources. Today with a click of a button, the CO is able to search a variety of knowledge stores.

The lessons learned library produced some very important lessons. First, he noted that during the 2004 operation, the battlegroup had problems using floppy disks to store data. It turns out that the sand from the island was corrupting the magnetic medium. Their solution was to use Universal Serial Bus (USB) thumb drives in lieu of floppy disks. Next, he discovered that in 1997 there had been a problem with the Status of Forces Agreement (SOFA) for the neighbouring country of Cuba. Other issues were also highlighted, all of which were moved to the collaborative workspace and flagged for the Operations Officer's attention. The SOFA issue was a priority so it triggered an automatic message to the Operations Officer, who reviewed the message and prepared a note to the lawyer identified by the CO as an authority in the area.

It was now 1000 and the CO's staff college friend sent him an IM. He asked his friend a number of questions about the previous operation. After a few minutes, the CO received an IM from the COS J3 in Ottawa suggesting a Warning Order was being developed and would likely be signed off before noon. The CO parted company with his friend and they agree that if anything else developed they would *talk* again.

The CO sent an IM inviting COS J3 into the collaborative workspace and he provided an overview of his morning. COS J3 remarked that *he did not know how they did it in the old days*. He suggested that the CO drive from Kingston to Ottawa for an afternoon classified briefing – they agreed to meet at 1600. The CO signed out of his knowledgespace to tend to some personal issues before departing for Ottawa.

At 1120, the CO received a priority message on his cellular phone. The message was from the collaborative workspace and it stated that COS J3 had just uploaded the warning order. The CO signed into his knowledgespace, received the order, added some additional information and forwarded a message to his operations officer who knew exactly what to do based on standing operating procedures.

HERT's base camp in Haiti

At 1200, he grabbed his tablet PC along with a few other necessities and commenced the drive to Ottawa. At 1315, he was hit head-on by another vehicle and died instantly. At 1400, the COS J3 was notified of the tragic accident. After ensuring that all necessary arrangements were in place to help the CO's family, the COS J3 returned his attention to the operational mission at hand. Clearly, a new CO had to be appointed as the Prime Minister had just announced that the CF would be despatching the HERT within 24 hours.

The selection of the new CO was simple. Since 2006, the CF policy had been that all command positions must have identified successors. The nominated successor is informed of their selection and therefore is able to mentally prepare for transition. In this case, the successor was aware of her assumption of command in ten months and she had begun preparing to be a CO. Knowing that she would be the next CO, she had been thinking about the storm and wondering if HERT would be involved. She had also been thinking what she would do if she were CO. She remembered visiting HERT in Kingston and being briefed on contingency plans.

The new CO HERT was informed of her new position at 1500. As she lived in Ottawa, she was able to meet with the COS J3 later that day. In the meantime, she was given access to the collaboration space and was able to review her predecessor's work. She too, knew the battlegroup commander from 2004 and decided to make contact. The two agreed to discuss the impending mission. As soon as they met face-to-face, the CO realized that her friend was uncomfortable about something. Soon he began to describe the details of a tragic incident on the island. The sharing of this experience would turn out to be very important in the days ahead. In fact, the story was so powerful that the CO never forgot the words of wisdom from her friend. After the operation, during the after-action review, she noted that the *war story* had saved the lives of several soldiers – that is the power of sharing knowledge.

At 1815, CO HERT met with the COS J3, just 12 hours after her processor first heard about the disaster. She told COS J3 that was up to speed and ready to go. HERT deployed the next morning.

The speed of response for Op SAGE was the result of the COs' ability to rapidly connect to the data, information and knowledge they needed to make decisions and take actions – this is the essence of knowledge management. This is a story of the synergy of technology, leadership and culture; this is a story of the power of sharing.

About this Story

This is a fictitious story that describes the power of knowledge management in action. It was created with the permission of the managing editor of the Maple Leaf.

For More Information

For more information about using stories to spark organizational change please contact Dr. John Girard (john@johngirard.net). *Please contact Dr. Girard if you wish to distribute this story.*

Version Française

Il y a une version française de cette histoire, demandez au Dr. Girard (john@johngirard.net)

KM TODAY

KNOWLEDGE Management

SPECIAL EDITION:
HIGHER EDUCATION

JULY / AUGUST 2008

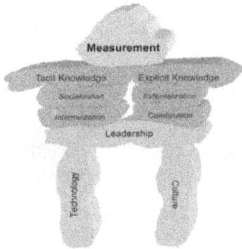

The Inukshuk: A view from the North - page 12

RRU Renews Online KM MA

The Director of Knowledge Management programs at Royal Rivers University, Victoria, BC, has confirmed that RRU will continue its knowledge management (KM) Masters of Arts program. The revised online program will build on the highly acclaimed package offered by RRU for more than a decade. New to the program will be an emphasis on the post-Nokana period espoused by

RRU continues on page 7

Minot State University: Leader in *Applied* Knowledge Management

Dr. Roderic Hewlett, Dean of Minot State University's College of Business (www.minotstateu.edu), described "applied Knowledge Management as core *business* for faculty and students alike." Dean Hewlett recalled that "in the early days [2004] some people questioned the value of the program; however, four years later, virtually everyone is united in the view that the program has added incredible value."

Today, most students and faculty are members of at least one community of practice or interest, and students participate in after action reviews, collaborate virtually, and spark change through storytelling. According to Dean Hewlett "the applied aspect of

the [KM] program is built on a solid academic foundation. Rather than simply exposing students to the theories of knowledge management, we create an environment in which we all may practice what we preach."

In addition to offering graduate and undergraduate knowledge management courses, Hewlett stated that "KM learner outcomes are integrated into many courses in the College." He proudly stated "that our combination of theory and practice provides a world class learning environment, one which is second to none." Dean Hewlett is confident that

MSU continues on page 2

Knowledge Management Modeling Research Continues at GWU

Great Western University's (GWU) Lead Professor for Knowledge Management (KM) announced that GWU will continue its ground breaking research in knowledge management. A team of researchers will investigate the

relationships between leadership, organization, technology, and learning. Early results are expected in the summer or fall of 2009

GWU continues on page 3

#3459697/23 5682   *Postage paid in USA*

DR. JOHN GIRARD
MINOT STATE UNIVERSITY
500 UNIVERSITY AVE W
MINOT, ND 58703

In This Issue:

KM World
Supplement
Knowledge in Education

Industry watch 6
Corporate taxonomy 8
University review 14
Personal toolkit 26

This is a fictitious story - to learn about using stories to spark organizational change, please contact Dr. John Girard (john@johngirard.net).

MSU (continued from page 1)

students are benefitting from the College's profound commitment to knowledge management

". . . our combination of theory and practice provides a world class learning environment"

Minot State's journey toward a knowledge environment commenced in 2003 when Hewlett rallied the Faculty to endorse three themes for the College. Two of the themes were well known at MSU: International Business and Entrepreneurship - in each of these domains MSU was an acknowledged leader, much as is the case today. Hewlett recalls that "The third, knowledge management, was less well understood; nevertheless, the Faculty collectively agreed that the foundations of KM were sound and we agreed that KM should become a College theme."

Over the next year the College recruited a KM faculty member to take the lead in the development of the core KM program. One the first tasks was to ensure that the team understood the tenets of knowledge management. Hewlett recalled "KM was new to many Faculty. We decided to offer some awareness seminars - these turned out to be very successful and really helped our team understand why it was important to integrate knowledge management into the College's core curriculum."

During the awareness seminars the Minot State team agreed on a clear, concise definition for KM. Simply stated, they believe *KM is creating and sharing organizational knowledge.* Although more than fifty definitions could be found in the literature, the MSU team desired a simple definition to help guide the

development of their program.

Unlike many KM programs of the early 2000s, MSU decided not to design a bespoke KM degree, but rather, opted to incorporate the knowledge theories, tools and techniques into all College of Business programs. Although commonplace today, such a novel concept was unheard of only four years ago. MSU's pioneering efforts are likely the reason this best-practice has been successfully replicated across America.

Time has proven Hewlett correct, as an after-action-review, or AAR in the KM parlance, clearly demonstrated earlier this year. AARs are now routine events at MSU; instructors use the tool to validate learner outcomes, students are encouraged to participate in AARs to improve the quality of programs, and the administration use AARs to ensure programs are meeting the stated goals. For example, the AAR of the KM theme demonstrated conclusively that students, faculty, and the administration were benefitting from the creative project.

KM is creating and sharing organizational knowledge.

Hewlett uses Storytelling as an example of how the applied nature of KM has been incorporated. The College's core Business Communication Course includes a module on the theory of Storytelling, which is team-taught by two faculty members - one an expert in communications and the other in KM - together they provide a unique combination of experience. But it does not stop there, as students are expected to apply the concept of storytelling in Senior courses, such as the College's International Management course. Hewlett is convinced that "the blended teaching

approach combining the incremental application of tools and techniques is a recipe for success."

"KM learner outcomes are integrated into many courses in the College."

When asked what he would do differently, Hewlett paused reflectively, and then stated "I wish we would have started sooner." Grinning, he continued: "the success of the program makes me wish more folks could have benefitted, had we started in 2003, we would have helped another cohort. That said, I am absolutely delighted with our results."

The College of Business' innovative program earned MSU the distinction of being the 2008 MIKE (Most Innovative Knowledge Educator) Award recipient for their outstanding application of knowledge management in an educational environment. When accepting the award, Dean Hewlett offered to share the secrets of their success with others.

About this Story

This is a *fictitious* story that describes the power of knowledge management in action.

For More Information

For more information about storytelling to spark change in your organization, contact Dr. John Girard:

john@johngirard.net

Use of this Story

The author is a believer in sharing ideas; however, he would like to know who is using his stories. Please contact Dr. Girard if you wish to distribute this story.

SEEN & HEARD

MSU College of Business' Student Newspaper

CONGRATULATIONS JOB CORPS EXECUTIVE MANAGEMENT PROGRAM GRADUATES!

12 MAY 2006 — MINOT STATE UNIVERSITY — SPECIAL EDITION

Conference a Huge Success

"An overwhelming success" is how Dr. John Girard, the Director of Job Corps Executive Management Program (JCEMP), described the recent JCEMP research conference. "I am absolutely delighted with the quality of research completed by the JCEMP Fellows," stated Girard. Asked if he was surprised by the quality, Girard grinned and replied "Not at all - I would have been disappointed if the Fellows had not exceeded the standard normally expected of graduate students." He continued "this was a very motivated group; early in the year they decided to work as a team to ensure all Fellows completed high quality academic research projects."

Dr. Linda Cresap, Dean of the Graduate School, described the conference "as a huge success," and said "I hope this [conference] will become an annual event and perhaps even a model for other graduate programs."

In total twelve JCEMP Fellows presented the results of their research to a panel of College of Business faculty members and Minot business leaders. After each oral presentation the Fellows were subjected to a battery of questions by the panel.

Class of 2006 - The First JCEMP Cohort to Graduate as a Group

For the first time in the history of the Job Corps Executive Management Program (JCEMP) all Fellows graduated as a cohort. The twelve members of the Class of 2006 commenced their journey in June of last year by attending a five-week session here in Minot. All twelve returned to Minot this week for today's Commencement ceremony, also a first for the program.

Dr. Gary Ross, Dean of the College of Business, described the milestone "as a tremendous achievement and a testament to the group's hard work, dedication and commitment." Ross described the Class as "an exceptional group of individuals that transformed into a high performance team."

After the Graduation ceremony the Program Director, Dr. John Girard, was seen *Job Corps hugging* each of the graduates, fulfilling a promise he made if the group graduated togther. He commented that "he was very proud of each and every graduate."

Speaking under the condition of anonymity, a group of graduates reported that the program was "easy peasy lemon squeezey" and that the "**praw**ject **prezen**tations were the best part of the course eh!" Dr. Girard suggested "they were speaking gibberish - obviously a result of stress."

This is a fictitious story. To learn about using stories to lead people into the future, please contact Dr. John Girard (john@johngirard.net).

APPENDIX 3

Virtual Worlds

A Walk Down Memory Lane

Reality is merely an illusion, albeit a very persistent one.

—Albert Einstein

Throughout this book, we have highlighted a series of active Second Life (SL) implementations. As mentioned, we recommend that you visit each of these to learn about the art of the possible. There are some amazing islands to visit. We also have highlighted that there were many good SL examples that have faded and although these existences are now inactive, we thought you could still benefit from the lessons learned from these early adopters.

Nissan Motor Company

Nissan Motor Company Ltd. is a multinational auto company based in Japan. Nissan left SL in 2001. They used their island experience to launch two brands, so it was a timing play on marketing new solutions: the real-life launch of the Nissan Sentra and Altima vehicle models. Their presence over 18 months consisted of two themed islands across four Sims (virtual islands).

The design of Sentra Island consisted entirely of a parking lot, a giant Sentra vending machine, a "Loop-d-Loop," and a circular road. Residents who come to this Sim could only do two things: operate the vending machine and drive their new free virtual cars. The launch of this island was linked to the real-life Sentra release, and for that purpose, the giant vending machine provides virtual Sentras free of charge. Like Sentra Island, Altima Island sold and gave away virtual Nissan products, thus encouraging users to operate Nissan vehicles throughout the grid. Two driving track Sims separated the islands. The Sim adjacent to Sentra was made up of a series of roads, weaving in and out of mountains. The next Sim over was at sea level and had only one road to the next Sim. At 300 meters above ground is a sky track on which users can record and try to beat their best time. Of all the corporate presences in SL, Nissan during its presence in SL stood out from the crowd because it has successfully created a reason for users to come back. Nissan designed their two islands to be engaging. The virtual cars they leveraged with their brand are a good example of integrated marketing. They used creative freebies; customer giveaways, including several test-driving tracks and generously sized sandboxes; and purchasable Nissan code. The Nissan Island's pioneering leadership will no doubt give rise to more giant vending VW machines dispensing product look a likes.

Cisco

Cisco is a multinational corporation based in San Jose, California. It designs and sells networking and communications technology and services. The island experiment was primarily used for Cisco employee training, customer interaction, presentations, and collaboration.

Cisco, although no longer active on SL, had invested in a series of islands on four Sims. Half of the site is aimed at residents and offers information about Cisco products and services. It included a feedback area, several amphitheaters, a technology center, and a plethora of informational kiosks and videos. The other focus of the site was a community-based interaction between customers and employees. This island included an extension of the Cisco Network Academy, offering training to employees. Many SL bloggers have written of Cisco's presence with interest because of their active business-to-business activities and their emphasis on interaction.

When active, there was always a lot going on at Cisco Systems' SL site. The various semiregular events included user-group meetings with keynote speakers, staff meetings, customer education and training, and presentations. They also had a very clear schedule of events online.

While Cisco did not offer their products online, they did showcase them extensively. Each kiosk display had numerous podcasts and feeds, along with 3D models of the products being displayed. All the product showcases lead to the web, with significant in-world product information. We expect Cisco to relaunch a virtual world (VW) experience, but likely behind their firewall with more access controls, or a potential reentry into SL leveraging their learnings over 2 years of active leadership.

IBM

IBM is a multinational computer technology and consulting corporation headquartered in Armonk, New York. The IBM VW presence includes virtual commerce, collaboration, client engagement, and research and development.

IBM entered SL with a tremendous splash and at the height of their online presence had over 50 active Sims. The IBM Business Center was broken up into a number of sections. These included the Conference Center, Activity Area, Support Library, Innovation Center, Briefing Center, Sales Reception, Chinese Pavilion, Japanese Pavilion, Information Trail, and Sandbox. IBM.com program director Joanne Bald has indicated that while return on investment (ROI) was not their primary goal, IBM broke even on its investment after 7 months in world. Also noteworthy is that IBM made SL history when it partnered with Linden Labs to host a portion of the VW on their own servers.

There were always a wide variety of events and experiences being offered through IBM's different initiatives across SL. On the Business Center Sim, the frequency of large events is low. However, one must keep in mind that IBM has a Sim elsewhere dedicated solely to events. In addition, throughout their island, they always had numerous opportunities to leave feedback submissions.

At one time at the height of their VW and SL activities, the company has a community of over 6,000 people working with VWs. The Business Center offered a place for IBM sales people, clients and partners to meet, learn, collaborate, and conduct business together. The center was staffed 24 hours a day, 5 days a week. Their avatars are teleservice representatives and are available in 16 languages. If residents are looking to purchase IBM products or services they can do so through the IBM staff, up until the exchange of private information that has to be done either on the web or by phone due to privacy issues. The fact that residents can sit down with IBM representatives demonstrates that the company is fully utilizing the potential of SL in its business model and is creating a one-on-one business environment similar to what would be expected in the physical world.

IBM is a high-tech corporation and their SL presence reflected it. Throughout their VW, IBM implemented video and audio feeds along with kiosks and games. On the Business Center Sim, there were interactive kiosks and teleportation maps with information that is available in five different languages. IBM uses the Sims for meetings and other collaborative interaction experiences.

IBM developed one of the richest and most mature approaches to exploring VWs and testing different design and experience approaches. Now that they have left SL visibly, we know they have access to SL behind their firewall, but no longer can the public see or access their virtual islands. For security reasons, and more control of who is given entry with permissions, IBM is continuing to be committed to VWs and is now also testing other immersive VW technologies, taking the rich insights and learnings from over 3 years of leadership and experience with the SL platform.

Telstra

Telstra Corporation is the largest provider of telephone services, mobile services, dialup, wireless, DSL, and cable Internet access in Australia. It is based in Melbourne, Australia. BigPond is Telstra's brand name for consumer broadband services. It had the title of SL's #1 most visited corporate location in 2007. In a press release, Telstra stated that SL is being used as part of their core business in distributing BigPond movies and music.[22]

Telstra began their SL presence with 11 Sims, all with names that played on the word "pond." By February 2008, they expanded to 17 Pond Sims, along with two "Telstra Experience" Sims. The environment included virtual recreations of landmarks such as the Sydney Opera House, the Sydney Harbour Bridge, and Uluru. Activities included dancing, exploring the Australian outback, shopping, climbing the Harbour Bridge, scuba diving at the reef, tutorials, free vehicles, and viewing movies.

In lieu of relying on large media events, BigPond held frequent general user-orientated small-scale events. These included a variety of social experiences such as dances and orientations. BigPond functions almost like a microcosm of the SL world. The Sims lacked an event schedule, which would be helpful for communication and community building.

Recently, Telstra completed the SL Telstra Experience Center, a virtual replica of the real-life building in which Telstra users test various products and services. This island is one that Telstra seems to be using more for internal purposes. The in-world note card that was given to SL users on the island stated,

> The Telstra Experience Centre build is more like a prototype than an end-user experience, and is a solid example of innovative SL use. Users of Real World Telstra broadband service also had the unique option of entering Second Life through the BigPond portal. To date, BigPond has brought in approximately 85,000 registered users through the BigPond.com registration process. This meant that BigPond imported its own user base into Second Life, and created a community based around their services. At the same time, the service, while active, stressed community and engagement through the social activities and offers. Also Big Pond had several residential Sims in-world, one example being the island "Pondune."

After several months in world, Telstra realized the importance of having staff in their Sims. At the height of their VW experimentation, Telstra had 24 hour in-world volunteer support. Telstra's 11 Sims were extensively detailed. BigPond Sim included audio and video that allowed for an immersive environment. The various islands contained all manner of interactive kiosks and display screens.

Kraft: Phil's Supermarket

This non-traditional effort illustrates how we're changing the way we market our products to build brand equity and remain relevant to our key consumers.[23]

—Lisa Gibbons, Kraft spokesperson

Kraft Foods is the second largest food and beverage company in North America.[24] They are based in Northfield, Illinois. Their original VW design had them showcasing over 70 new foods and beverages in SL.

Kraft experimented with innovative ways to support their brand and market presence by allowing consumers to interact with real products by viewing nutritional data, collecting and trading recipes, building product lists, preshopping for items, and attending virtual events. In line with the business applications of Web 2.0, Kraft's virtual island was designed to allow consumers to control and create their experience with the brand.

Phil's Supermarket was named after Phil Lempert, the food editor for the *Today Show*, known on television as the "Supermarket Guru." The island consisted of one Sim that has gone through some major transformations since its launch. The supermarket marked the first consumer packaged goods company to set up shop in SL. On the island, users attended cooking demos, took part in educational food forums, experienced special events, examined the packaging of various Kraft foods, and downloaded recipes and nutritional information. Residents were able to transport to seven different areas: the main entrance, Maxwell House Café, Rick's Wine cellar, Produce and Organics, Kraft Kitchens Cooking institutes, Consumer Panel Research, and Phil's Food Forum. The environment was fairly simple—a flat island on which the various sections of the supermarket were laid out. In the various food "departments" residents could click on floating packaging to receive note cards outlining nutrition information.

Food is a very difficult experience to transpose into the virtual realm. Since residents cannot actually taste the products, other brand experiences are crucial. As such, event density is very important for Kraft's in-world presence. In the promotional Machinima video created just before the launch of Phil's Supermarket, Phil Lempert announced that events like in-world forums and cooking demos would be daily occurrences.[25] Boards throughout the island announce upcoming events and the like. At present, there are invitations for feedback regarding future events, but no visible upcoming events. The cooking demos, Q&As, and forums that took place were great examples of how a consumer packaging company could interact with consumers in a virtual environment, despite the fact that VWs do not allow for much more than virtual representations their packaged goods.

The educational aspects of Phil's Supermarket were innovative—recipes and nutritional information are things that residents could enjoy, especially given SL demographics. There were always lots of freebies scattered about as well. For instance, in an effort to promote DiGiorno pizza, Kraft featured a DiGiorno Football Sweepstakes along with umpire gestures, jerseys, and helmets, for a period of time. However, the rec-reated food on the shelves throughout the island could be much more interactive—beyond the interactive Coca-Cola bottle.

Community is a focus of this SL presence. As the press release stated, "Phil's is all about building a food based community in Second Life." To go along with the SL Sim, Phil Lempert launched a website: http://www .philssupermarket.com. General information about their SL presence, upcoming events, and contact info (among other things) were always available there. This certainly added to the community experience sur-rounding the Phil's Supermarket theme. In fact, the island was set up well for community interaction. Kraft is continuing to experiment with VWs but in environments with more controls.

Harvard Berkman Center

Harvard made its foray into SL, in tandem with the Beyond Broadcast conference. The conference focused on the changing face of media and addressed gradually dissolving traditional boundaries. For this event, Harvard Law's Berkman Center set up an island in SL. The Sim features a replica of the Ames Courtroom, an outside presentation area, a sandbox, and a several other features.

Since the end of the conference, however, Harvard has used SL in a new way. Charles Nesson, his daughter Rebecca, and Gene Koo are teaching the course titled "CyberOne: Law in the Court of Public Opin-ion" online in the SL Sim. According to Nesson, the teaching possibilities in VWs are much greater than those offered by web studies alone.[26] On Berkman Island, the professor can present lectures, show videos, interact with students in real time, and conduct mock trials. Since the start of the course, CyberOne has organized several trials (i.e., Bragg vs. Linden Lab/ Philip Rosedale trial) on Berkman Island.

Ohio University

Ohio University, one of the hundreds of educational facilities in SL, actively explored the educational capabilities of VWs. They began in SL in 2006 with two islands but purchased five more in February of 2007. At the end of 2009, they had two developed Sims on the main SL grid and one on Teen Second Life. Their blueprints were based on how best to serve traditional college students, adult and distance learners, high school students, and middle school students in a convenient and engaging fashion that would allow for both synchronous and asynchronous learning experiences. The goal of Ohio University's in-world presence was to provide an attractive and engaging metaphor for Ohio University's real-world campus and extend the university's mission into the VW. The islands have a number of buildings and a welcome area. The major buildings consisted of a student center, a learning center, and an arts and music center. Throughout its online history, Ohio University provided many offerings that ranged from virtual classes to organized educational games.

Many of the university courses taught online were also free to the general SL public. To showcase the SL presence, Ohio University's website had a class taught by Katherine Milton, the director of the college of Fine Arts' Aesthetic Technology Lab. Her experimental media class met once a week in real life and once a week in SL. The online course was also monitored by seniors and graduate students who evaluated the media as both "a venue for performance and art and as a platform for creative expression."

The school also actively promoted several experimental games and activities, specifically the Nutrition Game, the Software Engineering Process Game, and Groupthink. In the Nutrition Game, the player received instructions on a note card explaining the rules. The player then chooses three meals, simulating breakfast, lunch, and dinner, and three different recreated fast food restaurants on the Sim. Each player's goal is to stay within his or her calculated calorie budget. Once the game is finished, the player receives detailed information on how the options he or she chooses affects his or her long-term health. The player is then prompted to fill out a feedback form on the experience. The game is a great example of how virtual learning is so engaging, creative in its design, fun to play, and informative. These games were designed to test different modes of education in VWs.

Ohio University was one of the most innovative and pioneering educational organizations testing how to leverage VWs for online learning and new models for student and teacher engagement.

Other Educational SL Active Sims

- Education is one of the most viable applications of VWs in SL. For example, Santa Barbara City College's "Explore It!" showcases careers in the technical industries (such as multimedia) for use by educators across the world.
- Athens Academy is a Greek community dedicated to learning within the environment of SL. It aims to offer free education-focused classes and events.
- National University of Singapore to enable learning, teaching, sharing, and social interaction.
- The Council on Library and Information Resources (CLIR, formerly the Digital Library Foundation) enables new research and scholarship by developing an international network of digital libraries.

These can all be found easily by visiting the SL directory under "Education": http://secondlife.com/destinations/learning.

ABN AMRO

ABN AMRO is a Dutch bank, based in Amsterdam, Netherlands. Between 1991 and 2007, it was one of the largest banks in Europe. RFS Holdings BV, a consortium of Royal Bank of Scotland Groups, the Government of the Netherlands, and Banco Santander, currently owns it. Daan Jitta, the senior vice president, said,

> [Second Life] could be important in the future and we need to learn about it. It's a medium to communicate with clients, and employees and prospective employees. We get lots of feedback and it puts us in close touch with our customers.[27]

ABN AMRO, while active, had four main islands: Hall of Fame, Trade Globe, ABN AMRO, and Paintball. During the summer of 2007, they owned 27 Sims, a series of which were aimed at a growing Dutch SL community. In April 2008, ABN announced that it was working with Active Worlds to create a service that allows users to build within VWs.

This would allow ABN to host VWs behind their firewall, currently not possible on SL.

Since 2006 to mid-2009, ABN held investor meetings every first and third Thursday of the month. These sessions were active and highly accessible by members of the ABN investors group and by those with invitation. Banks have been at an immediate disadvantage in SL because of security and privacy concerns. Nevertheless, they offered an impressive breadth of service. ABN AMRO was able to use the VWs as a platform on which to have a dialogue with their customers. ABN employed a full-time consultant, who worked 36 hours a week and was fluent in both Dutch and English to act as greeter at their main Sim. She was there to answer any general banking-related questions and to answer anything about the SL Sim itself. Because of privacy issues ABN AMRO cannot offer any personal banking services in SL.

ABN's investor meetings provided an excellent example of how SL community-building tools can be used. While certainly not cheap, the bank experimented with community-based islands and learned from the experience.

Although ABN AMRO Island is no longer active, they were the most progressive investment banking (IB) and capital markets bank in the world testing out VW investor experiences.

Starwood Hotels and Resorts

Starwood Hotels and Resorts was one of the first "real life" brands to enter SL with the launch of their Aloft Island in October 2006. Starwood is one of the world's largest hotel companies; it owns, operates, franchises, and manages hotels, resorts, spas, residences, and vacation ownership properties under nine brands. The VW launch of Aloft generated user feedback that was used to make modification to the hotel prior to the real-life build in 2008. By 2007, the virtual version of the hotel had come, gone, been revamped, and gone again. However, the purpose behind the VW build as a market research tool and pre–real-life test-bed remains quite innovative.

Electric Sheep Company did the build for the hotel, and Aloft tracked the progress on their blog (http://www.virtualaloft.com). As the project neared completion, the Sim was made accessible and feedback was encouraged. Essentially, this fishing for feedback is what many bloggers found successful about Starwood's initiative in SL. Between October 2006 and January 2007, Starwood continued to hold events and receive feedback from young, tech-savvy users. While this was going on in world and online, Starwood staff continued to work on their real-life prototype in a warehouse in New York. As well, developers posted photographs of the real world prototype in the virtual Starwood hotel.

At the start of May 2007, Starwood launched a redesigned and improved Aloft. The new island was based on the market feedback accumulated during the first foray into SL. This is an important point as it illustrates the use of SL for gaining valuable market research and minimizing business risk. Having finished what they set out to do in SL, Starwood recently donated their island to the Canadian online not-for-profit community TakingItGlobal, headquartered in Toronto. Within the next 4 years, VWs will become an imperative sales channel. The next generation of consumers belongs to Generation Virtual. This is a market segment native to the web, and their VW experience associated with products will be the most important influence on consumption. Like real life, the VW brand experience will become as important as the product itself.

APPENDIX 4

Helix's Innovation and Social Enterprise Research

In this appendix is an extract from Helix's recent report on innovation and social enterprise. For more information, please see http://www.helix-commerce.com.

Cisco—At the top of our list for collaboration innovation is Cisco. From the ground up since its inception, Cisco has embraced a host of social networking tools: Cisco WebEx provides instant messaging (IM), audio- and videoconferencing, wiki-like shared collaboration spaces, and more. C-Vision is Cisco's YouTube–like tool; We Are Cisco has a Ciscopedia (an internal Cisco wiki-like directory) that allows sharing of experience, expertise, and personal interests. In addition, wikis, blogs, and videos on demand (VOD) have become everyday tools for communication and collaboration. The most recent Cisco TelePresence is a video conferencing technology on one level and a collaboration and social networking tool on another. Cisco has discovered that these tools add tremendous ROI to the bottom line efficiencies and effectiveness of their organization. Cisco Canada recently won the top employee of Canada award and attributes much of it to creating a socially and forever connected worldwide community passionate about customer value and learning.

Google—Google's mission is to organize the world's information and make it universally accessible and useful. Their core values support innovation practice, working within a strong collaboration culture that inspires talent to take action. One of their core values reflects business goes virtual by stating,

> *You don't need to be at your desk to need an answer.* The world is increasingly mobile: people want access to information wherever

they are, whenever they need it. We're pioneering new technologies and offering new solutions for mobile services that help people all over the globe to do any number of tasks on their phone, from checking email and calendar events to watching videos, not to mention the several different ways to access Google search on a phone. In addition, we're hoping to fuel greater innovation for mobile users everywhere with Android, a free, open source mobile platform. Android brings the openness that shaped the Internet to the mobile world. Not only does Android benefit consumers, who have more choice and innovative new mobile experiences, but it opens up revenue opportunities for carriers, manufacturers and developers.

IBM—After Drew Neisser stated IBM could potentially be bigger than Facebook in the corporate setting, Colette Martin from Forbes went on record shortly after stating that IBM's use of enterprise 2.0 is world class:

> IBM's strength lies within the enterprise. Providing the tools to keep large global companies and their employees connected— within the walls of the company—is where IBM is likely to excel in this market. This is not the first time IBM was using a tool internally long before the rest of the world—e-mail, instant messaging, and intranet technologies were all used internally within IBM long before they were even given names. They arose out of the necessity to be connected. They were—and are—the basis for what we now call social media tools.[28]

IBM has worked very hard stay ahead of the competition in the design and deployment of market leading innovations in social software. Rated by Gartner as the leading innovator, with their Lotus Connections and Lotus Quickr solutions, you can learn a great deal of how they are developing new ways of working as they are always working as a living lab or incubator of new ideas.[29] A great example of one of these research projects getting rolled into our products most recently is their automated recommendations strategy developed in Lotus Connections 3.0. To see this at work, go to greenhouse.lotus.com.

Microsoft—There is tremendous support internally to use Microsoft SharePoint collaboration and social networking toolkits internally but more importantly promoting a culture for employees to develop personal brands and to be evangelists using blogging and microblogging toolkits to help change the world.

OpenText—a provider of enterprise content management software that brings two decades of expertise supporting 100 million users in 114 countries. They recently hired Eugene Roman, former chief information officer (CIO) of Bell Canada, who is currently CTO for OpenText and is actively involved in thinking and shaping their collaboration and social innovation for new product offerings. Eugene has always had a passion for connecting people using social communication and leveraging open space innovation approaches to increase employee dialogue to innovate more effectively. An active bee farmer and wine maker in addition to his roles at OpenText, it is no surprise that OpenText is like many of the leading vendors jumping into the social collaboration bandwagon to extend product value and relevance to customers. In June 2010, OpenText announced a family of social media offerings that enable businesses to securely apply the value of social media to solve core business challenges, such as improving customer engagement or promoting team productivity.[30]

- OpenText helps its customers realize practical and measurable business benefits such as faster time to market, higher customer retention, or greater team productivity, while helping to reduce compliance, security, and privacy risks. They see by integrating social media into their solution offerings that they can help add more value to meeting client needs.
- To support its customers as they seek to take advantage of the early-days social media explosion, OpenText has stepped up quickly by adding blogs, wikis, and other native Web 2.0 capabilities to its OpenText ECM Suite.
- They recently acquired the Vignette Community Applications and Services now coined. OpenText Social Communities is an enterprise social media solution that empowers organizations to engage with their customers, employees, and partners.
- The OpenText Social Communities consolidates social applications, such as video galleries, photo galleries, slideshows,

comments, ratings, forums, blogs, wikis, download management, event management, and idea management with user profiles, microblogging, social bookmarking, and group and moderation support.

- They also have recently released OpenText Social Workplace to offer employees an elegant way to network and interact with each other and excel in how it supports a team's ability to form, organize, and collaborate on projects as an easy-to-deploy shrink-wrapped solution.

- According to Info-Tech's "Collaboration Vendor Landscape" report, OpenText Social Workplace "provides a collaboration product in the workplace that is as intuitive as the collaboration tools employees use at home." The report further notes, "This solution minimizes information overload, a problem that plagues knowledge workers in modern organizations of all sizes." The report can be downloaded at http://campaigns .opentext.com/forms/InfoTechCollaborationPaper.

SAP—Recently named one of the top-10 "most engaged brands on the Web" for its engagement with customers and partners through its social media channel, as well as through Facebook, Twitter, wikis, and blogs, SAP continues to add new services and features to the SAP community network to enhance the user experience for its more than 1.7 million global members. Highlights from the SAP Report are as follows:

- The world's most valuable brands are experiencing a direct correlation between financial performance and deep social media engagement. SAP will now serve as an OpenID provider, which will enable easier access to the large network of partners and other resources offered by the SAP community network.

- Additional collaboration platform enhancements improve overall performance and collaboration through the addition of ratings and improved search capabilities providing members increased value from the community network. "SAP's innovative 'community' programs help it to engage deeply and build long-term loyalty with both customers and partners, while enlisting their feedback on industry-specific needs and solution requirements," Ovum analysts Warren Wilson and Nishant Singh wrote in a recent report. "The community programs tend to foster stability in challenging economic times and growth opportunities as the economy rebounds."[31]

Procter & Gamble—P&G is a role model in opening up product and customer connections. They finished their global internal social networking strategy to open up usage of diverse social tools like Facebook. They are finding that with real-time access to customers that use their products on Facebook has improved their level of customer intimacy knowledge for product requirements and also helping their employees to feel connected to their end customers, as they have often been further removed in the value chain to dynamic customer real-time dialogue. Their current CEO actively blogs on a weekly basis, and major investments are under way to improve the user interface experience of the intranet to improve the collaboration experiences at P&G.

Molson Coors—Molson Coors views social media as an integrated solution. Like the company's organizational culture, social media is a medium to portray a companywide message. Devins (2009) has explained that social media is about having conversations, a feature that distinguishes it from the core marketing group (see chapter 8).

HSBC—HSBC Brazil won the top intranet site award in 2009 by Neilsons for their innovative strategy connecting employees more effectively leveraging collaboration and social connections. Developed by TerraForum, under the leadership of Dr. Jose Claudio Terra, whose lifelong journey has been dedicated to knowledge management creating more collaborative and healthier work environments.

Charles Schwab—Unveiled in 2008, they jumped on the social networking bandwagon with the release of Schwab Trading Community, an online community fostered on its active trader clients. The closed environment is offering traders the opportunity to communicate, blog, share experiences, and connect with other traders. Schwab is adapting the concepts of community building and virtual communities to benefit active traders. They have taken some of the best social networking features and functions and provided to their clients in a closed environment. Schwab's online trading community allows traders to blog, establish discussions with fellow active traders, and attend live webinars on trading topics like

"Top Risk Management Strategies for Volatile Markets" and "The Latest on Technical Analysis Tools."[32]

Deutsche Bank—One would not think of a German back to necessarily be avidly using Twitter feeds to communicate key capital market messages, but with over 80,000 worldwide employees of Deutsche Bank, it has already made strong inroads, with 30,000 employees "approved" for Enterprise 2.0 tools. They initially tried to use Gmail and Yammer for enterprise chat but were later shut down by regulatory compliance. So they have now develop a microblogging platform that would be "lightweight and easy" for teams to start using. The service, called "The Wire," is much like an internal Twitter feed, based on Statusnet, which allows teams within Deutsche Bank to update each other easily. This has been growing successfully. However, the reason we added Deutsche to a bank to watch is their innovative uses of Twitter in capital markets.[33]

J.P. Morgan—J.P. Morgan has been experimenting using Facebook in their capital markets organization to attract university graduates to join their organizations, using social networking customized experiences integrated with a more hip external facing website leveraging video, learning simulations, and other forms of social interaction. Rated as one of the top investment bankers (IB's) attracting the best and the brightest, J.P. Morgan is putting its brand to work in powerful new ways.

ING Direct—ING is known for their innovation on the World Wide Web as they are a world-class electronic bank. The Canadian operation is led by Peter Aceto, CEO, who is passionate about open and collaborative communication. One of the most active Twitter CEOs in banking in the world, Peter has found that Twitter has allowed him to externally speak to employees and customers in ways that were simply not possible. He feels more connected and his employees can share an idea with him and know that he will respond by the end of the day. With an active social media external presence in diverse media channels, they are now innovating to open their first ING Café in Canada that has a community center with intelligent digital signage. Imagine Twitter feeds in real time in the community center customized to content relevant to community discussions at hand. Imagine having a relaxed local coffee brand working at an Internet workspace to make private calls before doing your banking. ING is leading the banking world in thinking of how to integrate a sense of deeper local connectedness using design, technology innovation, and social community models for creating the future of banking.[34]

Electronic Arts (EA)—Headquartered in Redwood City, California, EA is a global leader in interactive entertainment software. The majority of their customers and employees are part of the Millennial and Generation X demographics (age 25–40), so they tend to be heavy users of social computing in their personal and professional lives. To better enable their employees to achieve a healthy balance between their personal and professional lives (a core job satisfaction criteria for Millennials), Electronic Arts created EA People, an internal social networking site built on the SharePoint My Site, which provides the familiar features of a Web 2.0 social network within the umbrella of the enterprise. Employees can customize their own site by selecting one of the master templates that reflect EA's major games and by adding SharePoint Web Parts like photo libraries. There is even a Facebook Web Part that uses Facebook's Web Application Interface API to enable secure interchange with the outside system. EA employees tend to work mostly with people from their team, so it can be challenging for a developer to find other developers on different teams to help with a problem. Because everyone on EA People has a My Site, it is faster and easier for employees to find the right resource exactly when they need it.[35]

EA also recognizes the importance of recognition to these new Millennials and created a Web Part to aggregate all the contributions the user has made on articles and blogs so employees can get recognition for their contributions. This aids in the motivation and retention of a productive group of workers who values the opportunity to express themselves and make an impact at work using the technologies they know from their outside lives.

RBC—RBC has a core value and appreciation of innovation at its core, and social media innovations have been applied in diverse ways over the past 4 years, from their innovation challenge that uses social media with university students to ideate on the bank of the future with major prizes up to $5,000, and also an opportunity to be spotlighted for recruiting. Their social media infrastructure uses diverse tools like Microsoft SharePoint, Lotus Connections, and in some areas uses next generation Web 2.0 tools like Jive and Igloo. Their overall portal for their presentation layer is WebSphere, which is used to integrate the diverse collaboration footprints. They have a strong visionary leader with Avi Pollack, who leads their social and collaboration strategy, is a lawyer by training, and is a former entrepreneur now wearing corporate shoes.

Bank of America—They have put in place a robust social media regulatory compliance policy and security software using Socialware and are now using Twitter internally for customer service communication. This will help unlock the grid lock of many organizations across the world to realize social networking is simply another communication channel—it just happens to be the fastest growing, and customers prefer Internet-based communication over other forms, like e-mail or hard copy.

MTS Allstream—MTS is the third largest telecom company in Canada, and it stands out due to its focus on employees and striving to create a culture that is a connected community. The company has standardized on Microsoft SharePoint for its collaboration tools, have developed customized tools for ideation, and are now using microblogging with Yammer to enable short burst communication needs. (See chapter 8.)

RIM—In 2010, RIM made a strategic decision to invest heavily in a global eCollaboration program to provide improved infrastructure to meet the rapidly growing needs of its $15 billion organization, a growth from 2009 of 35%. With the increased competitiveness of the smart phone market, RIM sees scale and employee productivity can be increased by investing in next generation social networking and collaboration tools. They have standardized on the IBM Lotus Connections collaboration and social networking platform, with external social media channels active in both Facebook and Twitter to increase their customers, employees, and reach (See chapter 8).

Toronto Dominion (TD)—TD has over 2,300 retail locations across Canada and the United States. Their vision is to be the better bank and be the best-run, customer-focused, integrated financial institution, with a unique and inclusive employee culture. To support their vision they have appointed a social media vice president, Wendy Arnott, who is guiding their corporate communications and social media strategy programs worldwide, with leaders from lines of business to ensure Gen X and Y's preferred ways of working manifest into access to social networking tools. To date, they have actively experimented in using Facebook (TD Money Lounge) to share financial tips and techniques with university students and also provide helpful applications in the Facebook platform like

SplitIt to manage joint expenses for students living together. Currently they are just starting to test a corporate wide pilot, like RIM, selecting the IBM Lotus Connections platform to connect internal employees together leveraging social networking tools integrated with Microsoft SharePoint toolkits. TD has also successfully actively experimented using podcasting in its retail branches to bring the local markets closer to one another. Powered by Pollstream, retail customers in local TD communities can promote local church, school activities, or post public safety messages. TD has a long heritage brand of being one of the friendliest banks signified by their green chair image of "bringing comfort." They have more than 2,300 retail locations in Canada and the United States and serve over 18 million customers worldwide. Their brand promise is about attracting and retaining the best employees in the business and provide customers with outstanding service and convenience. That's how they are building the better bank, one that *Euromoney* magazine named Best in North America.[36]

Notes

Chapter 1

1. Amazon.com (2009).
2. Cyran (2011).
3. Shift happens (2009a).
4. Shift happens (2009b).
5. Did you know? (2009).
6. Socialnomics (2009b).
7. Socialnomics (2009b).
8. Socialnomics (2009b).
9. Socialnomics (2009b).
10. Socialnomics (2010).
11. Virtual business (2009).
12. Virtual business (2009).

Chapter 2

1. Here comes everybody (2010).
2. See Girard and Girard (2009).
3. Written by Heidi Collins, Dr. Cindy Gordon, and Dr. Jose Claudio Terra—see Collins, Gordon, and Terra (2006).
4. Macsai and Wilson (2009).
5. Alexa: Facebook.com (2010).
6. Facebook (2010).
7. Facebook (2010).
8. Inside Facebook (2010).
9. Inside Facebook (2009).
10. Inside Facebook (2010).
11. LinkedIn (2010b).
12. LinkedIn (2010a).
13. Blog (2009).
14. Mullenweg (2009).
15. Sobel (2010).
16. Macsai and Wilson (2009).
17. Twitter (2010).
18. Smith and Rainie (2010).

19. Alexa: Twitter.com (2010).
20. Compete: Twitter.com (2010).
21. Compete: Wikipedia.org (2010).
22. Wikipedia (2009).
23. Compete: Wikipedia.org (2010).
24. Wales (2009).
25. Li and Bernoff (2008a), p. 9.
26. Tapscott and Williams (2006), p. 11.
27. Li and Bernoff (2008b).
28. Bernoff (2008).
29. Girard and Girard (2009).
30. Fulmer (1999).
31. Alexa: Wikipedia.org (2010).

Chapter 3

1. Leadership (2010).
2. Leadership (2010).
3. Leadership (2010).
4. The storytelling chapter in *A Leader's Guide to Knowledge Management* was written by John Girard and Sandy Lambert.
5. Snowden (2002), p. 3.
6. McDougall (2011).

Chapter 4

1. Welsh (2007), p. 3.
2. Forrester (2010).
3. Isaacs (1999).
4. Isaacs (1999).
5. Cindy Gordon is coauthor.
6. Weise (2010).
7. Watson Wyatt (2006).
8. Koys (2001).
9. Welsh (2007), p. 3.
10. Weise (2010).
11. Frost and Sullivan (2009).
12. Frost and Sullivan (2009).
13. Frost and Sullivan (2009).
14. Salire Partners (2010).
15. Salire Partners (2010).

Chapter 5

1. LightSpeed Venture Partners (2010).
2. LightSpeed Venture Partners (2010).
3. Keegan (2010).
4. Keegan (2010).
5. Helix Commerce (2010).
6. Wikipedia (2011).
7. Damer (1997).
8. Damer (1998).
9. Virtual Worlds (2009).
10. Eon Reality (2009).
11. Peddie (2010).
12. Peddie (2010).
13. Peddie (2010).
14. Oliveri (2010).
15. Oliveri (2010).
16. Ashby (2010a).
17. Ashby (2010b).
18. Helix Commerce (2010).
19. Helix Commerce (2010).
20. Helix Commerce (2010).
21. Wagner (2007b).
22. WebPro News (2009).
23. Saloman (2007), p. 5.
24. Keegan (2010).
25. Zohar (2011).
26. Keegan (2010).
27. Keegan (2010).
28. Second Life (2010).
29. Helix Commerce (2010).

Chapter 6

1. Verety (2008).
2. NightHawk (2009a).
3. NightHawk (2007).
4. NightHawk (2009b).
5. Friedman (2006).
6. Xpitax (2009).
7. Xpitax (2009).
8. Etsy (2009a).

9. Etsy (2010).

10. Li and Bernoff (2008b).

11. Bernoff (2008).

12. Etsy (2009b).

13. Etsy (2009c).

14. Cisco (2010b); Gordon (2011).

15. Verety to close doors (2010).

Chapter 7

1. Howe (2006).

2. Howe (2008).

3. 99 Designs (2009a).

4. 99 Designs (2009b).

5. 99 Designs (2009c).

6. 99 Designs (2009a).

7. Netflix (2009a).

8. Netflix (2009b).

9. Netflix (2009c).

10. Ideas for Good (2010).

11. Mentos (2010).

12. EepyBird (2010).

13. National Geographic (2009).

14. Photo-crashing squirrel (2009).

15. United breaks guitar (2010).

16. Ayres (2009).

17. Dave Carroll Music (2009).

18. Li and Bernoff (2008b).

19. Sashin (2010).

20. TripAdvisor (2010a).

21. TripAdvisor (2010b).

22. Sashin (2010).

Chapter 8

1. Gordon (2010). For great photo of the idea, see http://tinyurl.com/collabdie

2. Symantec Study (2010).

3. Molson Coors (2010, November 15 interview).

4. Molson Coors (2010, November 15 interview).

5. Molson Coors (2010, November 15 interview).

6. Molson Coors (2010, November 15 interview).

7. Molson Coors (2010, November 15).
8. Moffat (2010).
9. Devine (2009).
10. MTS Allstream (2010).
11. MTS Allstream (2010).
12. Helix and Innovation Social Enterprise Research (2011)
13. IBM (2010).
14. Howe (2006).

Chapter 9

1. Helix Commerce (2010).
2. Helix Commerce (2010)
3. Helix Commerce (2010).
4. Frenzoo Report (2009).
5. Modaiva Fashion Week (2010).
6. Second Life MarketPlace (2011).
7. http://secondlifegrid.net/casestudies
8. http://metaverse.stanford.edu/metaverse-u-1-0-archive/speakers/speakers
9. Helix Commerce (2010).
10. Ibid.

Chapter 10

1. IBM Innovation Survey (2009).
2. French & Raven's five bases of power (2010).
3. Petrecca (2010, November 18).
4. McKinsey (2010).
5. Microsoft (2010).
6. Intelligent city. (2011).
7. http://www.intelligentcommunity.org/index.php?submenu=AboutUs&src
   =gendocs&ref=Mission&category=AboutUs
8. Council for Economic Planning and Development (2011).
9. CATA Alliance (2011).
10. Alexa: Wikipedia.org (2010).
11. Howe (2008).
12. Sashin (2010).
13. Howe (2006).

Appendixes

1. Denning (2001).
2. Stories & storytelling (2005).
3. Kaye and Jacobson (1999), p. 50.
4. Chartier, LaPointe, and Bonner (2005), p. v.
5. Denning (2004).
6. Forman (1999), p. 1.
7. Neilson and Stoffer (1999), p. 1.
8. McKee and Fryer (2003), p. 51.
9. Denning (2004), p. 150.
10. Bell (2004).
11. Neilson and Stouffer (2005), p. 26.
12. Baum (2000), p. 159.
13. Mai and Akerson (2003).
14. Forman (1999).
15. Allen (2005).
16. Allen (2005), p. 64.
17. Matsui (n.d.), p. 7.
18. Matsui (n.d.), p. 7.
19. Snowden (2002), p. 3.
20. Snowden (2002), p. 3.
21. Denning (2004), p. 127.
22. Helix Commerce (2010).
23. Helix Commerce (2010).
24. Helix Commerce (2010).
25. Helix Commerce (2010).
26. Helix Commerce (2010).
27. Helix Commerce (2010).
28. Martin (2010).
29. Gartner Group (2010a,b).
30. OpenText (2010).
31. SAP Report (2010).
32. Schwaab (2008).
33. Bakely (2010).
34. Aceto (2010).
35. Electronic Arts (2009).
36. TD Bank (2009).

References

21 Effective Quotes of Charles Darwin. (2007). Retrieved August 2010, from http://greathumancapital.wordpress.com/2007/03/15/21-effective-quotations -of-charles-darwin/

99Designs. (2009a). 99 Designs: About us. Retrieved December 28, 2009, from 99 Designs: http://99designs.com/help/aboutus

99Designs. (2009b). 99 Designs: How it works. Retrieved December 28, 2009, from 99 Designs: http://99designs.com/help/howitworks

99Designs. (2009c). 99 Designs: Interview Mark Harbottle. Retrieved December 28, 2009, from 99 Designs: http://99designs.wordpress.com/2009/12/15/ 99designs-interview-mark-harbottle

Aceto, P. (2010, October 7). Interview research with Dr. Cindy Gordon.

Alexa: Facebook.com. (2010). Retrieved December 21, 2010, from Alexa: http:// www.alexa.com/siteinfo/facebook.com

Alexa: Twitter.com. (2010). Retrieved December 21, 2010, from Alexa: http:// www.alexa.com/siteinfo/twitter.com

Alexa: Wikipedia.org. (2010). Retrieved December 21, 2010, from Alexa: http:// www.alexa.com/siteinfo/wikipedia.org

Allen, K. (2005). Organizational storytelling. *Franchising World, 37*(11), 63–64.

Amazon.com. (2009). Amazon Kindle is the most gifted item ever on Amazon. com. Retrieved December 27, 2009, from Amazon.com: http://phx.corporate -ir.net/phoenix.zhtml?c=176060&p=irol-newsArticle&ID=1369429

Ashby, A. (2010a). Edmonton Oilers to launch virtual world for kids. Retrieved January 17, 2011, from Engage Digital: http://www.engagedigital.com/2010/ 12/23/edmonton-oilers-to-launch-virtual-world-for-kids

Ashby, A. (2010b). University of Sunderland to use virtual world in cultural study. Retrieved January 17, 2011, from Engage Digital: http://www.engagedigital .com/2010/12/22/university-of-sunderland-to-use-virtual-world-in-cultural -study

Ayres, C. (2009, July 22). Revenge is best served cold—on YouTube. *The Times*. Retrieved December 20, 2010, from *The Times*: http://www.timesonline.co .uk/tol/comment/columnists/chris_ayres/article6722407.ece

Bakely, M. (2010). Fierce IT Deutsche Bank uses social networking to unite employees. Retrieved October 4, 2010, from Fierce Finance IT: http://www .fiercefinanceit.com/story/deutsche-bank-social-media/2010-10-04

Baum, D. (2000). *Lightning in a bottle: Proven lessons for leading change*. Chicago: Dearborn.

Bell, S. (2004, April 2). Trust vital for e-commerce. *Computerworld* (New Zealand). Retrieved October 4, 2010, from http://computerworld.co.nz/news.nsf/news/FCA480238A04B632CC256E68007288E0

Bernoff, J. (2008). Social technographics defined. Retrieved December 18, 2009, from Forrester: http://www.forrester.com/Groundswell/ladder.html

The Big Money Facebook 50. (2009). Retrieved December 1, 2009, from *The Big Money*: http://www.thebigmoney.com/articles/-big-money-facebook-50/2009/11/30/big-money-facebook-50

Blog. (2009). Retrieved November 11, 2009, from Wikipedia: http://en.wikipedia.org/wiki/Blog

CATA Alliance. (2011). The iCANADA declaration. Retrieved from http://www.cata.ca/Advocacy/iCanada/default.aspx

Chartier, B., LaPointe, S., & Bonner, K. (2005). *Get real—the art and power of storytelling in workplace communities*. Canada.

Cisco. (2010a). Cisco collaboration business case. Retrieved January 17, 2011, from Cisco: http://www.cisco.com/en/US/solutions/ns1007/collaboration_business_case.html

Cisco. (2010b). TelePresence. Retrieved January 17, 2011, from Cisco: http://www.cisco.com/en/US/netsol/ns669/networking_solutions_solution_segment_home.html

Compete: Twitter.com. (2010). Retrieved December 21, 2010, from Compete: http://siteanalytics.compete.com/twitter.com

Compete: Wikipedia.org. (2010). Retrieved December 21, 2010, from Compete: http://siteanalytics.compete.com/wikipedia.org

Council for Economic Planning and Development (CEPD). (2011). iTaiwan 12 Projects. Retrieved from http://www.cepd.gov.tw/dn.aspx?uid=5631

Cyran, R. (2011, January 6). No-show Apple dominates convention. *International Herald Tribune*, p. 18.

Damer, B. (1997). *Avatar: Exploring and building virtual worlds on the Internet*. Berkeley, CA: Peachpit.

Damer, B. (1998). *Avatar: A virtual world timeline*. Retrieved from http://www.vwtimeline.com/presentations/07-MiscPresentationVersions/bcs-london.ppt#256,1,Slide 1

Dave Carroll Music. (2009). Dave Carroll Bio. Retrieved December 20, 2010, from Dave Carroll Music: http://www.davecarrollmusic.com/about-dave/bio

Denning, S. (2001). *The springboard: How storytelling ignites action in knowledge-era organizations*. Boston: Butterworth-Heinemann.

Denning, S. (2004). Telling tales. *Harvard Business Review, 82*(5), 122–129.

Did You Know? (2009). Retrieved December 23, 2010, from YouTube: http://
www.youtube.com/watch?v=6ILQrUrEWe8

EepyBird. (2010). EepyBird: About us. Retrieved December 20, 2010, from
EepyBird: http://www.eepybird.com/about.html

Electronic Arts (2009). *Collaboration 2.0: Inside Electronic Arts.* Retrieved
December 10, 2010, from http://mikeg.typepad.com/perceptions/
2009/11/collaboration-20-inside-electronic-arts.html

Emerson, A. L. The effects of employee satisfaction and customer retention
on corporate profitability: An analysis of the service-profit chain. Retrieved
July 3, 2010, from Employee Satisfaction Research: http://cuprofessional
.com/uploads/EmersonISMDissertation.doc

Eon Reality. (2009). How large is the virtual reality market size? Retrieved January 17, 2011, from Eon Reality: http://eonrealityblog.wordpress.com/2009/
09/25/how-large-is-the-virtual-reality-market-size

Etsy. (2009a). Etsy: About us. Retrieved December 17, 2009, from Etsy: http://
www.etsy.com/about.php

Etsy. (2009b). Etsy launches the virtual labs! Retrieved December 18, 2009, from
Etsy: http://www.etsy.com/storque/etsy-news/etsy-launches-the-virtual-labs
-622

Etsy. (2009c). How does Alchemy work? Retrieved December 18, 2009, from
Etsy: http://www.etsy.com/help_guide_alchemy_overview.php

Etsy. (2010). Etsy: Press kit. Retrieved January 16, 2011, from Etsy: http://press
.etsy.com/press-kit.html

Facebook. (2010). Facebook statistics. Retrieved December 21, 2010, from Facebook: http://www.facebook.com/press/info.php?statistics

Forman, J. (1999). When stories create an organization's future. *Briefs, 15,* 1–4.

Forrester. (2010). What's the social technographics profile of your customers?
Retrieved December 22, 2010, from Forrester: http://www.forrester.com/
empowered/tool_consumer.html

French & Raven's five bases of power. (2010). Retrieved December 22, 2010,
from Wikipedia: http://en.wikipedia.org/wiki/French_%26_Raven's_Five
_bases_of_Power

Frenzoo Report. (2009). Retrieved from Evri: http://www.evri.com/organization/
frenzoo-0x39cc83#

Friedman, T. L. (2006). *The world is flat: A brief history of the twenty-first century.*
New York: Farrar, Straus and Giroux.

Frost and Sullivan. (2009). Referenced in research noted in: *Cisco: The return
on collaboration: Assessing the value of today's collaboration solutions.* Retrieved
December 22, 2010, from: http://www.cisco.com/en/US/solutions/collateral/
ns340/ns856/ns870/c11-597613-00_return_collab_wp.pdf

Fulmer, W. E. (1999). Buckman laboratories (a). Harvard Business School Cases, 1–16.

Furness, A. T. (1998). *Creating better virtual worlds*. London: Elsevier Publishing.

Galland, L. (2010). ADHD is on the rise. Retrieved November 9, 2010, from *Huffington Post*: http://www.huffingtonpost.com/leo-galland-md/adhd-is-on -the-rise-_b_783381.html

Gartner Group. (2010a). Changing patterns of work. Retrieved August 5, 2010, from http://www.gartner.com/it/page.jsp?id=1416513

Gartner Group. (2010b). Gartner magic quadrant on social software. Retrieved August 5, 2010, from http://www.readwriteweb.com/enterprise/2010/10/ gartner-magic-quadrant-2010-fo.php

Girard, J. P., & Girard, J. L. (2009). *A leader's guide to knowledge management: Drawing on the past to enhance future performance*. New York: Business Expert Press.

Google Core Values. (2011). Retrieved August 5, 2010, from http://www .askstudent.com/google.list-of-google-core-values

Gordon, C. (2010). *Communities of practice: Leading Practices*. http://stores.lulu .com/helixcommerce

Gordon, C. (2010, November 11). Research interview by Dr. Cindy Gordon with Molson Coors Executives (Ferg Devins, Adam Moffat).

Gordon, C. (2011, January 9). Research interview by Dr. Cindy Gordon with Ayelet Baron, Cisco.

Hambrose, H. (2009). *The wrench in the system*. New York: John Wiley and Sons.

Helix Commerce. (2010). Retrieved on July 2010, from Virtual Worlds Publica-tion Report—Virtual Worlds: A Universe of Opportunity: http://stores.lulu .com/helixcommerce

Here Comes Everybody. (2010). Retrieved January 17, 2011, from Wikipedia: http://en.wikipedia.org/wiki/Here_Comes_Everybody

Heskett, J., Sasser, E., & Schlesinger, L. (1997). *The service profit chain*. Boston: Harvard Business Press.

History of massively multiplayer online games. (2010). Retrieved January 20, 2011, from Wikipedia: http://en.wikipedia.org/wiki/History_of_massively _multiplayer_online_games

Howe, J. (2006). The rise of crowdsourcing. *Wired, 14*(6). Retrieved January 15, 2009, from Wired: http://www.wired.com/wired/archive/14.06/crowds.html

Howe, J. (2008). *Crowdsourcing: Why the power of the crowd is driving the future of business* (1st ed.). New York: Crown Business.

IBM. (2010). Global Innovation Survey. Retrieved January 14, 2011, from http:// www-935.ibm.com/services/us/ceo/ceostudy2010/

IBM. (2011). *Social networking IBM research programs*. Retrieved from Center for Social Innovation: http://www.research.ibm.com/social/projects.html

Ideas for Good. (2010). About the challenge. Retrieved December 20, 2010, from Ideas for Good: http://www.yourideasforgood.com/about

Inside Facebook. (2009, December 11). Leaderboards: Facebook. Leaderboards for Tuesday, December 11, 2009, from Inside Facebook: http://pagedata .insidefacebook.com

Inside Facebook. (2010, December 21). Leaderboards: Facebook. Leaderboards for Tuesday, December 21, 2010, from Inside Facebook: http://pagedata .insidefacebook.com

Intelligent city. (2011). Retrieved July 3, 2010, from http://en.wikipedia.org/ wiki/Intelligent_city

Isaacs, W. (2008). *Dialogie: The art of thinking together*. New York: Crown Business Publishing.

Johnson, S. (2001). *Emergence: The connected lives of ants, brains, cities, and software*. New York: Scriber Publishing.

Kaye, B., & Jacobson, B. (1999). True tales and tall tales the power of organizational storytelling. *Training & Development, 53*(3), 45–50.

Keegan, V. (2010). Virtual worlds: Is this where life is heading? Retrieved from http://www.mg.co.za/article/2010-08-22-virtual-worlds-is-this-where-real -life-heading

Knowledge at Wharton. (2009). Virtual worlds: Mapping a new business reality. Retrieved from http://knowledge.wharton.upenn.edu/10000women/article .cfm?articleid=6094

Koys, D. (2001). The effects of employee satisfaction, organizational citizenship behavior, and turnover on organizational effectiveness: A unit-level, longitudinal study. *Journal of Personal Psychology*, no. 54: 101–114.

Leadership. (2010). Retrieved on December 19, 2010, from Wikipedia: http://en .wikipedia.org/wiki/leadership

Li, C., & Bernoff, J. (2008a). *Groundswell: Winning in a world transformed by social technologies*. Boston: Harvard Business Press.

Li, C., & Bernoff, J. (2008b). *The Social technographics ladder*. Retrieved December 18, 2009, from Forrester: http://www.forrester.com/Groundswell/images/ groundswell_figure_3-2.jpg

LightSpeed Venture Partners. (2010). Blog. Retrieved from http://lsvp.wordpress .com/2009/08/30/2-5bn-market-size-estimated-for-virtual-goods-in-the-us -by-2013

LinkedIn. (2010a). LinkedIn: About us. Retrieved December 21, 2010, from LinkedIn: http://press.linkedin.com/about

LinkedIn. (2010b). LinkedIn: Home. Retrieved December 21, 2010, from LinkedIn: http://www.linkedin.com

Macsai, D., & Wilson, Z. (2009, December 1). Facebook and twitter offer businesses opportunities and challenges. *Fast Company*. Retrieved December 29,

2009, from Fast Company: http://www.fastcompany.com/magazine/141/when-brands-go-social.html

Mai, R., & Akerson, A. (2003). *The leader as communicator: Strategies and tactics to build loyalty, focus effort, and spark creativity.* New York: AMACOM Division American Management Association.

Martin, C. (2010, November 29). Can IBM compete with Facebook in social media? *Forbes.* Retrieved November 29, 2010, from Forbes: http://blogs.forbes.com/work-in-progress/2010/11/29/can-ibm-compete-with-facebook-in-social-media/

Martinez, M. (2009). Swarm theory and web communities. Retrieved March 26, 2009, from http://www.seo-theory.com/2009/03/26/swarm-theory-and-web-communities

Matsui, B. (n.d.). Action mapping, a planning tool for change. Retrieved August 2, 2006, from the Claremont Graduate School: http://www.prel.org/products/Products/ActionMapping.htm

McDougall, D. (2011). The Future of iRETAIL. Interview with Dr. Cindy Gordon.

McKee, R., & Fryer, B. (2003). Storytelling that moves people. *Harvard Business Review, 81*(6), 51–55.

McKinsey. (2010). McKinsey research on collaboration within in the networked enterprise. Retrieved from http://www.mckinsey.com/mgi/mginews/use_web_2_business.asp

Mentos. (2010). Retrieved December 20, 2010, from Wikipedia: http://en.wikipedia.org/wiki/Mentos

Mitham, N. (2007). Automobile timeline. Retrieved June 1, 2007, from KZero: http://www.kzero.co.uk/blog/?p=685

Modaiva Fashion Week. (2010). Retrieved from http://www.modaviafashionmarketing.com/fashionweek.html

Molson Coors. (2010). Annual report. Retrieved from http://www.molsoncoors.com

Molson Coors. (2010, November 15). Interview research by Dr. Cindy Gordon and Alex Blom (primary research case study).

MTS Allstream. (2010, October 15). Interview research by Dr. Cindy Gordon (primary research case study).

Mullenweg, M. (2009). Mullenweg: 10 blogs to make you think. Retrieved December 21, 2010, from CNN: http://www.cnn.com/2009/TECH/11/11/wordpress.blog.mullenweg/index.html

National Geographic. (2009). The daily dozen. Retrieved December 20, 2010, from *National Geographic*: http://ngm.nationalgeographic.com/your-shot/daily-dozen?startgallery=116&image=9

Neilson, R., & Stouffer, D. (2005). Narrating the vision scenarios in action. *The Futurist, 39*(3), 26–30.

Netflix. (2009a). About Netflix. Retrieved December 28, 2009, from Netflix: http://www.netflix.com/MediaCenter?id=5379

Netflix. (2009b). Netflix Prize. Retrieved December 28, 2009, from Netflix: http://www.netflixprize.com//index

Netflix. (2009c). Netflix Prize leaderboard. Retrieved December 28, 2009, from Netflix: http://www.netflixprize.com//leaderboard

NightHawk. (2007). NightHawk teleradiology. September 23. *Lab Business Week.* Retrieved December 12, 2009, from NightHawk: http://www.nighthawkrad .net/admin/editor/uploads/files/Lab%20Business%20Week%20-%20 article%20-%2009.23.07%20w%20header.pdf

NightHawk. (2009a). NightHawk radiology services. Retrieved December 12, 2009, from NightHawk: http://www.nighthawkrad.net/index.php?page =sub&id=107

NightHawk. (2009b). NightHawk technology. Retrieved December 12, 2009, from NightHawk: http://www.nighthawkrad.net/index.php?page =technology

Oliveri, D. (2010). The most popular virtual worlds for tweens. Retrieved January 17, 2011, from Suite101: http://www.suite101.com/content/the-most-popular -virtual-worlds-for-tweens-a271136#ixzz19Kd2cCRL

OpenText. (2010). OpenText expands social media offerings to help businesses drive bottom line results. Retrived from http://www.opentext.com/2/global/ press-release-details.html?id=2371

Peddie, J. (2010). CAD report. Retrieved from http://www.jonpeddie.com/ publications/cad_report

Petrecca, L. (2010, November 18). Offended moms get tweet revenge over Motrin ads. *USA Today.* Retrieved December 22, 2010, from USA Today: http:// www.usatoday.com/tech/products/2008-11-18-motrin-ads-twitter_N.htm

Photo-crashing squirrel leads to social media win for Banff Lake Louise tourism. (2009). Retrieved December 20, 2010, from Reuters: http://www.reuters .com/article/idUS208716+08-Sep-2009+PRN20090908

Reichheld, F. (1996). *The loyalty effect.* Boston: Harvard Business School Press.

Salire Partners. (2010). Research report on ROI of collaboration. Retrieved from http://www.google.ca/search?sourceid=navclient&ie=UTF-8&rlz=1T4GGIH _enCA263CA263&q=In+another+research+study+conducted+in+early +2010%2c+Salire+Partners+published+a+report+on+the+operational+ROI +of+collaboration

Salomon, M. (2007). Business in Second Life: An introduction. Retrieved May 2007, from Smart Internet Technology CRC: http://www.smartinternet.com .au/ArticleDocuments/121/Business-in-Second-Life-May-2007.pdf

SAP Report. (2010). SAP named one of the top-10 global brands for engaging social media; continues to improve SAP community network services to help members gain better insight through collaborative innovation. Retrieved August 18, 2009, from SAP: http://www.sap.com/press.epx?pressid=11708

Sashin, D. (2010). iReport global challenge: Earth's most fascinating places. Retrieved December 20, 2010, from CNN: http://edition.cnn.com/2010/IREPORT/12/15/global.challenge.irpt/index.html

Schwab. (2010). Schwab's online trading community. Retrieved from http://www.schwab./public/schwab/active_trader/ . . . /trading_community

Second Life. (2010). Eureka—the destination guide blog. Retrieved January 17, 2011, from Second Life: http://blogs.secondlife.com/community/community/eureka

Second Life MarketPlace. (2011). Retrieved from Second Life Market Place: https://marketplace.secondlife.com/products/search?search%5Bcategory_id%5D=3

Shift Happens. (2009a). Retrieved December 27, 2009, from Shifthappens: http://shifthappens.wikispaces.com

Shift Happens. (2009b). Shifthappens: History of the presentation. Retrieved December 27, 2009, from Shifthappens: http://shifthappens.wikispaces.com/History+of+the+Presentation

Smith, A., & Rainie, L. (2010). Overview: The people who use Twitter. Retrieved December 21, 2010, from Pew Internet: http://pewinternet.org/Reports/2010/Twitter-Update-2010/Findings/Overview.aspx

Snowden, D. (2002). Complex acts of knowing: Paradox and descriptive self-awareness. *Journal of Knowledge Management, 6*(2), 100–111.

Sobel, J. (2010). WHO: Bloggers, brands and consumers—day 1 SOTB 2010. Retrieved December 21, 2010, from Technorati: http://technorati.com/blogging/article/who-bloggers-brands-and-consumers-day/

Socialnomics. (2009a). Retrieved December 27, 2009, from Socialnomics: http://www.socialnomics.com

Socialnomics. (2009b). Statistics show social media is bigger than you think. Retrieved December 27, 2009, from Socialnomics: http://socialnomics.net/2009/08/11/statistics-show-social-media-is-bigger-than-you-think

Socialnomics. (2010). Social media revolution 2. Retrieved December 23, 2010, from YouTube: http://www.youtube.com/watch?v=lFZ0z5Fm-Ng

Stories & storytelling. (2005). Retrieved August 2, 2006, from Ivy Sea: http://www.ivysea.com/pages/Storytelling_portal.html

Symantec Study. (2010).

Tapscott, D., & Williams, A. D. (2006). *Wikinomics: How mass collaboration changes everything.* New York: Portfolio.

TD Bank. (2010). *Euromoney* names TD number one bank in North America. Retrieved January 25, 2011, from TD Bank: http://www.td.com/ar2009/pdfs/ar2009.pdf

TripAdvisor. (2010a). TripAdvisor: About us. Retrieved December 20, 2010, from TripAdvisor: http://www.tripadvisor.com/pages/about_us.html

TripAdvisor. (2010b). TripAdvisor: Fact sheet. Retrieved December 20, 2010, from TripAdvisor: http://www.tripadvisor.com/PressCenter-c4-Fact_Sheet.html

Twitter. (2010). Twitter is the best way to discover what's new in your world. Retrieved December 21, 2010, from Twitter: http://twitter.com/about

United breaks guitar. (2010). Retrieved December 20, 2010, from Wikipedia: http://en.wikipedia.org/wiki/United_Breaks_Guitars

Verety. (2008). Verety: Welcome. Retrieved December 12, 2009, from Verety: http://www.verety.com/about_welcome.asp. No longer available, see http://web.archive.org/web/20080730012121/http://www.verety.com/about_welcome.asp

Verety to close doors. (2010, March 15). *The Pierce County Tribune*. Retrieved December 20, 2010, from *The Pierce County Tribune*: http://www.thepiercecountytribune.com/page/content.detail/id/501403.html?nav=5003

Virtual business. (2009). Retrieved December 27, 2009, from Wikipedia: http://en.wikipedia.org/wiki/Virtual_business

Virtual Worlds (2009). Virtual worlds popularity spikes. Retrieved July 15, 2009, from http://www.engagedigital.com/2009/07/15/virtual-world-popularity-spikes

Wagner, M. (2007a). Five rules for bringing your real-life business into second life. Retrieved August 21, 2007, from *Information Week*:

Wagner, M. (2007b). Is Second Life just a big chatroom? Retrieved May 30, 2007, from *Information Week*: http://www.informationweek.com/blog/main/archives/2007/05/is_second_life_1.html

Wales, J. (2009). An appeal, from Wikipedia founder Jimmy Wales. Retrieved from Wikipedia: http://wikimediafoundation.org/wiki/Appeal2/en?utm_source=2009_Jimmy_Appeal1

Watson Wyatt. (2006). *Watson Wyatt human capital index: Human capital as a lead indicator of shareholder value, survey highlights*. Rochelle Park, NJ: Author. Retrieved March 2006, from http://www.watsonwyatt.com/research/resrender.asp?id=W-488&page=3

WebPro News. (2009). Second Life: Alive and kicking. Retrieved March 2009, from http://www.webpronews.com/topnews/2009/03/16/second-life-still-alive-and-kicking

Weir, A. (2010, December). *Crowdsourcing: The Genie is out of the bottle*. McMaster University, research paper.

Weise, C. (2010). *The return on collaboration: Assessing the value of today's collaboration.* Retrieved from Cisco: http://www.cisco.com/en/US/solutions/collateral/ns340/ns856/ns870/c11-597613-00_return_collab_wp.pdf

Wikipedia. (2009). Wikipedia: About. Retrieved November 11, 2009, from Wikipedia: http://en.wikipedia.org/wiki/Wikipedia:About

Wikipedia (2011). Intelligent City Definition. Retrieved April 17, 2011, from Wikipedia: http://en.wikipedia.org/wiki/Intelligent_city

Xpitax. (2009). Retrieved December 17, 2009, from Xpitax: http://www.xpitax.com

Zohar, M. (2011, August 3). Interview with Dr. Cindy Gordon. Virtualization regarding Scencaster.

Index

Note: The *italicized t* following page numbers refers to tables.

Announcing the Business Expert Press Digital Library

Concise E-books Business Students Need for Classroom and Research

This book can also be purchased in an e-book collection by your library as

- a one-time purchase,
- that is owned forever,
- allows for simultaneous readers,
- has no restrictions on printing, and
- can be downloaded as PDFs from within the library community.

Our digital library collections are a great solution to beat the rising cost of textbooks. E-books can be loaded into their course management systems or onto students' e-book readers.

The **Business Expert Press** digital libraries are very affordable, with no obligation to buy in future years.

For more information, please visit **www.businessexpertpress.com/librarians**. To set up a trial in the United States, please contact **Sheri Allen** at *sheri.allen@globalepress.com*; for all other regions, contact **Nicole Lee** at *nicole.lee@igroupnet.com*.

OTHER TITLES IN OUR STRATEGIC MANAGEMENT COLLECTION
Series Editor: **Mason Carpenter**

www.ingramcontent.com/pod-product-compliance
Lightning Source LLC
Chambersburg PA
CBHW060340200326
41519CB00011BA/1993